Emil Bo␣

Genesis

Creation and the Patriarchs

Floris Books

Translated by Maria St Goar

Originally published in German under the title *Urgeschichte*
by Verlag Urachhaus in 1934. Seventh German edition 1978.
First published in English by Floris Books in 1983.

ISBN 0–86315–000–4

Printed in Great Britain
by Billing & Sons Ltd, Worcester

Contents

Preface   7

Creation and History
1 Creation: The Great Cycles of Time   11

Primordial Time and Revelation
2 Adam – Paradise – The Fall: Lemurian Humanity   23

3 Primordial Revelation: Provision for the Human Spirit   41

4 Cain – Seth – Enoch: Atlantean Humanity   47

5 Noah – Job: Transition to the Post-Atlantean Time   67

The Age of the Patriarchs
6 Gilgamesh – Nimrod – Abraham:
   Between Babylonia and Egypt   86

7 Melchizedek: The Hidden Sun Mystery   108

8 Lot – Abraham – Isaac:
   Between Legacy and Promise   125

9 Jacob: The Babylonian Legacy   141

10 Joseph and his Brothers: The Egyptian Destinies   160

References   177
Bibliography   181
Index   185

Acknowledgements

Unless otherwise stated, all quotations from the Bible are from the Revised Standard Version with kind permission of the National Council of the Churches of Christ (New Testament © 1946, 1971; Old Testament © 1952).

Where the context required it, Bock's own translation has been translated into English. These are marked *B* after the reference.

Preface to the fifth German edition, 1958

This book has a history. Twenty-five years ago, in the year 1933, when in the tumultuous present it became evident what spiritual controversies must be fought out, the author decided to venture a comprehensive Christian spiritual history and its preceding stages as implied in the Old Testament. In the years 1927 to 1929, in twenty-five instalments, he tried to contribute to a new comprehension of the Gospels; from 1930 to 1933, in forty-two instalments, the books of the New Testament appeared in a new translation with appropriate commentaries. In this work it had been his aim to penetrate through the layer of imagery, particularly determining the style of the first three Gospels, to the actual historical foundation of the unheard-of event of salvation, where history can no longer be taken as a sum of individual facts, but a constant mystery-drama, a style, will and revelation of higher powers.

Now the intention was to describe history as such — something that had also become possible on the basis of impressions gained from two journeys to Palestine — with regard to the patterns of supersensory occurrences in human destiny. Beginning with the Old Testament, the author wanted to continue with early Christianity, understood here in a broad sense. It was to be as the dawn of a new age in the setting of the last pre-Christian centuries; the life of Jesus; the 'three years'; and finally the quiet and frequently deeply submerged continuation of the primal Christian spirit up to and including the present age.

Originally, only one volume was planned for the description of the spiritual history as it emerges in the Old Testament. But it became clear that the originally planned arrangement would be much too compact and difficult to understand. It was more advantageous to proceed only as far as the age of the patriarchs in the first volume and to divide the remaining material into two additional volumes.

The conditions of the times demanded that the publication be given as much weight as possible. Publishing a work on the Old Testament in the years 1934 to 1936 was an integral part of the spiritual battle which the co-workers and congregations of The

7

Christian Community in Germany had to wage in those days against the spirit-hostile terrorism of those in power. A positive work on the Old Testament made clear that spiritual values of mankind were being fought for in that area which above all others was the target of hate-filled fury of persecution.

Unfortunately, the original plan to deal with the Old Testament in *one* volume unfavourably affected the first volume, now appearing in its fifth printing. Descriptions were required which, in the present age, are bound to make a strange impression at first. It would have been better to render them in much more detail. But later on too, when new printings were necessary (the first volume was out of print within a year) it was not possible to give a new form to the too compressed text and it seemed advisable to proceed first with the complete work.

And thus it has remained, not only when the other two volumes about the Old Testament were published in 1935 and 1936, but also when the first four volumes on early Christianity were added: the first two in 1937 and 1939, the later two in 1948 and 1954, after the years of prohibition during which all our literature had been forbidden. But since the complete work is now available, with all but the first volume in a more detailed style, comprehension is offered for the first as well. This is now issued with only insignificant alterations.

From the preface of the first edition (1934), the following may be repeated:

These 'Contributions to the Spiritual History of Mankind,' which begin with contemplations of the Old Testament, represent an attempt to employ the living light of Rudolf Steiner's spiritual science for a comprehension of the great directions and impulses of historical evolution, as well as an elucidation of the biblical records.

In so far as their method is concerned, the considerations that are begun here must be a venture. On one hand, since they try to avoid the prevailing materialistic habits of thought, they cannot proceed in contexts based exclusively on external sources. On the other hand, they cannot flow from the sovereign vision of spiritual research available to Rudolf Steiner. The attempt must be made to combine the knowledge of the external sets of facts and the imaginative-mythical occult traditions — to which belongs the apocryphal material of legends — with living in the anthropo-

PREFACE

sophical thought-content. Anthroposophy gives a key to both. In unfolding the spiritual world panorama, it offers the possibility of perceiving the spiritual backgrounds everywhere; and it gives insights of its own concerning certain converging points and riddles of historical evolution. In this way, it is possible to penetrate to an inward perception of the historical figures and processes so that one supports the other and makes it evident. Naturally it was not possible always to start from the very beginning. Nor was it necessary to develop all elements of the spiritual scientific world view from the ground up. Instead, the aim was to formulate the basic concepts and descriptions as concretely as possible so that they are comprehensible through themselves and will yet refer him who seeks a well-grounded knowledge of them to the corresponding study of Anthroposophy. Where a total world conception is unfamiliar, only the patient co-operation between author and reader will lead further. Much will only become completely comprehensible as the descriptions proceed. The whole explains the detail. But to sense and recognize the totality of historical evolution in all details signifies the discovery of the sources of enthusiasm, of which Goethe says that it is the best of what we have of history.

The reason we begin with the Old Testament's description is that if it is rightly understood, one's sight is thereby directed to the spiritual-cosmic maternal womb of humanity's history. Just as one cannot figure out the riddle of the human being, if the question concerning 'unbornness' is not added to that of immortality, one must not only ask where mankind is heading, but also whence it comes if one wants to discern the inner motivation and breath of history. The contributions beginning here also seek to show that the New Testament is more fully understood, if the Old Testament has yielded up its depths. It is not without reason that the Christian Bible includes the books of the Old Testament.

Emil Bock

Creation and History

1 Creation: The Great Cycles of Time

As humanity made the transition from the dream knowledge of the Orient to the wakeful thinking of the Occident, the historical form of thinking and the sense of history were born.

The wisdom of the ancient Orient beheld earthly happenings as if from divine heights, sunk in contemplation of the ever-turning cycles in which tranquil, unending duration with its rounds and repetitions, not yet the stern step of time and evolution, held sway. Only the western spirit can recognize the goals of will concealed in mankind's evolution and experience time as a real factor. In place of the cycle of timeless tranquillity, the forward path of progressive evolution begins, with its breathless striving and fear of time's all too rapid flight.

The significance of the Old Testament is that it builds the bridge from the non-historical eastern to the historical western world conception. 'The ancient Hebrew world-view . . . gives the first impulse for a historical outlook . . . The Old Testament is the first great example of a historical approach to events. Hence it bequeathed to the Occident the heritage of such a historical approach.'[1] The spark of will penetrates. Humanity awakens to an evolution brought about and guided by the divine, a path to goals set by the gods.

The study of history in common use today, which is proud of the scientific approach of the past few centuries, certainly feels superior to a historical representation like the one in the Old Testament, especially in its first books. The method is based on an exclusive faith in 'outer sources'. An event is acknowledged as true only if reliable contemporary findings or information about it exist. The start of a historical development is placed in the time of the oldest information available. The evaluation the Old Testament receives on this basis is obvious, for, with divine unconcern, it reaches far beyond the realm of provable history into

11

primal times. How can the description of epochs, of which no source material can exist, withstand the historical criticism of today? One may enjoy the Old Testament as edifying religious fiction, but for the scientifically disciplined historian, such documents are of no account.

Moreover, because other ancient writings are known — for instance, the history of the Chaldeans written in Greek by Berossus — which relate the history of single nations to the world's creation, it is assumed that ancient writers did not yet possess a view of the entire human race. What true historic value can ancient creation myths have, if they stem only from the naïve style of a writer who poetically dates his own people's history back to the gods?

In reality, we have an important original model of true historical writing in the Old Testament. The history of mankind no more begins upon earth than does the life of the individual human being. The birth of physical man is preceded by the growth of the soul-spiritual entity in supersensory spheres. Therefore mankind's destinies in the realm of earthly densification and embodiment are preceded by aeons in which human beings together with the creator-beings of higher realms, worked on the physical world as on the living garment of God.

In earth history, celestial history continues. This is why all historical writing, though it may be based on the best of 'source materials', must remain incomplete and blind, unless it is aware of the supersensory, super-historical sphere of real spiritual beings.

As a prophet envisions the future still slumbering and growing in the spirit realm, so the true historian must be capable of reading the books of the past inscribed in the cosmos. He must have the faculty of retrospection. True myths are windows of retrospection; they reveal the history prior to history.

In the Old Testament we watch earthly history emerge from heavenly history. The prenatal destinies of mankind and earth itself appear to us. A text speaks to us which can unveil a spiritual-physical primordial history. We witness the 'coming-into-its-own' of history, which, before it becomes *historical* history, is creation: *cosmic* history; then the development of primeval humanity: *mythological* history. Just as the source, so also does the goal of the Old Testament belong to the spiritual realms as an all-embracing human-cosmic goal. The intention is not to describe the history of a single nation. The history of the Israelites is

1 CREATION

depicted only because through them the body of God who is to become man is prepared for mankind and for the whole earth creation. It is the concrete Messianic goal that breathes the onward-moving sense of time into the books of the Old Testament and makes them the first documents of a historical world conception. The developments described by the Old Testament are not completed within it. They demand to be continued in the books of the New Testament all the way to the Revelation to John. The last book of the Bible is the lofty recording of prophetic preview, just as the First Book of Moses, Genesis, is the classical book of spiritual retrospection, or prophecy in reverse. And between retrospection and preview, between Genesis and Apocalypse, lies the path of history. The creation myth and the prophecy of the future represent the balance of historical existence.

The more western cultural development became entrenched in materialism and abstraction, the less the beginning of the Old Testament was understood. The ancient oriental clairvoyance, that knew of rounds and cycles of evolution, was completely forgotten. A one-sided way of thinking arose that conceived the 'beginning', of which the story of creation speaks, as the very first beginning of all, and the arising of the world described there as a 'creation out of nothing'. If history is imagined as a straight line, then there is indeed only *one* beginning. For a view, however, that includes the knowledge of cosmically ruled rhythmic cycles and cyclic epochs, there are ever-new primal beginnings, similar to the circling of the sun that brings forth a new morning after each night.

The Old Testament is, however, hesitant in mentioning the rounds directly. At the beginning, where history still has cosmic character, the cycles are clearly visible. The seven days of creation obviously designate great cosmic cycles of time. (That they are not identical with what we call a day — something Origen pointed out — is shown by the fact that the creation of the sun, which determines our days and years, is put as late as the fourth day.) Later, when history enters its rightful realm, the cycles become veiled and the line of forward progress is visible above all else. An example of how hints of cyclic figures continue to be felt in the Old Testament is the title-like headings, where the '*tholedoth*', the 'evolutionary cycles', are mentioned; though in the usual translations they have been completely obscured ('generations' or 'descendants' in the Revised Standard Version).

13

1. 'These are the evolutionary cycles of the heavens and earth when they were created' (Gen.2:4*B*).
2. 'This is the book of the evolutionary cycles of Adam' (Gen. 5:1*B*).
3. 'These are the evolutionary cycles of Noah' (Gen.6:9*B*).
4. 'Now these are the evolutionary cycles of Terah' (Gen. 11:27*B*).
5. 'Now these are the evolutionary cycles of Perez' (Ruth 4:18*B*).

The cyclic element is visible where the prenatal condition of humanity and a people still re-echoes. The lineal dominates where the earthly biography, the mystery drama of earthly history, enters in. At the end of the Bible, in the Revelation, as a mark of the breakthrough from the historical into the spiritual, the cyclic element is reattained in great profusion on a new level. Contrasting with the seven days of creation in Genesis stand the fourfold sevens: the letters, seals, trumpets, and vials of wrath.

It is an abstract misconception to believe that the biblical creation story describes the first beginning of all earth existence. The world had long since been there. In earlier aeons, our earth planet had already gone through the mightiest of evolutionary developments. Also it is not as if man had not existed before the Elohim said: 'Let us make man'. Man had been evolving for aeons of time as a soul-spirit being. The divine creative word did not call forth existence out of nothing. It called the earth forth to new existence and development after the earth had once again rested from its cyclic evolution, and bestowed on it a definite form as the new beginning of a sequence of forms now to be passed through. Not the creation of all aeons is referred to; what is meant is the beginning of one specific aeon; that in which, through densification of earth's substance, earthly will and earthly destiny become possible in a narrower sense. What follows will show that the biblical creation story focuses on the advanced point in time in which this aeon fully comes into its own after having completed all cosmic recapitulations. Thus, the new element of man that now originates is none other than the seed of the outer form that we bear today as physically incarnated beings. The name 'Adam' does not refer to the first man, but to the first earth-man. Into the earth-sheath, growing denser and forming itself in stages, the eternal soul enters with the breath of God. Until then it had been embedded, alive and active, in the divinely ensouled air element. Not the beginning, but the earthly incarnation of earth and man is brought about by the divine creator Word.

In the rich legendary traditions woven around the Old Testament,* the aeons preceding the creation of Adam are mentioned in a great variety of ways as if they were generally-known facts. The imaginative picture of seven primeval kings is explained at one point in the following way: 'These kings represent the seven former worlds that were created and existed long before our world was there, which, therefore, can be called the "eighth king".' Or it says that Enoch had already attained a high rank 'in the very first world that preceded the world of Adam'. 'A thousand worlds the Lord had created at the beginning. Then, he created still more worlds, and he continued to create and destroy worlds, until he created our world.'[2]

The opinion predominates that while Hellenistic-Judaic philosophers such as Philo and the Talmudists and cabbalists, who kept alive the legendary traditions, represent the concept of primordial aeons, Genesis itself asserts a creation out of nothing. The biblical account, however, clearly presupposes an earlier existence, and Talmudic teaching rightly refers to this: 'Two things are there that were not created. These are the wind and the water . . . as is said: the wind† of the Lord hovered over the waters.'[3] Since it actually reads: 'The wafting spirit of the Elohim brooded (raying warmth) over the waters,' the third element, that of warmth, is often designated as already existing. 'Three things were already there before the world: water, wind and fire.'[4] The aeons of fire, of air, and water, the ladder of elements by which our planetary existence descended from super-physical realms, were already over when the aeon of the fourth, the earth element, arose out of cosmic night. It is into the evolving of this actual earth aeon that Genesis allows us to look.

* As our studies continue, we shall frequently quote these apocryphal and legendary traditions of which a main part has been collected in several volumes by M. J. bin Gorion. Fantastic and playful as this wealth of stories may appear, in them there is reflected some of what was handed down as ancient occult knowledge in certain esoteric theological schools in order to complete and clarify the more exoteric stylized books of the Old Testament canon.

† The Hebrew word *ruach*, like the Greek term *pneuma*, designates the outer as well as the inner aspect: air and spirit.

To determine the exact point at which the Old Testament begins in the great revolving stream of evolution, one would need a kind of huge chart of time on which could be retraced everything resulting from the retrospection of the seers.

A comparison of the biblical story of creation with the creation myths of other peoples might bring us nearer our goal. We should have to avoid the usual form of these comparisons, most of which, quietly denying the myth's value in regard to historical truth, only aim to establish literary dependencies or common sources in the different traditions. But one who has realized that all genuine creation myths of mankind date back to times when the capacity of clairvoyant retrospection was still widespread understands the concurrences as well as the differences between the various sequences of portrayals. In some myths the same thing is beheld, in others different aspects are visualized. No seer claims to describe everything. Each describes either in a more imaginative or more inspired way, a segment out of the great world tableau of the primordial ages of the past. Even where the various myths appear to contradict each other, they complement one another in reality.

The more complete our collection of creation myths of all peoples, however, the more we should find ourselves like a man with a great number of coloured stones, who can only form them into the mosaic picture he is told to make, when he has the complete plan. The thought alone that truth and harmony connect all creation myths is too abstract and vague to give us a concrete plan for putting in order and fitting together the many images of retrospection. Here, we need a world conception based on the reattainment of the capacity of exact spiritual vision of the past, and related to the clear, modern historical manner of thinking.

Anthroposophy fills this gap. It gives us the grandiose map of time become spiritual space, on which we can find the locality of biblical Genesis. It shows us the rounds that our earth planet has completed in its development. At the same time, it describes the inherent meaning, composed of progress and purpose, that orders together all the large rounds, along with the smaller ones of which they consist.[5]

We are told that the earth has already passed through three great planetary conditions before becoming earth in the actual sense. Each time, between two such great rounds of evolution, there is a return into the cosmic night of the spirit sphere.

In the first of the great cycles, the soul-spirit beings who belong

1 CREATION

to our planetary existence, including man, go through the first stage of incarnation. They begin to weave a garment and a bodily sheath, and thereby attain to the level of the mineral kingdom. But at that time, nothing like the hardness, solidity and impenetrability of the stony minerals of today existed. Material densification of that world existence progressed only to a moving, weaving fire element. Warmth substance was the only corporeality that existed. This first condition of embodiment of our planetary existence is designated as the *Old Saturn*.

In the next aeon, as a stage of further condensation, the air element is added to that of warmth. Out of the dark, brooding cosmic warmth, the light was born. A greater wealth of possibilities for embodiment was offered to the hierarchical beings as well as the human souls still engulfed in deep sleep. Creation as a whole, however, did not reach beyond the level of the plant kingdom. By no means did individual, contoured plants already exist. The world moved in an ethereal totality of plant states. Though blossoms and plant forms did light up and sparkle forth out of this weaving primeval plant existence, there was not as yet the abundance of the physically tangible phenomena that surround us today. This second planetary world condition is called the *Old Sun*, since what is sun today, together with the earth, moon, and the other planets, was contained within it, forming one cosmic body.

In the third cosmic aeon, as a further densification, the element of water is added to that of warmth and air. To the light is added tone, the cosmic Word. This aeon is dominated by a significant separation. Duality comes into being when the sun's shining etheric being separates from the corporeality of the planet. This causes the watery body of the earth to proceed by degrees in its condensation. It attains the stage of the soul-bearing animal-kingdom, without, however, producing individual bodily forms. In a gradually diversifying animal corporeality, still in the fluid element, man finds the next stage of his incarnation. His deep cosmic sleep slowly lights up to a dream-like picture consciousness. This embodiment of the earth is called the *Old Moon*, since earth and moon still formed a unity.

Only then follows the real *Earth* condition of our planet, in balance between sun and moon. For the moon, to prevent earth from becoming too hard, had separated from it. Gradually, the firm earth element was added to the fiery, the airy and the fluid

17

elements. Life ether united with the light and sound ethers, and corporeal existence reached the human stage. The rudiments of man's upright form of today that walks over the earth surrounded by animals, plants and stones, developed. Into the dream-weaving picture consciousness, there dawned the wakefulness of thought.

Each great cycle has its own primal beginning, when it arises out of the cosmic night of rest. This means that it begins the whole world existence anew, and repeats the past world conditions on a new level in greater compactness in the first of its smaller cycles.

Therefore the fourth great cosmic cycle is at first occupied with the earth's coming into its own in its subcycles. Again, the densification process out of the fire element begins in a dark Saturn-like round, the *Polarean* cycle. Once again, in the *Hyperborean* cycle, the air-earth lights up as sun, and in the middle of this cycle, the sun separation is repeated. Once again, the water-earth that is one with the moon gives birth to the resounding cosmic Word in the *Lemurian* age. In the middle of this cycle, the crisis of the earth's over-densification is resolved by the exit of the moon. Finally, in the fourth smaller cycle of the *Atlantean* age, the earth comes into its own with the clear formation of a contoured physical corporeal world. The fifth smaller cycle, the *post-Atlantean* age, in which we have been developing for about ten thousand years, represents Earth's first great step into the future.

After the Polarean age, which was still almost wholly spiritual, the cycles, as they assume an increasingly clearer spatial form, draw a great cross upon the earth. The scene of the Hyperborean era was far in the north of our earth globe, though everything concerning humanity still took place in the sphere surrounding the earth. It was the Greeks who gave to those regions, into which Apollo, the spiritual being of the sun, always disappeared from them for half the year, the name 'Hyperborea', 'land above the north'. In the next epoch, advancing humanity chose as the scene of its destiny the southern half of the globe. Ancient Lemuria was a continent in the regions covered today by the Indian Ocean, which slowly condensed out of the watery element between what is now Australia and Africa and reached as far as India and Asia Minor. Old Atlantis, the first continent to resemble those of today, arose in the region of our Atlantic Ocean. It extended westward to America as well as eastward to the western parts of Europe and Africa. Covered with heavy mist, finally densifying to solid

1 CREATION

ground, the Atlantean continent emerges in manifold ways in the memory of mankind. Plato, in connection with Egyptian priest-wisdom, mentions it. Germanic mythology points to the primeval times of Niflheim (home of the mist). So, as the focal point of evolution shifted from north to south in the transition from the Hyperborean to the Lemurian era, the transition from the Atlantean to the post-Atlantean age was from west to east.

The changes of the earth's corporeality that brought an end to the sun world of Hyperborea must have been the beginning of the cooling-off phenomena, which finally, during the ages of the last solidification, led to the glaciation of the far northern regions and found late echoes in the so-called ice ages. The lunar world of Lemuria was destroyed by great volcanic catastrophes, and the first rich earthly culture of ancient Atlantis perished through tremendous floods.

In this world view, the cyclical and linear historical elements find their synthesis. In great and small cycles and in manifold ways, the law of repetition, reflection and intensification is manifest as in the movements of a mighty symphony. Smaller cycles, repeated in greater, offer the possibility of retrospection into the great cosmic cycles. Yet the whole revolving, evolving world flows together in the clear purpose-filled path leading to awake, self-conscious, free man. History is born. We have thus gained the spiritual 'map' of which all genuine creation myths describe one portion, and on which the times and realms can be rediscovered, to which the Old Testament points in the beginning.

The biblical story of creation starts where the aeons of fire, air, and water have already incorporated their substances into the earth's development, and where the divine tone of the cosmic Word, is already resounding in the earth-sphere. We are transported in Genesis into the *third* round. This is not the great round of the Old Moon, but the corresponding smaller cycle within the earth aeon, the *Lemurian epoch*, through which, as through a window, the repetition of the great round of the Moon condition with its subcycles becomes visible. The primal beginnings arise for retrospective vision. The great cycles of the days of creation that have brought about this stage of densification and embodiment, light up quickly one after the other. We are transposed into the middle of the Lemurian time and see how creation reaches the human stage. In the figure of Adam, we recognize humanity of the Lemurian epoch, previously human in soul-spirit realms, in its

19

progress towards human existence in earthly corporeality. The images of backward vision in Genesis are assigned their right place; they become legible through the comprehensive world view of Anthroposophy stemming from a modern perception of spirit.[6] Bridges of understanding are built between the results of backward vision of the Old Testament seers and the findings of Anthroposophy. They have been arrived at independently of each other, and yet confirm and clarify one another.

Those interested in theology will not always receive from this book what they are looking for. The problem of literary genuineness is not the primary issue here, that of spiritual truth is. It is not that we reject all textual criticism and want to canonize the existing traditional text version. But as far as is possible from ancient traditions, the scriptures are still sufficiently intact to be able to lead us to the realities within them.

The question of authenticity of the texts cannot be of prime importance, since our studies by no means stem solely from the biblical text. It is customary to read all that can be said about the Bible exegetically out of its text; indeed, the rule has been made that nothing may be added to the Bible. The prevailing habits of thinking will therefore accuse us, 'You do not interpret, you interpose.' Our method of description is, however, to approach the Old Testament only after having worked for a long time with all the means at our disposal, the most important being anthroposophical research on the facts of the earlier historical epochs. When, in the descriptions of the Bible, we rediscover and recognize what we have already accumulated as intuition or knowledge, then the images of the Old Testament and the concepts won through Anthroposophy mutually clarify, enrich and confirm each other. From it all, the spiritual truth affects us in an ever more genuine and living way.

The real historical development of mankind by no means begins with the figure of Adam. Mythology arises as the link between creation and history. Earth's history is *cosmic* until Adam; *mythological* from Adam to Abraham and beyond; it only becomes *historical* with Moses. It is important that not only cosmic, but also mythological, history demands to be read and grasped differently from actual history. Though Genesis devotes only a few pages to it, the realms of development between Adam and Abraham are perhaps a thousandfold that of the time represented in

1 CREATION

all the remaining Old Testament. Almost every word here signifies millennia.

One habit of thinking, which actually veils the magnificence of the first chapters of the Bible, is the popular opinion mentioned earlier that the Old Testament is merely an Israelite-Jewish folk history. It must be clear that the beginning of what is conceived today as race only commences after Noah; it is not until Abraham that the history of the people of Israel begins. Names like Adam, Enoch and Noah shine forth out of ages when there could be no question of today's racial contrasts. A detailed description of the antediluvian era — quite erroneously pictured as primitive, and therefore disregarded, but in truth the *magna mater* of humanity — will therefore follow.

From the cosmic to the mythological, and then to the historical era, a great contraction occurs in the measure of time. The Babylonian lists of kings by Berossus relate a series of royal rulers from the times prior to the great flood and ascribe to each of them an average of 30 000 years of rule, which presents modern thinking with quite insoluble riddles. Then the periods grow smaller until the final dynasties of the individual kings number only a few years, indeed in one case only forty days. Similar dimensional time-contractions appear in the biblical representations. Beginning with Abraham, the measure of time is human. Until Abraham, it is superhuman and divine.

We must not think that behind the decrease of years designating the life-spans of the patriarchs, only quantitative changes are implied. Where the Bible reckons with such vast measures of time, the figures of persons, images and names must be qualitatively valued and understood differently from where the historical dimensions are already similar to ours.

The Bible describes human figures throughout, but they have different significance earlier and later on. If, in truly historical times, we look at figures of people like Moses, Joshua, David and Solomon, we find in these persons themselves the historical realities referred to. Names like Adam, Cain, Seth, Enoch and Noah, on the other hand, conjure up imaginative figures whom we are supposed to look through as through transparencies. Each figure is simultaneously a whole humanity; each event is also a picture of cosmic transformation and stages of evolution. Although it makes no distinction in its descriptions, the Bible at first shows mythological and only much later historical figures; therefore, in its first chapters, it requires of the reader of the history of mankind a capacity of insight equal to the power of spiritual vision out of which flows its historical narrative. But even where creation and mythology pass over into history, the books of the Old Testament demand to be read with an awareness of their supersensory visionary origin.

Primordial Time and Revelation

2 Adam – Paradise – the Fall: Lemurian Humanity

High on the ceiling of the Sistine Chapel in Rome, Michelangelo painted the creation of Adam in the way his artistic sense could perceive it. A wonderful balance between the divine and the human, between Creator and the created, prevails in this work of art. The finger, hand and arm of God project their life into the finger, hand and arm of man. Man truly arises as the image of the Godhead. Though Adam is lying upon the solid ground of the earth, while the creator-beings hover in the wind-swept realm of the air, the mantle of the Godhead billowing in the wind reflects buoyancy towards the earth realm and therein reveals the shore of the only just solidifying corporeal world. And the recumbency of man, who as yet has not awakened to his upright form, appears also to be floating. Indeed, the form and position of one leg and foot of both man and God are only distinguished by the shade of dreams and the touch of wakeful life. And what about the clearly defined contour of Adam's form? It is none other than the form of God. Can we picture Adam's body filled with the same material substantiality of form that we are accustomed to in our corporeal existence today? Then, the divine beings in the wafting mantle would have to be also imagined in such physical corporeality. This work of art leads us away from the human level that conceives of both bodies as having earthly form. Instead, from the level of the divine creator form, it subtly directs us to seek even the body of man in the spiritual realm of pure form.

This vision, classically depicted by Michelangelo, corresponds to the first of the two pictures in which the seer of Genesis shows the creation of man (Gen.1:26; 2:7). The twofold representation is not due to different sources having been interwoven in the text of Genesis, as theology believed for a time and still does to an extent now. Two primordial metamorphoses of earthly human development, separated by vast spans of time, are represented.

We are looking back into the first half of the Lemurian epoch of our earth aeon, and follow Rudolf Steiner's detailed description in *Cosmic Memory*. The conceptions that we have to form here must be completely divorced from what we are used to and what is similar to the view that the earth today offers to our senses. It is not so very long ago that the earth was still one with its own atmosphere; and only gradually, like sediment, a denser nucleus formed within the still completely soft, fluid and aeriform earth. We must probably picture to ourselves that this core formation occurred under a certain influence of the fire element, particularly in that area of the earth where, within the denser fluid nucleus, the beginnings of the Lemurian continent were forming. There, the earth was ablaze with volcanic glow in many places. But, because at that time the solid earth minerals did not yet exist, what we observe today in a volcano can only vaguely illustrate the densifying influence of the volcanic fire. Today, a volcano spews forth fiery masses, which then harden into solid lava, thus causing a rigid crust formation on the softer ground. In the Lemurian age the inner fire of the earth, like today's geysers and solfatara, could only spew out boiling water and steam, and later boiling mud. But as this cooled down, a greater density and earthboundness of the planet's body occurred.

In this earth environment, living beings in today's form are unimaginable. They could not have endured for an instant. Yet the ancestors of the plant, animal and human kingdoms did exist in a germinal and not yet individualized corporeality, adapted to the earth's condition of that time. It consisted of the elements that made up the planet's corporeality. The plants and animals existed as species in archetypal form, hovering above their corporeal realm. This is what the biblical story of creation refers to when it says that the Elohim had created plants and animals 'each according to its own kind'. And it is no contradiction when, after the creation of plants, we read 'When no plant of the field was yet in the earth and no herb of the field had yet sprung up' (Gen.2:5). The species of plants existed, but no individual plants; there were animal species, but no single forms.

The time came in the course of the earth's formation, when the

2 ADAM – PARADISE – THE FALL

Elohim could create man. But at his creation, Adam was not the only man in the universe. In the wafting mantle of the Godhead, Michelangelo depicts a multitude of human beings, while the one man is being created in the image and likeness of God. Mankind was already in existence in a soul-spirit condition. It is the earthly human form that newly arises, the beginning of an individual earthly dwelling. But the house which the creator-spirits prepare for him is not yet made of solid earth substance. Man's form comes into being as an ethereal body, into which only the archetype, the spiritual-physical 'pure form' of the physical body, is woven. Physical eyes could by no means have perceived it. This is the content of the first Adam-creation referred to also by Michelangelo.

The Bible says that the primordial image of the human form was hermaphroditic, combining both sexes. What later became separated into two sexes was still a unity here: 'The Elohim created man in their own image. In the image of God they created him. Male-female they created him' (Gen.1:27*B*).

If the Adam humanity thus coming into existence is given the power of propagation (Gen.1:28), it signifies that as a result of the soul-spiritual element still holding sway over the bodily element, it was possible for the first earth man to produce his like from within, to build bodily sheaths for other human beings still within the earth's circumference. But man is still far from being able to work upon the world surrounding him. He works upon himself as today he regenerates himself in sleep, since human consciousness of that time can also be compared to deep dream-permeated sleep. Although the first creation of man has been recounted, the Bible can say, 'and there was no man to till the ground' (Gen.2:5). A further solidification of his body is required before the very first rudimentary beginnings can arise of what we term man's work upon physical nature.

Condensation progresses and the creator powers who mould the terrestrial globe let the human form keep pace with this cosmic incarnation process. The second creation of man takes place. It is no longer said that the divine creative power creates him; the forming and animating of his body is described. The Greek Bible translates the corresponding Hebrew word with ἔπλασεν (*eplasen*), using the verb from which our word 'plastic' derives. For the first time, the substance is designated out of which the human form is fashioned: 'the dust of the earth'. There is significant unison between the name of man, 'Adam', and the term for earthly matter, *adamah*. 'Adam' is no individual name but neither does it mean 'man' in general. It specifically refers to 'one formed of earthly substance'.

The physical body has now really begun to condense in the visible, tangible realm of matter. His clearly outlined earthly sheath causes man to form an individual life and soul body from the common cosmic life and soul existence: through the divine breath, man becomes a soul possessed with individual life (Gen. 2:7).

But still one must be careful not to picture the human being who has now arrived in the realm of earthly matter as similar to the physical man of today. Man did not yet possess the upright form, neither was his organism so richly differentiated; he certainly did not possess hands, the royal instruments of free activity. These can only develop after the upright force has become effective in the human body. Some lower animals that crawl on the ground are a cosmic memory of those primordial forms of the human being fashioned out of earth substance. Only gradually did man become a warm-blooded being: generating his own warmth for the first time, when forced to assert himself against his environment as solid substance cooled. Within the fiery fluid element — a condition that cosmic memory has retained in the fish form — man had had no need of his own warmth. The capacity of hearing was the first of his sense organs to develop through the tone ether of the cosmic Word that resounded through the universe like the humming in a shell. Man's eyes were not yet open. His soul, however, lived inwardly in a world of coloured images like dreams, that awakened surging feelings within him, yet also informed him of what surrounded him.[7]

After this second creation, the images of Genesis show us how the Adam humanity is assigned a locality as the realm of further development, where the tempests of the planetary evolution do not reach. The picture of the peace-filled paradise garden arises before us. The place is located 'in Eden in the east'. 'Eden' is a Sumerian word meaning 'the desert'. The garden is thus an island of life in a dying world. Man becomes Adam Kadmon (from the word *Kedem* meaning 'east'), bearer of a physical body that still carries the imprint of its pure divine origin, who is surrounded by a vast circumference of an already hardening material world.

2 ADAM – PARADISE – THE FALL

What is meant by the garden of paradise? The answer is found only by means of the law of repetitions of great and small evolutionary rounds. Through the small round of a region of life surrounded by a desert, we look back into great primordial aeons.

Once the entire earth was a garden of paradise. That was in its cosmic sun condition, the second of the great rounds, when sun and earth still permeated each other. One could call the Old Sun *the great cosmic paradise*. At that time, its entire body, woven out of warmth, light and air, was at the stage of the plant kingdom, shining in cosmic purity. Rudolf Steiner describes it in the following way:

> . . . we must not imagine that there were plants on the old Sun in their present form . . . Imagine a gaseous sphere, and within it weaving and sprouting light, living light, which causes the gaseous vapour to shoot and sparkle in radiant blossoms, while at the same time below there is an effort to check these luminous outbursts, an effort to make the Sun cohere round its centre. Then you have the inweaving of light, warmth and air in the ancient Sun evolution . . . At the time when the air, warmth and light sphere of the Sun was in its full splendour, when light, playing in the surface of the airy globe, threw off the sparkling blossoms of plant existence, these physically gaseous forms were actually the same as the plant species which can still be found today, though only in spiritual realms . . . Man was himself living a plant existence, and his bodily form was among those light forms in continuous play in the gaseous globe.[8]

The Old Sun is the home of what Goethe beheld and described as the archetypal plant (*Urpflanze*). It was a world of pure archetypes. Again following Goethe, this sphere could be called 'the realm of the mothers'. When Plato speaks of the world of living ideas of which all things are born later on, he too indicates the Old Sun condition of our earth. The light-filled purity and innocence, which we still find in the plants, was the property of all creation, including the human being, in that aeon.

When the cosmic development progressed to the Old Moon and Earth conditions, the pure sphere of the great cosmic paradise vanished until the sun condition was repeated in the second round of the Earth aeon, the Hyperborean epoch. Thus, the next small cycle became reality. We could call Hyperborea the *small cosmic paradise*. Here, compared with the Sun condition, are increasingly compact dynamics, and contours are becoming more earth-like.

Though the air element represents the greatest density attained, it is as if corporeal existence were pressing toward terrestrial solidity in all things so that geographical determinations for the Hyperborean region, 'the land beyond the north', are possible. A sunlit shining garden of luxuriant though not yet earth-rooted plant-beings must have covered the Arctic. Perhaps the petrified palms found in Spitzbergen point, like later witnesses, to the sun condition of those northern regions. As on the Old Sun, man and animal wove within plant-corporeality; but having completed the Old Moon condition, the kingdoms of plants, animals and human beings contrasted more with one another. In Hyperborea the image was reality: man together with the animals dwelt in the garden of cosmic innocence. This was the Golden Age, because the sun itself shone and sparkled through all earthly substance.

An event occurred in the middle of the Hyperborean era terminating the paradisal condition: sun and earth separated. A cosmic expulsion from paradise took place: earth had to leave the sun sphere of resounding, living light. Light and darkness separated and the dark earth substance received the sun's blessings only from outside. Limited to a much smaller volume, the earth rushes forward more urgently on its way to solidification.

We sense countless telluric transformations as a result of the sun's separation. Something like a tremendous primeval ice age must have occurred that caused a shifting of the warmth element from the poles to the region of the equator.[9] If the earth had been of solid structure at that time, one could speak of a gigantic rift from north to south, which would have been caused by the sun's withdrawal from the earth's body. All north-south polarities that our earth exhibits originate now; and as the Hyperborean era comes to an end, the stage of human progress shifts from the northern to the southern hemisphere. Geologists call this part of the earth covering the south of Asia, and the seas between Australia and Africa, Gondwana.

Is there no more room for the paradise of the Old Sun condition? Here we come to the garden of Eden, the island of life surrounded by a wasteland, of which Genesis speaks. Paradise finds its next smaller reality in the Lemurian age. What we could term the *great earthly paradise* evolves after the two cosmic paradises. How can we picture this?

From the north southward, the sun world of Hyperborea hardened and died away. As a result of a special compression of the fire element, the volcanically seething world of Lemuria developed in the south. On the border of both worlds at the northern edge of Lemuria, as a last southernmost emanation from Hyperborea, a sphere may have survived, which was capable of preserving an echo of the paradisal Sun condition. Staying with the somewhat drastic image of the north-south rift one could say: a vestige of the departing sun was left behind in the body of the earth. One region remained where the ethereal world of the sun could be reflected and continue more intrinsically than elsewhere in earth existence. This garden of the sun was assigned to Adam Kadmon, the young earth humanity, as a dwelling place. Divine grace erects a sun-bridge for man from the luminous heaven of the old solar existence into the world of dark lunar solidification. Man is allowed to remain for a time near the divine beings, who had actually bade the earth farewell, along with the sun. All around this island of nearness to God reigns desolation: chaotic life to begin with and volcanic seething, which leads in later epochs into desolate rigidity and produces the great deserts that exist on earth today. On this island, man is allowed to condense and solidify his body without being drawn into the tumultuous seething and solidifying process that sets in all around.

To form at least a faint concept of the spatial, geographical location of this earthly paradise, we may refer to the indications offered by the Old Testament. Four streams, Pishon, Gihon, Hiddekel (Tigris in the Greek) and Euphrates, branching out from a common source, give life to the great garden, and bear forth its emanations into the world. The two latter streams are clearly recognizable. The Gihon has always been traditionally equated with the Nile. It appears, however, that Havilah, the land of gold, around which the Pishon river flows, points to Arabia and Hindustan. But how can we speak of a common source for streams that flow in such opposite directions?

This is a riddle only if we stop at present-day conditions of compactness of the planet earth. In the Lemurian epoch, when the earth's body itself was still liquified and in motion, the streams could not have had the structure that a river assumes when it has to force its way through the earth's hard ground. The four streams of paradise can therefore only refer to streams within an ocean-like moving whole — similar to today's Gulf Stream. If we relate rivers of today to the four biblical names, they can only faintly indicate a region on earth, constituted in an entirely different way in the Lemurian age. Today, only a high mountain plateau could be the common source of several streams. Considering the world's consistency at that time, we must recognize that the image of the paradisal head-water region indicates a central fountainhead of forces. By means of a direct ethereal driving force, it was able to send far-reaching streams in all directions. The 'mountain' on which paradise was located was a dynamic 'plateau' concentrating cosmic-ether forces.

If, with a view to the maps of today, we accept the biblical names of the rivers as reference points for the paradise region of Lemuria, its location is determined in the south-west by the Gihon-Nile, in the north-east by the Euphrates and the Tigris, and in the centre, around which the Pishon flowed, by Arabia. The idea of a larger region emerges, but within it, our attention is drawn to a centre of radiation in the west of the whole area, where Palestine later came into being. This is in accord with the ancient traditions, which are certain that paradise extended from the east into the Promised Land.

For the imaginative consciousness that found expression in the legends, Palestine and particularly Jerusalem was the most ancient province of the world and also the site of Adam's creation. 'The Holy Land was created first of all, and the rest of the whole world after this.'[10] Throughout all the ages, when men beheld the sacrificial rock of Moriah, which later became the foundation stone of Solomon's temple and which is still held sacred today by Jews and Muslims, they had a feeling of a primordial beginning, of a foundation stone of the whole of world evolution. It was as if a remnant of Saturn had become visible on earth, a monument to the Saturn-like Polarean first round of the earth, where in its surging fire, creation only reached the stage of the mineral kingdom. 'The Lord had a special love for Adam, the first man. He created him at a pure and holy place. From what place did he take man? It was the place of the Holy Temple. It is said the Lord took a shovelful of earth from the ground on which the altar stood and made of it the first man.'[11] The *Treasure Cave* says: 'God formed Adam . . . out of the four elements . . . and he stretched himself and stood in the midst of the earth. And he set his feet on the place where in time to come the cross of the Redeemer would be erected. And thus was Adam created in Jerusalem.'[12]

The place of man's creation was also at the gate of paradise that spread out eastward, 'towards morning' from there. When Adam entered the garden, he walked, as it were, from Saturn to Sun, recapitulating the aeons of the earth's evolution. We shall have to discuss later why, when he left the garden, outside its gate he came upon the lunar terrestrial element instead of the holy primal weaving that once ruled there. 'After God had driven man out of Eden, man went and sat down in front of the Mount of Moriah. From there, his body had been fashioned; to that place he returned.'[13]

Although the possibility became ever less for the existence of a non-earthly realm within the earth, the paradise island was not destroyed all at once. A few places remained distinguished by their qualitative ethereal nature from their environment and these could be called *little earthly paradises*. Some regions of Asia Minor, from Galilee to Syria and Babylonia, were until recent times held to be the earthly location of paradise. In historical times, one of the most famous 'paradises' was the Oasis of Damascus. But it is useless to puzzle over the mystery of which was the genuine paradise. All of them are fragmentary remnants of a super-terrestrial shining, living island of the sun that once spread from Palestine north-east, east and south-east, in the midst of an earth existence that grew ever more moonlike. Today, there remains scarcely more than a hint, only a faint memory, of what had once survived there of a pre-physical condition of earth.

The ancient road that runs from Judea to Galilee and then continues as the Via Maris from the Sea of Galilee to Damascus and on to Babylonia, the path on which Abraham came from Chaldea into the land of the Jordan, on which Jacob travelled to the land of Laban, and on which later Paul went to Damascus, may well be an indication of the direction of the primeval migration concealed in the biblical words: 'Yahweh Elohim planted a garden eastward in Eden, and there he put the man whom he had formed' (Gen.2:8*B*).

For long periods, the young Adam Kadmon humanity worked on its corporeality and on the plantlike environment in which it was still deeply and harmoniously embedded (Gen.2:15).

The earth as a whole was increasingly entering a tremendous crisis. The earth planet was in danger of hardening into a moon. The condensation appeared to degenerate into lignification and calcification. How would this crisis be solved? A great cosmic separation was preparing. At first, the effects of the crisis reached the Adam humanity, dwelling in close proximity to the gods within the sunlike protected region, only in a diminished, hence beneficial way. Man's bodily sheath became denser, its integration with its surroundings decreased more and more. Hence, the inner nature ceased to be all-powerful over external nature and the imminent cosmic separation threw an advance shadow, which created its reflection in the human being. Among human beings, the separation into the two sexes began to develop. Instead of the bisexual human being, the male and female gender made their gradual appearance in differentiated human bodies. The Bible indicates this in the image of the creation of Eve. Slowly, the capacity for self-propagation diminished. But as the human being's universal preoccupation with the external surroundings decreased, soul forces were freed that could now turn inward. Man utilized only part of his forces for the formation of his corporeality and that of his descendants. This made possible the beginnings of an individual inner soul life. And in defending himself against the weight arising with the densification of matter, man activated the vertical force and attained upright form. Now, in addition to the organs of movement, he could develop the organs of creative activity, namely the hands.

During this time, the number of human beings incarnated on earth decreased more and more. It was as if souls could not cope with the lignifying earth and therefore chose other cosmic spaces instead of the earth realm. From the terrestrial standpoint, this is shown in that the old form of reproduction and birth subsided owing to the separation of the sexes, while the time had not yet come for the new form to take place through the union of the two.

As a solution of the great cosmic crisis, a mighty telluric event in the middle of the Lemurian epoch completely changed the body of the earth. The long-impending cosmic separation became reality. As in a final contraction and intensification of its volcanic force, the earth thrust out the moon. Thus, the surplus of hardening forces that threatened to suffocate the earth was diverted. From outside, the moon now works beneficially upon the earth. The earth finds its balance between sun and moon. The repetition of the Old Moon age is completed. The earth at last comes into its own.

The event of the moon separation is known to natural science. Professor E. Kayser says: 'Actually, moon and earth form a double planet that rotates around the sun in common point of gravity. Originally, both bodies must have formed one cohesive mass from which the moon was separated only later.'[14] But the fundamental importance that this cosmic separation holds for the right consideration of all palaeontological, geological and geographic problems will only be recognized if the external facts of the earth's layers and the outlines of the continents are not presupposed in the later conditions of solidity familiar to ourselves.[15] For that age, there can be no question of a rigid, crystallized form of the earth's rock and mineral ingredients. Everything is still in a state of flux. Though the lignification and hardening process progressed in frightening proportion, it was still far from becoming solid ground and rock formation. It is only through the moon separation, which, to use the geological terminology, falls into the Mesozoic era of earth's evolution (Jurassic and Triassic periods, chalk formations), that a clear separation begins into land and sea masses, and the continents start to form.

If one pictures earth substance in a still half-fluid state, then the moon's exit from earth is not quite so unimaginable. Rudolf Steiner once described that it could help form an idea to recall how a smaller drop separates from a large drop.

We have to be careful to distinguish between the one mighty cosmic catastrophe and the process which occurred both before and after it in some areas of the earth. The place of the great moon exit must be sought in the region where the Pacific Ocean is today. Guenther Wachsmuth points out that in contrast to all other oceans the floor of the Pacific lacks the sial layer, because, along with the main bulk of its substance, the moon took away this upper layer of the earth's crust, thus leaving behind a 'wound'.[16]

Along with the formation of the continents, now beginning, the accompanying process must have shown on the earth's body where traces of the transition from the Hyperborean to the Lemurian condition existed. Most noticeably in the southern hemisphere, today's global map makes evident the recurrent tendency towards the triangular form of the continents. South America, Africa, and India all end in a sharp angle pointing south. The well-known geographer, Eduard Suess, traces this form-tendency back to a whole system of deep faults and rift valleys that meet mostly in pointed angles and that the earth's body bears as marks of great catastrophes of transformation.[17] Through the shapes of the big continents in the southern hemisphere, one can indeed look back into the dynamics of that great cosmic event in the time of the Adam-humanity in the middle of the Lemurian epoch.

Now, among the big triangle shapes, there lies a small, particularly well-shaped triangle — in a sense a model and prototype — namely the Sinai Peninsula; leading again to the region around Palestine as a centre of forces of the great formative processes. At the southern point of the Sinai Peninsula, two particularly important and descriptive rifts meet: the great East African Rift and the Syrian Rift, which, coming from Asia Minor and Syria and continuing into the Red Sea, make Palestine the land with the lowest elevation on earth, and because of this, a truly unique country. Considering both rifts together, E. Kayser says: 'In no part of the world . . . have such enormous and deep rift valleys been detected. If the above rifts are connected, this would result in a fault zone of no less than seven thousand kilometres. It is correct to say that this is perhaps the biggest, most outstanding gash on the face of the earth.'[18] Guenther Wachsmuth, who can point to the triangular tendency as essential proof of the teaching concerning the ethereal formative forces, has brought the Syrian Rift and its southern continuation as the most significant tear in the earth's countenance into close connection with the processes that convulsed and formed the earth organization during the moon separation.[19]

Owing to the special condition of the region assigned to it, the Adam humanity survived the mighty eruption. Paradise is like a great Noah's ark and bears mankind across into a new period of the earth.

The moon separation, however, must have entailed two consequences for mankind. On one hand, the cosmic nightmare of the peril of lignification is now over: human beings can once again incarnate on earth in greater numbers and fashion their world. On the other hand, the realm of paradise could not be for ever spared the tumultuous transformations of the earth's surface, which now more than ever surged up from south and east as a result of the mighty upheavals within the earth's interior.

For the second half of the Lemurian epoch, spiritual research describes a lofty germinal condition of cultural life, irradiated by the glow of mankind's morn, in the Adam colony, which is the advancing part of humanity.[20]

As yet, man's every stirring of soul is instinctive; this implies that only the inspiring consciousness of higher beings is the source of all soul-life and action. The capacity of thinking is still distant; everything is will and feeling, but in them man is borne by gods. The male human beings primarily develop the will — still completely extending upward into divine forces — to which the kingdoms of nature, having remained pliable, are obedient. The leaders among the human males appear like powerful 'white magicians'. In the element of feeling, the human females early on develop an imaginative conceptual life, colourful and intense, the germinal beginning of memory, which in the Atlantean epoch is to take the place of instinct. They are therefore capable of being the leaders of the masculine forces. Where matriarchy and the woman's role of leadership were in force[21] among nations until historical antiquity, an echo of the primeval Lemurian culture has survived longest. As yet, all man's activities tend more to artistic creation than laborious work. Solemnity and harmony stream from divine realms into the human being's ways and doings still undisturbed by self-will. Divine grace pulsates particularly in the very first rudiments of speech, which mankind attains toward the end of the Lemurian epoch. Higher beings impart the word element, borne by themselves until then, to men. The divine Word becomes human language.

What spiritual research states concerning the location of this development still holds true:

> The place on earth in which this stock of a coming race of men was developed was especially suited for this purpose. It was one where the then still turbulent earth had become fairly calm . . . While it was to develop a hot climate, it was by and large free of volcanic activity.
>
> Human nature could unfold more calmly and peacefully here than in the other regions of the earth.[22]

But the tempests of evolution approached the protected realm more closely.

Before the moon separation, the earth's rapid lignification had produced quite curious forms in the kingdom of living beings. While human beings in their delicate, pliable corporeality were only capable of surviving in small numbers in an especially protected region, animal species which had descended earlier than man into solidification could exist on the remaining surface of the earth. They were a true pictorial expression of the gigantic crisis in earth evolution. It is the time when the great dragon monsters of prehistory develop: the ichthyosauri, plesiosauri, dinosaurs, and so on, whose skeletons or fossil remains are found in the Mesozoic layers of the earth.[23] One cannot imagine that man existed side by side with these sons of chaos and of the nether world. Indeed, no trace of the human being has been unearthed in the rock strata where these animals are found, for at that time man's body was as yet not physically dense enough to leave remains like those of the already harder animal bodies. Then too, decimated to a small number, humanity found itself in a different region of the earth; indeed, one could almost say in view of the different nature of this region: in another sphere.

An image frequently recurring in the mythologies of people has its reality in that age. A defenceless human form is on an island, threatened by a monstrous dragon out of the surrounding, surging sea. The Adam humanity found itself in this condition just before the moon separation. The realm of peace was surrounded by a surging, dangerous world, in which dragons existed, and which is symbolized in the hardened dragon form. The myth of Lucifer's fall is connected with the origin of these monstrous dragon-like creatures in Lemurian prehistory. The first great 'battle with the dragon' took place in the superterrestrial spiritual regions at this time.[24] Beings who should have accompanied the normal path of mankind's destiny could not await their time, and developed a premature will of their own in the supersensory spheres. This will longed for corporeal densification, which at that time existed neither in heaven nor on earth. Through the Michaelic power, the guardian of pure spirit will, the forces of self-will were thrust down to earth, where they became the causes of an intensified hardening process. And on earth the dragon forms appeared as images of the self-will that had been cast out of the heavenly heights. This is the prototype of Michael's battle with the dragon that recurs in all epochs. In heaven, the dragon is defeated and thrust down to the earth, where he then appears as man's enemy and tempter (Rev.12:9,12).

The moon crisis is a great attack of the dragon against earth and mankind. By means of the moon separation, this attack is warded off with divine help. But the tempter does not rest.

Just because of the moon's removal from the earth's body — although the earth as a whole is freed from the danger of complete calcification — a vast death process commences. Around the lunar fissure, the earth turns into a region of ashes and slag left by an incalculable world conflagration. Something like a counter-paradise arises. Just as paradise was the remnant left by the separating sun, so, at the point of the moon's exit, a landscape forms that is covered with moonlike substance, a remnant of the moon. It is probably not incorrect to assume that the so-called great 'desert plateau' that includes the deserts of Africa, Arabia, Asia and Australia, which in fact form a circle around the areas of the Lemurian continent, has a connection with the great world cataclysm.[25]

Within this plateau, the desert in southern Palestine — in the Sinai Peninsula and in Judea around the Dead Sea — occupies a special place of significance. It is not of great expanse, but quali-tatively it seems to be of archetypal nature, just as the Sinai Peninsula is archetypal for the form of the southern continents. It is no flat, sandy desert, but one of ravined mountains. Around the southern part of the Jordan Valley and the Dead Sea it drops deep into the earth and makes an impression as of a nether world. The desolate masses of cretaceous rock, frequently sitting directly on top of volcanic porphyry, truly give an impression as if a segment of the moon had adhered to the earth. While this region received its present form only in much later times — we shall refer back to this when considering Abraham's era — we do not go wrong in supposing that the main archetypal character, for which we could designate the desert of Judea *the* desert, dates back to the middle of the Lemurian epoch. Hell advances to the very portals of paradise. Can the paradisal region survive, when in its vicinity the earth tears apart and the nether world looks up out of the open abyss?

The dragon force of solidification, born of premature self-will, surges closer and closer to the Adam humanity. The tempter's power approaches now, not outwardly as gigantic dragon-like animals, but in a more inward manner. The introduction of the forces of densification into his corporeality held drawbacks for the human being, but it also enabled him to fashion his body into an instrument of a completely new consciousness. As long as he inhabited a body that remained free of the impact of material substance, an abundant picture-consciousness welled through his soul and brought him divine revelations. But this was not his own. He was only the arena of a consciousness appertaining to the gods. The hardening of his organs, in particular his head, entailed the loss of the divine magical power and the old picture-consciousness, but as into a crystallization point, into these surging images could fall the seed of self-consciousness. Man's consciousness became less abundant and mighty, but he could experience it more as directed and brought about by himself, and thereby begin to experience his own being.

The myth of the Fall depicts the point in evolution when the human being yields to the allurement of the new consciousness which, in the inner life of imagination and ideation, the female human being had already approached more closely. Man thus lays the first foundation for a self-aware individual nature within himself, but he thereby allows the hardening forces, embodied in the external surroundings as dragon and serpent, into his own being. The threatening influences of solidification gain admittance into the formerly protected island of the paradise region. The solar and godlike forces, which could remain present in this one spot on earth till now, had to recede into supersensory spheres. The remnant of the sun sphere leaves earth. The myth of man's expulsion from paradise is not to be thought of as human beings having to leave a region that nevertheless would have had continuance on earth. Paradise itself comes to an end, and one day men find themselves on desolate, hard soil in the very same place where once the garden of the sun-ether sphere flourished. The Fall is a cosmic event. The curse addressed to man: 'Cursed is the ground because of you' (Gen.3:17) in itself represents the loss of paradise from one aspect.

Man finds himself and the earth changed. 'In the sweat of your face you shall eat bread' (Gen.3:19). The relationship between human beings becomes different, for the old manner of procreation and birth becomes extinct. The new consciousness is acquired at the price of losing sovereignty over nature. Henceforth, for the purpose of procreation, the two sexes have to co-operate externally, and only the female gives birth. To Eve come the words: 'In pain you shall bring forth children' (Gen.3:16).

The image of the expulsion from paradise also points in all likelihood to migrations westward into the regions of the Atlantean epoch, which saved the most advanced part of humanity and the culture so far attained. The whole Lemurian continent finally fell victim to the raging fires of the earth's interior and the eruptions of volcanoes active everywhere. The flaming swords of the cherubim flash forth, who now stand as guardians at the gate of

2 ADAM – PARADISE – THE FALL

paradise which has withdrawn from earth. Legendary traditions mention that after the Fall man returned to the site of his creation, to Jerusalem. Once, the holy Saturnian age had pulsated there. Now the desolate maw of the earth opened, with the lunar world of the Judean desert. Surrounded by desert, glistening today as from a nether world towards the sightseer standing on the heights of Jerusalem, the Dead Sea is still occasionally called by the ancient name of the 'Kadmonite Sea'. Perhaps this is due to a memory of times when the portals still stood open to the Tree of Life in the land of Adam Kadmon. Returning to the site of primeval beginning, man finds that his home has turned into wasteland. The island of the blessed is no more. Tragedy enters the destinies of earth-humanity.

In the attempt to form approximate historical conceptions of the fate of the Adam humanity and the region designated as paradise, we have repeatedly come up against the problems of *Palestine's geography*. Palestine always appears to have been a kind of median centre of gravity for evolution: in the time between Hyperborea and Lemuria as well as later on between Lemuria and Atlantis, and again between Atlantis and Asia, the matrix of the post-Atlantean cultures. Even today, it holds a key position between the three great continents of Asia, Europe and Africa, both geographically and in regard to the character of the land. The strip of land between the Jordan Valley and the Mediterranean, illuminated by the Homeric sun that also shines upon Greece and casts the breath of Europe and Greece over the coast of Asia Minor, not only looks across to Europe but essentially belongs to it. The land east of the Jordan has the dimensions and the mystique of the Asian Orient. The south, extending from the Judean desert and the Dead Sea into the Sinai mountain range, has the grave intrinsic darkness of the African continent. In summarizing it may be permissible to express an idea that resulted from seeing the Palestinian landscape and which grew increasingly in definition and certainty. At first it proved fruitful in the comprehension of the Gospels; but then, more and more clearly it seemed to hold a key to the great cosmogonic secrets that we circle around in the historical penetration of humanity's beginnings.

A fundamental ethereal-geographical polarity dominates Palestine. Probably nowhere else on earth is there a soul-contrast of such forceful impact as that between Galilee and Judea. The landscape around the Sea of Galilee is rich in ethereal forces and even today, in spite of the dusty, withered condition of the formerly Oriental cultural region, it is filled with a completely other-worldly, sunlike ethereal element. In some places, where the secret of Galilee is present, particularly on the north-west shore of the lake and on the summit of Mount Tabor, one cannot help but feel transported from the realm of physical phenomena near to the sphere of primeval phenomena. One does not experience *just any* lake or mountain. What is beheld here seems in the most wondrous way to be identical with its own spiritual archetype. And the more imaginative Christian tradition did again and again designate the Sea of Galilee as the lake of lakes and Mount Tabor as the mountain of mountains. The ancient Russian *Book of the Dove*,[26] for example, speaks of the 'mother of all lakes', and the 'mother of all mountains'. The realm of 'the Mothers', the sphere of primeval archetypes, which comprised the essence of both paradises — the Old Sun and the Hyperborean existence — and diffused itself as spherical radiance within the earthly paradise of the Lemurian epoch, seems to open. Galilee is the sphere of miracle; laws of existence are discernible there that completely differ from the ordinary laws of nature. Perhaps the faint trace of the ancient paradise region has survived there; in the most southern and western, and perhaps most archetypal of the small earthly paradises, which once may have extended beyond the Oasis of Damascus to north and east.

From the south, the hard desert and dead topography of Judea opposes the traces of paradise. If, in Galilee, one seems at times to have been transported into the sun sphere, in the low-lying gorges of the Judean desert, confronting the fantastic rock formations, devoid of human, animal or plant life, which surround the life-threatening brine of the Dead Sea, one cannot but feel now the land of the moon: of the Fall; earth has fallen into the depths of hell. It is as if, here, a moon remnant had been left hanging on the edge of one of the rifts, when the earth was freed from the threat of calcification.

The two seas, the Sea of Galilee and the Dead Sea, exhibit the contrast between life and death. Through them, the symbols of the sun and moon epochs and perhaps even actual traces of the sun and moon separation confront each other. Paradise and the nether world meet. One understands more and more why, since ancient times, this land has been called the centre and navel of the world, and why the great events of the old and new covenant, from Adam to Christ, had to take place here. The soil of the Promised Land does in fact reveal a concentration and quintessence of the whole planetary evolution of our earth.

3 Primordial Revelation: Provision for the Human Spirit

In the mythical picture of Genesis, Adam and Eve are shocked over their nakedness after having eaten of the Tree of Knowledge. This indicates both the acquisition of a dense physical sheath and the loss of a light-filled divine one. 'What was Adam's clothing? The cloud of the Lord enveloped him always. But when he ate of the fruits of the tree . . . the Lord's cloud vanished from him and he beheld himself naked and bare.'[27] A time arises when man feels himself stripped of the radiant aura and glory which formerly surrounded him.

'After Adam's creation', so says the second chapter of the *Treasure Cave*, 'when the angels beheld his magnificent appearance, they were moved by the beauty of his looks. For they saw that the form of his countenance was aflame in glorious brilliance like the sun's orb; his eyes' brilliance like that of the sun, and his body's radiance like that of a crystal.'

The idea of the paradisal body of light has always claimed attention in the ancient, still imaginative theology. In a conversation with his students, J. Albrecht Bengel was once asked about 'the light nature of Adam's body in his state of innocence'. Bengel answered:

> It is certain that Adam's integrity, indeed illustriousness, was most excellent in his state of innocence; for example, as the face of a lively, happy man shines with vivaciousness; and as St Stephen's countenance emitted a radiance . . . it could not have been otherwise but that likenesses of the magnificence of Adam's soul had to be in his body as well. God is light; since Adam was made in the image of God, he also had to have the nature of light and from it emanations must have shone forth out of his body, particularly from his countenance.[28]

The cloud of light, in which paradisal man was clothed, represents not only a state of existence but also a state of consciousness.

It is hard to form an idea of man's consciousness before he had a solid bodily sheath. Nothing is found in it of the wakeful egoity of today's thought-consciousness. Yet it would be quite wrong to assume that primitive conditions prevailed at the beginning of the human spirit's development. The opposite is the case. Humanity sets out with a divine revelation consciousness. Thoughts of the gods envelop man and stream like a spiritual breath of air in colourful images through his soul. At the same time, those swirling images must have contained a primordial musical element. Even while man does not yet possess an organ of sight, he can hear the resounding cosmic Word through the ear of his entire corporeality. The germinal beginning of human consciousness upon earth is *primordial revelation*.

Until recent times all sections of mankind were aware of the fact of revelation. It was one of the most important pillars of ancient theology. Only when world conceptions became coldly abstract and materialistic did it pass into oblivion. The presumptuous theory was formed that humanity rose from a spirit-devoid animalistic darkness to the unsurpassed mental clarity of scientifically disciplined intellect.

A knowledge of primeval revelation has been most vividly and unerringly retained where it was recorded in pictorial form. We arrive herewith at the particularly important picture-concept of the Book of Adam which says that an archangel brought to Adam, dwelling in paradise, a book in which could be read the loftiest cosmic secrets.[29]

Countless books of wisdom and secret writings of antiquity have been depicted as versions of this Book of Adam in order to connect them to primordial revelation. A particularly valuable example that has come down to us is the Syrian *Liber Adami* by the Mandaeans in which secrets of the starry heavens, the kingdoms of nature and the human being are recorded in solemn ritualistic language and abundant mantric repetition.[30] Also preserved in the Syrian language, the *Treasure Cave*, the present-day version of which originates from the great Eastern theologian Ephraem of Syrus, is described as the 'Christian Book of Adam'. In imaginative pictures it presents the history of the world and its redemption. Another book going back to primeval traditions, *The Agriculture of the Nabataeans*, belongs to the literary issues which the concept of the Book of Adam found in historical times.

3 PRIMORDIAL REVELATION

It refers all the way back to Adam as one of the greatest initiates.* As late as the Middle Ages, many spiritual streams, for example the Cathars, maintained that they were in possession of the Book of Adam, and thus laid claim to be acting in direct continuance of primal wisdom.

According to Talmudic traditions, it was the Archangel Michael who gave the book of primordial wisdom to Adam: 'From it, Michael gave to Adam the foundations of knowledge and Adam became wise.'[32] But to begin with the sun-radiant wisdom of God streams around man more in the form of light and power than it arises consciously within him as his own. Man is still close to his prototype, by means of which he is an image of the Godhead and at the same time a sum total and concentration of the archetypes of all the other kingdoms of creation. The human being is a microcosmic repetition of the macrocosmic surge of ethereal archetypes that once filled the whole of the earth planet in its Old Sun condition. The prototypes of all of creation's beings find their essential centre, their quintessence, in the human being and radiate around him as in a paradisal auric body of light. It is man himself in whom the single pages of the book of archetypes are bound together into one volume. In his own nature, man bears the Book of Life which the archangel of the sun bestows on him.

It is because of this that the Adam-being actually stands as Lord in the midst of all creatures. The images that lit up in God's creative consciousness, and thereby consolidated into existence, light up also in the Adam-being and, pulsating through him as magic will, make him co-creator. The book, which is man, does not consist of written but of spoken words. Even before the existence of an articulate language in today's sense, all the manifestations of man's being are like name-giving words that resound from the 'book' as if it were read: the creative Word of the divine-creative powers re-echoes upon the earth.

---

* As an example of the way such occult writings are linked to the primeval cycles of humanity's evolution, we quote a section from the writings of the Arab philosopher al-Maqrizi: 'Abu Bekr Achmed Ali ben Wachshiya says in his book *The Agriculture of the Nabataeans* that he translated it from the language of the Kasdaeians. Three of their sages composed this book: Ssagrit, Yanbushat and Qutama. The first, who appeared in the seventh millennium of the 7000 years of Saturn — the millennium that Saturn and Sun have in common — started on it; the second, who flourished at the end of the same millennium, completed it; and the third, who appeared after 4000 years of the seven-thousand year sun cycle, rounded it off.'[31]

> Wherever Adam took out the Book and read from it, the earth trembled and swayed like a ship on the sea. If he spoke from it before a mountain, the mountain melted like wax. If he spoke from it before the ocean, the sea left its boundaries like an overflowing vessel of water. When he spoke from the Book in front of a fire, the fire became ashes; and when he spoke from it before lions, panthers, bears and evil animals, they stood as if silenced . . . If he spoke from it before a tree, the tree yielded its fruit ahead of time.[33]

The already objectified imagination of the legend expresses exactly the same facts as does the clear description given by the spiritual researcher concerning the as yet marked fluidity and pliancy of nature and the magic primeval culture existing shortly after the middle of the Lemurian epoch.

This book of archetypes is lost from man's being through the Fall and with it his own inherent share in divine wisdom and power.

> So long as Adam was still in Eden, he sought in the Book and every day availed himself of the treasures of the Lord; the loftiest secrets were revealed to him, of which even the supreme servants knew nought. But when Adam . . . had transgressed against the commandments of the Lord, the Book flew away from him. Then Adam beat his head and stepped into the waters of the Gihon up to his neck. And the water made Adam's body spongy and his radiance was gone.[34]

Here, the most puzzling question arises. Why did the human being succumb to the temptation of eating from the Tree of Knowledge since he possessed the Book of Divine Wisdom? Though in his nature man possessed the Book of Life, and the radiant will of the cosmic Word inscribed therein shone forth from his being, his consciousness could participate in the effects of the book only in a deep dream-filled sleep. He could not yet read the book for himself. What was written therein streamed through his will, but as yet did not become the content of his cognition. So he coveted the ability to read it, and he ate of the Tree of Knowledge. He then possessed the ability, but the Book had vanished from him.

Yet man is not left without a 'book' after the Fall into sin. Legendary traditions relate that the archangel Raphael, endowed with healing powers, returned the lost book to him. But the book which he now possesses is a different one. Just as there is a Tree of Life and a Tree of Knowledge, so also a Book of Life and a

3 PRIMORDIAL REVELATION

Book of Knowledge. Man has exchanged the Book of Life for that of Knowledge. The two books are related as sun to moon. The sun rays forth its own light, the moon bestows only mirrored light. As long as man bore the actual archetypes of all existence within him, a self-luminous, sunlike world shone forth from him and determined his being. But he was only the stage for divine knowledge, not the subject of his own. Only after the divine ideas surging through him could rebound on mirror-surfaces in his being, could they also become the content of his consciousness. For this, man had to forfeit his state of being illumined — and weave dark density into his being. And so, from the Fall, the descent into matter, the exchange of the Book of Archetypes for that of mirror-reflections follows for man. The solar will-forces of existence grow dim, the lunar light of self-consciousness begins to fill the soul. It was probably at this point in time that man began to develop the organ of sight, his physical eyes. When the light of the spirit grew dim for man, he prepared himself for perception of physical light.

Vast, interpenetrating processes of evolution are concentrated in the pictures of the Fall into sin. The battle of the sun and moon forces for the soul of man lasts through long aeons of time: a battle in which the lunar world had to be victorious for the sake of the later development of man's individual being.

The biblical account describes a scene for us in which the Divine Power himself leads man to the forbidden Tree of Knowledge. It is the one in which man by divine command and through the power of God's nearness bestows names to the animal kingdom. This image is the biblical reflection of the miracle and power of the Book of Adam. By means of the Book of Life, man bears the archetypes, the 'names' of the animals, as essence within himself. The animals, who as yet do not exist at all in individual physical forms, permeate the ethereal-physical realm of corporeality only as species, as group-soul forms. Just as man can sense that he is perceived by the divine beings above him, they can feel themselves radiantly reflected and recognized by him, though he has by no means awakened to self-perception. If he is to progress to the faculty of *conscious* name-giving, the archetypes within him must first dim to mirror images. This takes place through the calcareous densification processes which the lunar element injects into the being of man.

Now a relationship begins between the human and the animal

kingdoms. A lecture of Rudolf Steiner throws light on the scene of name-giving in the paradise legend. It describes how certain formative forces proceeding from the moon become active in earthly calcareous processes, and on the one hand bring about the forms of the animal kingdom, on the other, the faculty of reflective thought in the human organism.

> Outside in space are the manifold animal forms; within us, in our intellect, are the thought-forms. These are, in fact, the animal forms projected into the spiritual . . . But as the animal kingdom needs the lime-formation to build up its forms in the outer world, so we need, as it were, a fine inner lime deposit, a lime formation, in order to become clever.[35]

In the scene of name-giving we see balance between sun and moon, between the Book of Life and the Book of Knowledge. Between the condition when light-filled man still bore within him the archetypes and names of the animals, and the later state in which their mirror images become discernible in his consciousness, the Fall into knowledge slowly commences, and while it makes of man an individual being, it pervades him at the same time with physical density and hardness.

Michael's power bestows on man the Book of Adam, the sunlike revelation; at the same time in evolution it casts the dragon out of the spiritual realms down to earth and mankind. Therefore, simultaneously with the gift of revelation man confronts the danger of obscuration. In the spirit realms, Michael conquers the power of premature self-will and the solidification connected with it. On earth, man must come to terms with it himself. Michael gives him only the weapon for this conflict, the primal revelation.*

Though the Book of the Sun has paled to the Book of the Moon through the power of the Serpent, man is able through the primal revelation to keep alive the substance of divine light in all earthly perception. The Book of Adam represents the great divine provision for consciousness. The history of humanity in the times of

---

* The *Treasure Cave* (chapter 3) speaks of the simultaneity of Lucifer's fall and man's investure with glory: 'When Satan was thrust from heaven, Adam was lifted up and drove into paradise in a fiery chariot'. The Revelation to John also points to the connection between the conflicts which arise for man through the fall of the dragon, and the armament he receives from the spiritual world for the battle. Here too the image of a book is used. In Chapter 10, a macrocosmic world of angels hands man a little book which he is to eat. Chapter 12 describes how the Archangel Michael thrusts the dragon from heaven to earth. The book and the adversary force confront man at the same time.

the Old Testament is one of gradual consumption, of using up the gifts of this Book.

Thus, looking back to the middle periods of ancient Lemuria, seeing the radiant island of the paradisal region, the seat of the Adam colony, rising out of the dark glimmering volcanic earth, one becomes aware not only of a site of cosmic innocence but also the source of a stream of wisdom from which mankind was to be sustained on its path of earthly destiny. Paradise is not only a protected area that remains related to the sun on an earth increasingly moonlike, it is at the same time the first great mystery centre of humanity. Behind the name Adam, which does point also to a certain individual, there light up, gathered around a supreme leader, figures of leaders whom the gods educate as their human successors and through whom, in time, the gods seek to be relieved of humanity's guidance.

In a cataclysmic cosmic thunderstorm and fire rain, the light of this primordial mystery centre threatens to go out and so must be guided to other regions of the earth not caught up in Lemuria's volcanic destruction.

The westward Adam-migrations begin, which are behind the pictorial image of leaving paradise. Through these migrations the quintessence of Lemurian culture is rescued and carried to where humanity is to enter upon its next great level of evolution, the regions of the Atlantean continent.

4 Cain – Seth – Enoch: Atlantean Humanity

In the paradisal dawn of humanity, death did not yet exist. Procreation occurred inwardly in the individual hermaphroditic human being and produced no dense bodies that retained any sort of independent form when the souls left them behind. Descending to earth and ascending again from it, the soul-spirit human beings followed in the wake of a lofty inhalation and exhalation process of Mother Earth. In procreating, earth-man placed himself at the service of earth's in-breathing. For the purpose of a sojourn on earth, man — together with the great Mother — beckoned and drew in a soul already inwardly close, placing forces from his own body of energies at its disposal. And when the soul again followed the earth's movement of breathing out and was inhaled by the extraterrestrial cosmos, it merely transferred its existence for a while to a different state without experiencing a tear or break in its still deep dream-consciousness. The delicate corporeal sheaths which had served on earth as its dwelling did not fall to the ground as a corpse, but were presently rewoven into the living, flowing totality of life of all fellow creatures.

Death's features were still completely like those of its brother, sleep. Just as we dwell outside our body with our soul-spirit being at night without experiencing a break in life, while we allow ourselves to be inhaled, as it were, by another world, so, in that ancient time, souls entered the extraterrestrial portions of their great cosmic course of life. The rhythmic transitions back and forth were actually experienced as no more than great breaths, in no way as a separation or loss.

So long as there was no death, man lived in permanence. He could only gradually awaken to the experience of time. In regard to this primeval age, it is also completely senseless to speak of man's life lasting for a certain number of years. Aside from the fact that the sun, moon and earth had first to come into a corre-lation resembling that of today in order to bring about periodic cycles and time measures of days, months and years as we know them, there was at first no fixed boundary for man's course of life by means of birth and death. When the soul left the earth, it resembled our falling asleep in the evening, knowing that we will awaken in the morning. Many great days of life spent on earth combined into a year of eternity. Man still had an aeon-like, eternal life in which many rings formed a chain. And inasmuch as such names as Adam and Eve not only refer to a whole group of human beings but also to certain individuals, it is indeed not absurd to speak of their life span as numbering thousands of years, if we want to use modern concepts of time at all.

It was only after the moon separation and the Fall into sin, when the new form of reproduction commenced, that death also took on a different appearance. The bodies grew denser, more substantial, and became subject to gravity; and the co-operation of the sexes, now clearly differentiated into male and female, was required for their procreation. The great Mother Earth was in-creasingly replaced by the human mother. What Mother Earth had contributed to man's birth by her fertile breath now changed into the labour pains by which a woman became a mother. And along with the pains of birth, the shudders of death became the lot of mankind. When the soul again left the earth, the body, born in pain, no longer remained as a living link in nature's surging forces. The corpse was a factor from now on, and man gradually learned to recognize decay.

The developments and transitions towards the end of the Lemurian epoch, so far alluded to, form a deeply moving drama, which unfolds before us if we penetrate through the Genesis images of the myth of Cain and Abel.

The birth of Cain is hidden in a veil of greatest secrets. After Eve has given birth to her first son, Genesis has her saying the darkly mysterious words: 'As husband I have gained Yahweh' (Gen.4:1).* This sentence points to a twofold divine blessing that played a part in Cain's birth. The first has to do with the great cosmic changes that have occurred in the earth's being. Mention has been made of the descriptions given by spiritual science concerning humanity's condition at the time of the moon crisis. Because earth was rapidly lignifying, becoming more and more moonlike, fewer and fewer human souls found it possible to sojourn upon it, and humanity dwindled to a handful of souls. The moon separation causes a powerful sigh of relief in the cosmos. A nightmarish weight is removed from the earth. Gradually, the number of human beings on earth increases as souls find their way back again from other planetary spheres. In every birth a cosmic blessing resounds, and as men turned to the moon now revolving around the earth, they sensed the spiritual power, the Father of Births, to whom they owed the new opportunity for life on earth. This cosmic blessing reverberates in the birth of Cain and the words Eve utters about it. Through the figure of Cain, who is the first-born of the new world-condition, we behold human souls descending again to the earth after the moon separation.

But yet another secret is connected with Eve's words. Not Adam, but a divine power is the father of Cain. The miracle of virginal birth envelops Eve as the mother of Cain. Legendary tradition expresses this in its own way: 'Her pregnancy was without suffering and the birth without labour pains.'[36] The curse, 'In sorrow thou shalt bring forth children,' inflicted upon Eve after the Fall, has not yet taken effect. If Cain is a first-born on one side, he is a 'last-born' on the other. Although the Fall has already

---

* The translation, 'I have gotten a man with the help of the LORD', arises from the perplexing riddle posed by the original text.

GENESIS

become reality, the hermaphroditic way of birth occurs one last time. Divine laws of life and the sun manifest themselves one more time upon an earth that has already passed through its moon condition, and what was formerly natural is considered a miracle after the new laws of nature have become effective.

Only with the birth of Abel, the curse of the Fall is fulfilled. In his figure we recognize the kind of humanity which owes its earthly existence to the duality of the sexes. The moon birth has taken the place of the sun birth. Only now, after the repetition of the sun and moon existence in the paradise of Hyperborea and Lemuria, does the time of the actual complete earth existence commence for mankind.

Comprehension of the great cosmic development also lifts the fearful myth of fratricide out of a primitive, merely human and moralistic conception. In the Fall, man had attained a knowledge of good and evil. As the germ of self-perception and self-consciousness began to form, he began to distinguish among the colourful, pictorial impressions flowing round him. One thing enticed him, another repelled him. With this arose the necessity for choice between one thing or another. Man ceased to be merely an organ of the higher divine will streaming through him; self-will was born, and through the activity of new mysterious forces of duality, a chasm opened up between God and man.

Abel bears the heritage of the Fall in his nature. He is the normal man of his time who knows good from evil, and who experiences himself separated from and placed opposite divine existence. In him lives the longing for reconnection of the severed elements, homesickness for the lost paradise. Thus, Abel is the first religious human being. Religion, reunion, and reverence for the being of God who no longer is united with man, is born in the Abel-humanity. Abel's offering is the beginning of religious history.

In Cain, the laws of primordial time are still effective. He is born of paradise, not the Fall, and therefore knows not what is good or evil. Forces of cosmic unity permeate him, although now he too shares a denser corporeal organization and the individualization connected with it. 'Cain' means 'the able one'. The magic forces of ability and will, which, in a divine manner, had been alive in man in the primordial time of paradise-Lemuria, now fill him in a more human manner. The Abel human being has surrendered the sunlike potentials of the will. In him they fade moonlike into forces of consciousness. The Tree of Life has withered in him in favour of the Tree of Knowledge. Cain inwardly bears the solar Tree of Life, but he carries it into the world of self-will. What becomes of the Tree of Life in a world which death has entered? Human magic arises — a two-edged sword. It can cause great benefits as well as great harm; it can bring about life as well as death. Abel knows good and evil, Cain does not, but he possesses the power to do good or evil in a superhuman way.

The biblical myth relates that Cain brought the fruit of the fields and Abel the first-born of the herd as offerings, but that only Abel's offering was accepted by the god Yahweh. Secrets of historical development are concealed within this image. With his sun-gifts from the plant kingdoms, Cain serves a divine spirit who has already retreated from the guidance of human evolution. The sun deity of the Elohim has turned the sceptre of development over to Yahweh, the spiritual being of the moon. Cain's gifts correspond to an already bygone aeon. They are no longer in keeping with the age. On the other hand, Abel's moonlike sacrifice of animals* corresponds with the spirit leading the present. Cain's magic will-power accumulates as wrath in a world which seems to play dead.

The tragedy Cain encounters is all the more revealed as through his offerings that have become untimely an important progress of cultural life nevertheless comes to expression. Cain is the creative human being in contrast to Abel, just because he does belong to a vanished world condition. Abel, while he is a man of the present, develops only the ability to nurture and preserve the old, not the power to produce innovations. Rudolf Steiner describes[37] how an important modification in man's diet is expressed in Cain's offering of the fruits of the field: to milk, as the old nourishment of the moon, is added that of the upper parts and fruits of the plants which are under the effect of the sun. In the spirit realm the sun element recedes, but in the formation of external life it produces a new impulse.

This important transition is not understood if milk and fruits are only considered in today's sense. Originally, milk was man's main sustenance. As long as the moon was still united with the

---

* During the Old Moon condition, creation reached the stage of the animal kingdom, as in the Old Sun condition that of the plant and in the Saturn condition that of the archetypal mineral kingdom.

earth, man absorbed milk from all surrounding nature. It was mainly the plant kingdom which lavished it on him. Man truly still sucked the breasts of nature. When the Ephesian goddess Artemis and the goddess Natura were later depicted as beings with many breasts, this contained a reminiscence of a world condition which still possessed full reality in the Lemurian age. The image of the cow Audhumla in Nordic mythology is also a retrospective look into ages when mankind passed through its initial state of infancy and was nourished on the maternal breasts of creation. The great garden of nature did not yet require cultivation by man. He was supplied with everything. Then the world changed and only the animal kingdom still supplied the nourishing milk. This ancient time, when man found his food without having to toil, is recalled in the occupation of the shepherd. Abel, the shepherd, preserves the old world in which 'the milk of human kindness' was man's only nourishment. Cain stands within the plant realm which is related to him. But it has changed and no longer yields on its own what man needs. It requires cultivation. Man must learn to plant, sow, cultivate and harvest. The Cain force devotes itself to this work. The settled existence of the man who tills the soil is added to the nomadic shepherd's life. To the moon nourishment that of the sun is added. Out of the old creative powers Cain builds on the future. Even though for the time being the age of the sun has come to an end, a seed of the sun is to be submerged in the ground of humanity's life, from which the lost world of the sun garden can newly sprout forth in time to come. For by placing the bloodless offering of fruit against the bloody animal sacrifice of Abel, Cain erects a prophetic sign. Though not the present, the future belongs to Cain. The fruits of the field point to bread and wine.

But tragedy holds sway between the man of magic and the religious man. Death has come into the world through the beginning of physical birth. As yet it is not fully revealed. He who still bears within himself the heritage of a deathless world tears the mask from the face of death. Killing is added to death. The old magic will forces reveal that the world has now become weak and limited, hemmed in between the boundaries of birth and death, subject to the transitory stream of time. Evil springs from the Cain-will, because the world now begins to absorb the contrast of evil and good. In the old world order, the Cain-will would have brought about the divine good. Now it is untimely and therefore harbours trouble. From now on, not only the suffering of Abel but also the horror of Cain over self-created harm exists in humanity. Should man cast off the sun-force of Cain, because by means of it he can create evil?

The Bible itself alludes to the tremendous value that would be lost, were the Cain element to die out. The divine power states that Cain's murderer would have to be cursed seven times more severely than the murderer of Abel (Gen.4:15). Progressing humanity on the whole becomes like Abel. Only a small segment of it bears the Cain force. If the old magic sun powers are lived to the full in the same way as the normal forces of Abel, infinite harm can arise through them. Humanity is confronted with a great risk.

In the ages when Lemurian life came to an end and the transition was made to Atlantis, an important turn in mankind's destiny was brought about. The Cain forces were withdrawn into segregated spheres of activity, where they could not cause unremitting recurrence of fratricide, but can be utilized and directed for the benefit of men. Esoteric points of departure for humanity's cultural development were established in the midst of general exoteric human existence. This was the origin of the mysteries.

When Genesis speaks of the unsettled, fugitive destiny that will henceforth be the lot of Cain's men, this indicates that a part of humanity has to renounce a personal homeland and must take homelessness upon itself in order ceaselessly to serve the progress of all mankind without regard for its own welfare and development.

The Cain humanity is confronted with mighty tasks in which it must transform its magic forces into arts. The plant world ceases to pour its gifts over man without his having to lift a hand. Along with the words, 'Thou shalt be a fugitive and wanderer upon the earth', Cain hears the stern prophecy: 'When thou tillest the ground, it shall not henceforth yield unto thee its strength' (Gen. 4:12). With ingenious skill the tiller of the soil must wring the yield from the earth, which formerly it gave on its own.

As man becomes more settled, the animal kingdom requires more than mere shepherding. Taming and breeding of animals is a task which appears along with the building of huts and houses. Jabal, the first of Lamech's three sons from the Cain generation, brings humanity the art of building houses and breeding animals, cattle herding as such (Gen.4:20).

The most unheard-of of the newly arising tasks is that of mastering inanimate substance, the youngest constituent of earth existence. When death gained entry into humanity, the element of death, the hard mineral kingdom of metals and rock, also gripped the earth's corporeality. Now the task is to force the dead into the service of life. The battle with death is taken up by Cain's sons, whose life forces threatened the lives of Abel's sons. Another son of Lamech, Tubal-cain, led those sons of Cain who make themselves masters of 'all instruments of bronze and iron' (Gen.4:22). And the third son of Lamech, Jubal, together with his people, transformed dead substance into an instrument of artistic activity. This is why it says that from him descended 'all those who play the lyre and pipe' (Gen.4:21).

Among the first fruits of the mysteries, in which the magic Cain-force is to be directed to the good, are primal beginnings of technology and art. The further development of technology, particularly in recent times, makes evident the two-edged aspect of the work undertaken by Cain and Tubal-cain. But Cain's sons are the men of daring, the courage of discovery, and the battle against the power of death.

As through a secret seal, the Bible, through a name, expresses the important turn that has taken place in humanity's history with the creation of the mysteries. Twice it mentions this name in connection with the Cain figure and thus allows a bright light to shine upon the image of the first construction of a city. Later, in the story of the Abel-Seth generation, the Bible refers back pointedly to this name. It is the name Enoch. 'Cain knew his wife, and she conceived and bore Enoch; and he built a city, and called the name of the city after the name of his son, Enoch' (Gen.4:17).

Enoch means 'the initiate'. It must be a primeval word of mankind, for its root is the same as that of the Egyptian word 'ankh', the hieroglyph of life, ♀, which, as the key of life and the seal of higher life beyond, represented by the rays of the sun, recurs a thousandfold in ancient Egyptian works of art. The double use of the name for the first son of Cain and the first city makes it evident that from now on humanity has as leaders personalities who have received their initiation and their mission for creative cultural activity in specific localities.

This signifies an important step in man's battle against the power of death. As long as death had not entered humanity, the divine beings themselves could be the leaders of men and dwell among them as if they were their own kind. But when human bodies densified to the point of being capable of death, divine beings could no longer reveal themselves to men in human form. The chasm came into being between man and God. Men were no longer distinguished from general humanity by virtue of the fact that as favourites of the gods they were deemed worthy of special association with them. In order to bridge the chasm between the human kingdom and that of the gods, and thereby to become leaders, human beings had to subject themselves from now on to certain disciplines and transformations of their soul forces. This was initiation. To be sure, the first beginnings of initiation during the transition from Lemuria to Atlantis may well have been in form entirely unlike initiation ceremonies in historical epochs among the various peoples. The most ancient and the later forms of initiation, however, would have had one thing in common; namely, that through initiation, the human soul dwelling on earth acquired the rights of citizenship in those spheres also, which it would otherwise enter only after death. Therefore, in all ages, the central part of initiation was guidance through death and resurrection. Mystical death is employed as the weapon in the battle against death. The initiation death, which the neophyte is led through, removes the sting from physical death, for it wrests from it the power of resurrection.

We now behold three stages of the death experience. At first, in primal ages, death has the same appearance as its brother, sleep. Through the Fall into sin, death assumes its characteristic gruesome form. With the founding of the mysteries, another brother of death takes its place beside it — the temple sleep, the mystical death — which makes itself resemble death in order to take from it its poison and wrest from death the spirit life.

Adjusted to the new development of the earth, the Abel humanity finds its great leader in Seth, who was born to Adam to replace Abel. Seth represents humanity's now timely level of consciousness in perfectly developed form: the life-filled realm of the sun-forces has withdrawn into superterrestrial spheres; only reflections of it can exist upon the earth, which originate as does moonlight from sunlight. The sun's power is reduced to mirroring itself in moon-wisdom. The Cain stream bears and nurtures the succession of the sun's powers; in Seth, a stream of wisdom that is different from the former places itself alongside it. Seth is mankind's first great teacher. The traditions connected with the figure of Seth have been summed up in the *Legend of the Rood* (Halliday).

To obtain relief for his sick father Adam, Seth sets out on the long journey and search for paradise. He finally arrives at its portal and is admitted inside. From the Tree of Life, he receives three seeds to take back to his father. When Adam died, Seth placed the seeds in his father's mouth, and a tree grew out of Adam's grave. From its wood many things were fashioned: the staff of Moses, the posts for the gate of Solomon's temple, the bridge over which Jesus carried the cross, and finally the cross of Golgotha itself.

With Seth's figure we already find ourselves on new territory, on a continent, the greater and central portions of which are today covered by the waters of the Atlantic Ocean, where mankind has begun a new evolutionary epoch. Perhaps, behind the image of Seth's pilgrimage to paradise, real historical journeys are concealed, through which human beings now inhabiting western lands sought to remain in touch with their home regions in order not to lose the 'light from the East'. In any case, through the Seth saga, we behold a humanity suffering from sickness and death, far from paradise, filled with homesickness and longing for its lost homeland of light. Paradise no longer is to be found on earth. The sun sphere has completely withdrawn to the spirit realm. Journeys and pilgrimages on earth can at most be an external support for the inward ascent to the spheres of the spirit which humanity must now aspire to.

Seth is capable of bringing down forces from the living spirit realm into the soul's realm of consciousness. Through Seth we can perceive that humanity again and again could partake of the forces of the Tree of Life through exalted leaders who were able to tread the path to the far removed home of light. What does grow from the seeds of heaven upon the earth? Do not the staff of Moses, the wood of the cross, belong to the Tree of Knowledge, which makes him who eats of it akin to death? The forces of the spirit realm can no longer live in mankind in their sunlike directness, only in their moonlike reflection. Branches from the Tree of Life are handed to man, but as soon as he has touched them, they are transformed into those of the Tree of Knowledge. The cosmos of power has passed over into the cosmos of wisdom, and from this the tasks arise which confront the Seth-humanity.

Seth is heir to the Book of Adam. In him, the succession of

primal revelations continues. It is told how Adam instructs the boy in the use of the book, which he preserves in the crevice of a rock. He teaches Seth to approach the book only 'in reverence, purity and sanctity, which is the path of all who know of the book and recognize its signs . . .'[38]

> And Seth clung with all his might to the book and strayed neither to the right nor to the left . . . And the wisdom of the holy book opened for him the portals of all perception and knowledge, and he comprehended what is good and what is evil, and knew that one must abhor evil and choose the good.[39]

No clearly discernible human figures rise above the morning mists of mankind's Atlantean epoch. Only as from a great distance we distinguish two leading streams, one concealing itself more, the other more active among men. The magic stream is the one of courage and risk. It mourns not for what is lost. It does not acknowledge the separation between good and evil, God and man. It forges earthly skills, human art, from divine forces. From its schools emerge smiths, builders and artists. The stream of wisdom senses the separation between above and below and knows how to differentiate between good and evil. It sends out teachers who show men the path of piety, and educators who guide the moral life through the first beginnings of what in later times was fashioned into the great principles of moral conduct.

Eventually, the Seth stream also has to establish mystery places and form a connection with the sphere of initiation. The holy legacy of primeval revelation requires care, protection and faithful transmission of its content. For unless, through initiation, the wellsprings of revelation are made to flow ever anew, the provision of primeval wisdom must in time become exhausted in spite of being most faithfully preserved. In their own way — and each word has meaning here — the imaginative traditions point to the origin of the Seth mysteries and their dependence, necessary in this regard, upon the Cain mysteries: 'And Seth fashioned a golden chest and placed the book therein, and laid all manner of spices by it, and hid the chest in a cave of the city of Enoch, which Cain, his brother, had built.'[39]

Within the Seth stream the name Enoch emerges, but not as yet expressing an essential ingredient of this stream. The development alluded to by this name reaches completion, when, among the sons of Seth themselves, a bearer of the name Enoch appears. This Enoch is the seventh in the successions of generations after

Adam, thus — the Letter of Jude in the New Testament emphasizes this particularly — an octave from Adam. The mystery and glory of the second Adam surrounds Enoch. His figure stands for all the lofty initiates of Atlantean humanity combined. When Genesis states that Adam remained alive up until the time of Enoch, this is an indication that the primeval wisdom of ancient Lemuria continued to be effective as living inspiration until the initiate wisdom of Atlantis became self-sufficient and found its own mature form.

Enoch is the next heir to the Book of Adam after Seth. The site where he is to find the holy book is revealed to him in a dream vision, 'and the way and means is made known to him in which to use it'. And Enoch betakes himself to the city of his own name, the son of Seth enters the city of Cain, and finds the golden vessel with the Book of Adam.[40]

We find only a few words about Enoch in the scriptures of the Old Testament. But already the essence of these words is such that an interpretation which assumes that the Bible knows little where it has little to say is wide of the mark. The sentence which Genesis utters about Enoch is, as it were, heavy with reverent silence. It is as if the Bible could only point delicately to a profound mystery: 'And after he begat Methuselah, Enoch walked with God three hundred years and begat sons and daughters. And all the days of Enoch were three hundred and sixty-five years. And since Enoch led a divine life, God took him and he was no longer seen' (Gen.5:22–24B).

Even through the numbers that Genesis relates, it conceals Enoch; for, among the names between Adam and Noah, the years allotted to Enoch are by far the fewest. But his number is of cosmic nature: Enoch's life numbers as many years as a year has days. Since whole generation sequences are summed up together in one name, the numbers mentioned here indicate very much longer time-spans than would be measured with them today. But Enoch's number is in any case that of a complete cycle of time, one great cycle of years, within the millennia of Atlantean life.

What Genesis mentions concerning Enoch's relationship to death has been the characteristic feature with which biblical traditions have expressed his special status: Enoch did not die but was taken away by God. Enoch's ascension to heaven — as that of Elijah later on — stands as an image in human consciousness, which, while it remains under the veil of mystery, reveals the possibility of victory over death.

The figure of Enoch is, however, not only of significance for the two streams connected with the Old Testament, Judaism and Christianity. All peoples in whom a concrete knowledge of primeval revelation has been retained are familiar with him and name him among the primordial teachers of humanity to whom their teachings are traced back. The Muslim Arab philosophers revere him under the name Idris, and list him and Seth, whom they equate with Agathodaimon, the primal benefactor of the ancient world, as inaugurators of all human knowledge and wisdom. Hellenistic traditions equate Enoch with the exalted messenger of the gods, who was called Thoth in Egypt, Hermes in Greece and Mercury in Rome. Egypt looked back to three Hermes figures. The third was the lofty founder and inspirer of Egyptian wisdom and culture. The greatest, however, was the first among the three, the 'three times great' one, 'Hermes Trismegistos'. The figure called Enoch in the Bible was beheld in him: the inaugurator of a much older and more extensive chapter of humanity's development. As the messenger of the gods, he had to convey the divine wisdom to earth and usher in a divinely inspired culture of primeval beginning. The 'hermetic writings', the secret books of Egypt, are traced back to him, of which late and distorted fragments are preserved for us in the Greek language. The former are said also to have derived from the Book of Adam which Enoch-Hermes possessed.

The images of the myths do not permit us to discern clearly contoured individual personalities even in the Atlantean epoch. It is as if through thick veils of mist bright lights spread their radiance far and wide and form great aureate figures, but the outlines of the figures from which the light emanates remain obscure.

But we would arrive at a false conception, if we only wanted to focus on the sources of light. Since the Fall, since the end of the Lemurian epoch, but particularly among the emergent Atlantean population, the principle of dissension and duality holds sway, and the battle between light and darkness has begun.

The principle of darkness is nourished by misuse of magic powers. But it is not as if Cain men and Seth men confront each other as servants of darkness and light. Though the magic stream of Cain produces accomplishments of a purely earthly nature, which thus prepare the way for a later development of egoism, humanity is still far from awakening to the ego, hence from aberrations of selfhood. The Cain sons' magic becomes dangerous when it leaks through to those who do not know how to master it, and particularly when it infiltrates the sphere of religious and cultic institutions, which the descendants of the Abel-Seth stream have begun to establish. Human egos themselves cannot as yet go astray, but, through misuse of magic in the religious and cultic area, they can attract and activate supersensory beings, who are opponents of the good gods. If the ancient magic powers are employed in the mastery of inanimate substance, earthly culture arises. If they are directed to the supersensory, black magic, demon worship, results.

Legendary tradition reports that even in the first generation of Seth's sons, hence still in the transitional age to Atlantis, the opposing stream came into being. It pictures Enosh, the son of Seth, as the first idolater and sorcerer. Also, it mentions a primordial flood, which came upon mankind as a result of its aberrations in the days of Seth, long before Noah and the Flood.

Once, so it is told, Enosh asked his father who had been Adam's father. When he heard that God had formed Adam out of earth, Enosh also took a clump of dirt and formed a human image with it. But through his breath, no living human being came into existence; the image was ensouled with a demonic power.[41]

Certainly, this legend was moulded at a much later time by the one-sided Jewish abhorrence of all things pagan, but perhaps it does point to how, once, through the untimely reversion to the magic forces of asexual procreation, cults came into being in which, instead of the benign creative spirits, those powers that have entangled man too deeply in matter were active. The saga of a flood in Seth's time may indicate reverberations of the fire catastrophes, which caused large portions of the Lemurian continent to sink to the bottom of the ocean.

According to imaginative legendary traditions, fearful changes occurred in the days of Enosh, as if the curse of the Fall were only now being completely fulfilled on earth and among men.

> Four things changed in the world at the time of Enosh. The mountains on which man had formerly tilled and sown seed now became petrified. Worms infested the bodies of the dead; never before had it been known what decomposition meant. Men became like apes in their appearance; the image of God was no more. And the evil spirits lost their fear of man.[42]

This also reveals the secret of the name 'Enosh', which correctly understood is in itself already an expression of the new deep fall of creation. Enosh means the 'man', but in the sense of 'only a man'. It contains a root, which in Greek becomes the word for illness (νόσος, *nósos*), and actually gives the name the meaning 'sick man'. 'Adam' also means 'man', but this designates man still close to the archetype of his earthly form. 'Enosh' is estranged from his archetype, the disfigured man. Henceforth, besides death, there is also sickness in the world.

From the beginning, the Enosh stream runs through Atlantean existence. Divine help for the threatened light, the new impulse of revelation, then appears in Enoch. The polarity of Enosh–Enoch is the expression for the great conflict of powers in Atlantean humanity which the Old Testament was able to coin.

Behind the name Enoch, we sense a lofty divine-human individuality, a leader of men, who guided and taught mankind through long eras of time. He was either incarnated himself, or inspired his followers and successors from out of the spiritual world. The abundant apocryphal traditions dealing with him contain a touching personal colouring. Still, in those ancient tales of Enoch, descriptions of an individual destiny intermingle with imaginations of a common fate. Human and superhuman elements meet in human images.

Enoch is described as representing an important new beginning. It says that until the days of his father Jared, the angels themselves descended from heaven to guide mankind on its paths. Then, Enoch, who had dedicated himself in seclusion to the 'divine life', to dialogue with God, for a long time far from men, was called upon to go forth to humanity, and to assume the office of the angel among them.[43]

Enoch had to leave the restricted realm of the mysteries. Human leaders had to continue to direct divine guidance. Starting with Enoch, human initiates began to guide humanity's destinies. In pictures gleaned from much later earth conditions, the legend looks back into the distant past:

> The Spirit of God hovered over Enoch, and he instructed men in the wisdom of the Lord and showed them his ways. Men also served the Lord all the days that Enoch was among them, and all came to listen to his wisdom. All the kings of men also, the first as well as the last, and their princes and judges, came to Enoch when

they heard his wisdom, and prostrated themselves on the ground before him.[44]

After Adam's death the sphere of the mystery centre slowly recalled Enoch. When the angel guidance had ceased, the people also experienced how the initiated human being gradually withdrew from their midst. The seclusion where Enoch kept company with God rather than men, increasingly bade him return. If he spent one day teaching among men, he remained absent from them three days. Then the times that he spent in seclusion grew longer and longer. And when he reappeared among men, the traces of divine life that shone on his countenance like rays of light became more and more powerful. At first he still appeared to men one day in the week; then only one day in the month; and finally only one day a year, 'until all kings and princes and all human beings longed to behold Enoch's face and hear his words'. But the greater their yearning for Enoch's countenance, the less could human beings endure the sight of the ever more brilliant light. Many died from the light, and finally only listeners with eyes cast down upon the earth gathered around the one who came more and more rarely.

Then Enoch became detached by one more degree from men. An angel assigned him to be a leader and teacher among celestial beings as he was hitherto among men. Once more, he powerfully addressed the people gathered around. His bequest to them was a lofty teaching of peace. 'And it came about as the people sat around Enoch and he spoke to them, they raised their eyes and saw the form of a horse descending from heaven, and the horse came down to earth in a tempest.'

Enoch mounted the horse and rode away. The crowd followed him, but day after day some remained behind until only a few were left who could follow him. 'On the seventh day it happened that Enoch drove to heaven in the tempest in a fiery chariot with fiery horses.' The group of the surviving faithful was found dead in the snow of the high mountains.[45]

By means of such descriptions we experience the sublimity of primordial revelation, but also its gradual disappearance from the human realm. The gods slowly withdrew their hand with which they guided mankind. Increasingly, humanity was left to fend for itself. But the Enoch legend ends in an image that contains a consoling promise. It is the image of the ascension to heaven, which is also alluded to in the brief text of Genesis.

4 CAIN – SETH – ENOCH

For one who knows that whole worlds of great significance are locked into the text of the Old Testament, the image of Enoch's being lifted up into the heavens is underscored by the sequence of names. That of Enoch's father, Jared, means 'the descending one'. Enoch follows Jared; the descending one is followed by the one who ascends. A power becomes visible in Enoch which in time can turn the descent of humanity into an ascent.

The image of Enoch's ascension points to the same secret as does his name, namely initiation. An ascension is interwoven into man's natural life in two different forms: through sleep and through death. In sleep, man's soul and spirit lift themselves out of their earthly dwelling and are carried near the spheres of heaven. But the weakness of man's inner being envelops his ascending soul like an impenetrable veil and holds its eyes closed. In death, the soul-spirit being of man rises to the heavenly sphere without the blindness of sleep. But the fruits of this ascension cannot benefit the life on earth any longer. The harsh hand of death, which holds man in its power, tears him away from earth.

The ascension learned and experienced by a soul strengthened in initiation is free of the limitations of sleep and death. The soul of man, which passes through 'mystical death', ascends into the spirit spheres without the blindness of sleep and powerlessness against the might of death. Without having to take leave of the earth and of its physical body, it enters the world beyond the grave and can return to earth with the gifts of heaven. Henceforth, such a soul possesses the key of life designated in Egypt with the word *ankh* closely related to the name Enoch. The initiate possesses the discretionary power of ascension, he can cross back and forth over the threshold. Enoch, 'the initiate' is the first bearer of a life that overcomes death. Thereby, he is the embodiment of the prophecy and promise of a power that in the future is to be made attainable by all men through the grace of God. From afar, Enoch's ascension points to the ascension of Christ.

Extensive imaginative descriptions of Enoch's lofty celestial journey have been preserved in the so-called *Book of Enoch*. They are apocryphal writings which, in their present form, only go back into the last centuries before Christ. We have two such Books of Enoch; one a voluminous text originally written in Aramaic, which is retained in Ethiopian texts; and a shorter one, originally in Greek, preserved in Slavonic texts of the Eastern Church.

The *Book of Enoch* was prominent in the theology of early Christianity. The literary expression of ancient wisdom was seen in it. St Augustine states at one point that on account of its being too old (*ob nimiam antiquitatem*), the *Book of Enoch* had been omitted from the canon of the Holy Scriptures.[46] Here, the tradition of the Book of Adam obviously is involved, of which it is said that Enoch possessed it. The *Book of Enoch* was reputed to be a variation of the Book of Adam, hence documents of primal revelation, into which are woven the new revelations that Enoch could bring from heaven to the earth.

A remark about the Book of Adam is needed to prevent misconceptions. It goes without saying that the book could not come into the possession of Adam, Seth and Enoch in a physically tangible form with lettered pages. The ancient traditions cite Enoch as the one who for the first time introduced written characters into human culture. The Egyptians and Greeks also consider Thoth-Hermes the inaugurator of writing. Therefore there could have been no written books prior to Enoch's time.

Anthroposophy even suggests that we understand the tradition of the origin of script only as an imaginative expression for that of formulated language as such. Toward the end of the Lemurian epoch, only the very first interjectional beginnings of language developed. Only in the course of the Atlantean evolution, mankind learned a language suitable for mutual confidences and communications. One cannot by any means apply conceptions gleaned from modern life to the times when a great teacher instructed human beings. Speaking and hearing can at most be considered as symbolic images for completely different processes between the teacher's soul and the souls of those receiving his instruction. Then, exalted divine messengers appeared, led by Hermes-Enoch, who bore the Word from the realm of the gods to men. They taught men to speak.

A supersensory sphere is thus indicated with the image of the Book of Adam.* Earthly scripts originated later as reflections of the supersensory script that can be read in the spheres of the stars. The *Book of Enoch* also existed in the supersensory sphere long before something like a faint shadow of it originated many thousands of years later through an external written record. Legend

---

* This is like the term 'Akashic Record', used by Anthroposophy in accordance with ancient terminologies.

relates that Enoch received the book along with his ascension, indeed, that heaven itself had been this book:

> The Lord lifted Enoch from the world below . . . and therewith the book was given to him, which is also called: The Book of Enoch. In the self-same hour the Lord showed him all the treasures of heaven.[47]

The *Book of Enoch* that has been preserved is strongly apocalyptic in character and in many instances its structure and individual images coincide with the revelations to St John, though they do not extend to such depths. The Slavonic book describes Enoch's ascension through the seven spheres of heaven. In the first heaven he is familiarized with the beings who bestow order and time upon the stars and are watchmen over the kingdoms of nature. The second sphere is that of the fallen angels; the third contains paradise and hell. The fourth is that of the rhythms which the cosmos receives from the sun; the fifth contains gigantic guardian figures; the sixth, choirs of angels and their fields of activity; the seventh, higher hierarchies who weave in light and fire. Then it says: 'Gabriel then tore me away like a leaf stripped by a storm and placed me before the Lord.'

Michael takes off Enoch's earthly garments and robes him in glory. And then Enoch has to inscribe all that was revealed to him in books fragrant with myrrh, 'all things in heaven, upon the earth and in the sea, the courses and places of all the elements, the seasons, the days' courses and changes, the commandments and teachings.'

Finally, he is directed to take the three hundred and sixty books to mankind, 'as the intercessor of my commander Michael; for thy handwriting and that of thy father Adam and Seth will not be destroyed until the end of time.'

The larger, historically better known *Book of Enoch*, has an over-abundance of images and in still stronger measure calls forth a feeling for the stream of the primal revelation which continued in Enoch, and is designated with the symbolic concept 'Book of Adam'. The 'Book of Angels' is a dramatic prelude to the whole text. The aberration of Enosh spreads over the earth. In an impure magic manner, angelic beings are drawn down into the human sphere and betray secrets to men for which the latter are not mature enough; until the archangels Michael, Uriel, Raphael and Gabriel order them to cease. Here as in Genesis an image emerges of the intermingling of sons of heaven with daughters of men.

Through betrayal of the mysteries, human beings learn the arts of the angels, and chaos arises. From the seclusion of his divine life, Enoch is dispatched to the fallen angels and reveals the coming judgment to them in mighty visions. They implore him to write a petition for their salvation. Enoch replies: 'You should really be pleading for men, not men for you.' He does, however, make himself the advocate of the unclean spirits and his journeys through the spheres of heaven, filled with innumerable visions, commence. All the dimensions of the might and life of the physical and super-physical cosmos reveal their secrets to him. His look penetrates not only into the inner core of the land of spirit but also that of nature. Enoch's world of imagery comes closest to that of St John's Apocalypse, where Messianic future times with their power struggles and spirit battles are revealed. Much of what is formulated in discreet conciseness in the latter spreads out in inexhaustible wealth of images in the former. Astronomical books alternate with those in which the whole history of mankind runs its course in imaginative rendering. It all culminates in the miracles accompanying Noah's birth, as if the sceptre of revelation were to be passed from Enoch to Noah.

Despite the severe distortion inherent in the late version of these books, they permit us to sense our way back into primordial times, when mankind had its teachers and was instructed by them during the first stages of its conscious earthly path.

The apocryphal writings touch upon the deepest mysteries concerning the figure of Enoch, where they designate him as the bearer of the being whom Paul later called 'the second Adam'.

> The light of the loftiest soul, which flew away from Adam when he was driven from the garden of Eden, ascended again and was preserved in a treasure chamber until the time Enoch was to come. Then this highest light of the holy soul came into Enoch, and Enoch attained to the same greatness that Adam possessed before the Fall.[48]

Frequently and in detail, Rudolf Steiner described the spiritual facts which form the basis of the pictorial tradition of Adam's pure soul of light. He relates that only a part of the Adam being entered into the course of earthly incarnations, and that the higher paradisal part underwent its destinies in the supersensory worlds until it physically incarnated for the first time in the soul of the Luke Jesus child, thus offering the purest soul sheath of humanity

to the Christ ego and making Christ the real 'second Adam'.
Further, we learn through Anthroposophy that on several occa-
sions in the aeons of its supersensory destiny Adam's *anima can-
dida** transmitted redemptive effects to humanity on earth by
means of serving the Christ being in the spiritual realm as his soul
sheath and mediator to the human realm. We are told of three
Christ events in pre-Christian times that have found their earthly
reflections in the great pre-Christian religions. Under the influence
of the second of these Christ revelations, humanity in the Atlantean epoch cultivated speech and the capacity for mental equilibrium.[49] Great initiates of the Atlantean era, the bringers and
teachers of the Word, must have been inspired and ensouled by
the 'loftier light soul of Adam' and through the latter by the Christ
being himself. This is what the legend concerning Enoch states in
exact imaginative form. Enoch is truly the messenger of the Logos,
the cosmic Word itself; the bringer of the Word, which first came
to mankind as speech, and later was to become flesh. Enoch is a
Christ prophecy become form. This is the innermost meaning of
the sublime descriptions so abundant in the apocryphal traditions,
which represent Enoch as Matatron, the celestial scribe and cus-
todian of the Book of Life in which are inscribed all human
destinies.[50]

5 Noah – Job:
Transition to the Post-Atlantean Time

The Hebrew Bible designates both Noah's ark and Moses' basket
of bulrushes with one and the same word, *tebhah*.† In fact, a
significant analogy exists between the two imaginations. In each
case an important young life is to be saved from the threat of
destruction. Just as one individual, Moses, was saved from the
infanticide ordered by the Pharaoh through being abandoned on
the Nile River in the basket of bulrushes, the ark of Noah had
made possible the survival of a young chosen branch of humanity
in the face of the great Flood. What begins as a destiny of mankind

---

* *Translator's note*. A term meaning 'pure soul' often used by Rudolf Steiner as
  well as Emil Bock.

† The Authorised Version uses the same English word, 'the ark of bulrushes'.

and whole nations later becomes individual destiny, as the age of egohood draws ever nearer in passing from the great cycles to the smaller ones.

We shall have to show later, in presenting the story of Moses, that the pictures of Noah's ark and the basket of bulrushes are the property of those mystery cults where, in historical times, in the coffin or chest of Osiris and Adonis, a symbol of initiation and the death and resurrection connected with it was placed before the public. Frequently, the Greek term λάρναξ (*lárnax*), meaning 'chest', is employed, which also appears as the name for the 'ark' of Deucalion in the Greek traditions of the Flood. In Cyprus, which was a centre of the Adonis cult until relatively late times, the name of the city of Larnaca recalls the ancient ritualistic custom, where during certain annual festivals the image of the god was hidden inside a chest and submerged in the sea for three days in order to demonstrate the mystery of death and resurrection.

The frequent representations of the ark on early catacomb paintings and sarcophagi sculptures are proof that this meaning of 'Noah's ark' remained alive until the era of early Christianity.[51] The proportions of Noah's ark and Moses' basket of bulrushes have moved close together here. Again and again, we see Noah arise from a coffin-like chest as a resurrected one. This chest in no way resembles a naturalistic conception of the measurements given in the Old Testament concerning the ark and the living creatures housed in it.

The images of Moses' basket as well as that of Noah's ark therefore point to much more than the mere saving of endangered life. What they do refer to is the intensification of life by the passage through a death and resurrection, attained by the special destiny of initiation. And before one can speak of the initiation of a single individual through his destiny, a whole branch of humanity passed through its destined initiation in times antecedent to the ages of single nations and individualities. This is the meaning of the biblical myth of the Flood: initiation of a whole chosen segment of humanity at a certain turning point of evolution by means of the power of the earth's destinies. Noah is the great priestly leader and hierophant in this initiation.

The myth of a great Flood has been retained by all peoples of the earth like a common recollection; more than sixty different flood sagas have survived. Each of them has a central figure corresponding to Noah. The Indians have Manu; the Greeks Deucalion; the Chaldeans have Xisuthros; the Babylonian Gilgamesh epos has Utnapishtim, who there has a surname, Atrachasis, meaning 'the primeval intelligent one'.

These various traditions seem to look back into different periods of the distant past. It has been found that in a large number of the mythological accounts, catastrophes are indicated that can be historically dated and identified as to their location.* Others, however, seem to focus on the most distant common fates of the whole earth and mankind. Yet all the traditions look back through the smaller cycles and repetitions into the larger cycle and primeval beginning. Through the more recent smaller flood events, they recall the great Flood, those tremendous water catastrophes, ten thousand years before the turn of time, which engulfed the Atlantean continent and along with it wiped out an entire stage of human consciousness. The flood sagas are not all equally transparent in regard to that distant age. Where transparency is at its best and retrospection clearest, the more recent, smaller repetitions recede into the background and the Atlantean Flood arises undistorted in a mighty imagination. This is to a large degree true of the Old Testament representation and the more fairy-tale-like sagas of India.

The Indian version of the Flood saga is especially important to us because of the name it gives the Noah-like figure. It calls the one who rescues life from destruction the 'great Manu'. The *Mahabharata* relates that one morning a fish swims up to Manu as he is bathing and speaks to him. The god Brahma himself is disguised in the form of the fish. It predicts the Flood to Manu, but promises that he will be saved on the ship he is to board when the Flood begins. Manu first cares for the fish in a container. Then, because the fish grows larger and larger, he places it in a pond, then in the Ganges river and finally the sea. The Flood commences and Manu boards the ship together with the seven holy rishis, the wise bards who are in possession of the genuine holy scriptures. Manu takes with him seeds of every plant. Then the fish swims up and, tying the hawser of the ship to its horn, hurries on towards the mountains. The ship lands on one of the highest peaks, and when the

---

* In order to understand the foundations of the age of Abraham, we shall have to speak in detail about the occurrences, already within historical ages, with which some flood sagas are connected.

Flood is over, Manu creates a new humanity and guides it according to divine laws.

For a conception of the Flood and the change wrought by it as a historical event in human existence, we now turn to the descriptions which anthroposophical research offers us concerning the life of Atlantean humanity and the transition to the post-Atlantean era.[52] In these, the name and figure of Manu plays a most important role. The great Manu was the leader of a mystery centre in old Atlantis, which stood out among all the others as a brightly shining place. All Atlantean mystery or oracle centres had the task of maintaining mankind's connection with the sublime spiritual being who once together with the sun, had left the earth behind but who, in the course of future development, intended to unite again with humanity. Most initiates of Atlantis, however, were unable to have direct contact with the sun being. They beheld him only in mirror images akin to moonlight and in the reflections of the planets. The direct sun revelations were received only in the circle around the great Manu, and thus the mystery centre of Manu, which was located on the eastern shore of Atlantis in the region where Ireland is today, was called the 'Christ oracle' or 'sun oracle'. The other initiation centres were to the sun oracle as the planets are to the sun. Each had its own colouring, its character and mission, by virtue of the various forces and talents of the groups of people belonging to it.

The expression 'antediluvian' is sometimes used to characterize a particular lack of culture and primitiveness. In reality, it would be completely wrong to imagine that the culture of mankind before the Flood was crude and primitive. All social life and cultural institutions arose directly from divine inspirations. The gods rather than men were the founders of Atlantean culture.

But the further the Atlantean age progressed, the more noticeable did major contrasts and dissensions become. Alongside the progressive mysteries, there were the decadent ones in which aberrations going back to the Enosh influence increased. The growth forces of nature and man, with which astounding wonders of cultural life were produced in the good mysteries because of the great pliability of all physical substance, fell into misuse there. Within the slowly developing communities, resembling states, greed for dissension and power arose.

The conflict of these opposing streams must have been expressed in dramatic distinctness through the differing configuration of men's bodies. The human form, which consisted of much softer and far more pliable substantiality than is the case today, was to a large degree the expression of the soul's qualities.

A man more filled with soul and spirit was of gentle build, mobile, expressive. One who was less spiritually developed had coarser bodily forms, immobile, not so plastic. Improvement in the life of the soul tended to draw man's members together; such a man would remain small in structure. Backwardness of soul, entanglement in sensuality, came to expression in gigantic bodily proportions.[53]

The time has arrived when, according to biblical description, tyrants and giants existed on earth (Gen.6:4).

Finally, all that opposed the good Atlantean mysteries as decadence concentrated itself into a gigantic calamity. Just as all soul-spirit forces could still influence the external configuration of the physical human body, so they also gradually invaded the formation of the earth's surface itself. The black magical abuse of forces of growth and reproduction, which emanated from the decadent mystery centres, finally took effect on the dense atmosphere of fog covering Atlantis, where water and air resembled each other more closely than is the case today. Tremendous storms and hurricanes were brought on which continued as tremendous water catastrophes and led to the gradual sinking of the Atlantean continent. The majority of human beings perished. Only small groups could save themselves through migrations eastward to Europe and Asia or westward to America into the new continents which only then began to assume their present form.

How did the sun oracle and its leader, the great Manu, conduct themselves in view of the ever increasing oppositional forces? It was Manu's task to prepare the future and to educate a small group of men in such a manner that they could be spared from all doom as the seed and germ of future humanity. Manu accomplished this by implanting into those souls fitted for it, a force which was to determine completely the human being in the post-Atlantean era: the power of thought. Lemurian humanity's greatness lay in the unfolding of instinct; that of the Atlanteans was the cultivation of memory; in the post-Atlantean era man was to become an independent personality and attain to freedom by means of the power of thinking. The name Manu itself expresses this. Through its root, *man*, which in Sanskrit appears in particularly clear form but is basically the common property of primeval human speech, Manu means 'the thought-bearer'. The German word *Mensch* and the English 'man' are derived from it and therefore express something of the royal dignity which thought grants to the human brow.

While the initiates of the other oracles, who received only the reflection of revelation, had to speak in symbolic images, the sun initiates, along with the power to receive revelations directly, also possessed 'the faculty to clothe their secrets in the form of human concepts'.[54] This made possible a significant advance in education, meted out to humanity by its leaders. Until then, human beings had been guided by divine powers and in accordance with divine laws, without being themselves aware of these forces and laws and certainly knowing nothing at all of the divine beings behind them. At most, men distantly sensed something of the world of the gods, when they beheld the initiates whom they experienced as messengers of the gods. Now, Manu taught his disciples to comprehend what until then had only been experienced. He no longer speaks *on behalf of* the gods but *of* the gods, directing the souls from things visible to what works invisibly behind them, and thus guiding them towards the element of thought. Pointing to the world of divine beings, Manu teaches man the first beginnings of thinking.[55]

Those human beings, who to the greatest extent had outgrown the old magical consciousness still totally entwined in the supersensory, were ready for Manu's teaching. Their souls were no longer a stage for the nature forces to act upon in benevolent or sinister manner, to the same degree as those of the other human beings. Instead, they had the potential for intellect, the capacity of soul equilibrium, inasmuch as they could distinguish matters and therefore were free to choose.

When the storms of destruction were unleashed upon the life of Atlantis and culminated in the great Flood catastrophe, an undisturbed continuation of the sun oracle's mission was no longer possible. The great Manu with his chosen followers moved eastward into remote regions of Central Asia, where the Gobi is located today, in order to form a well-spring for the thought-bearing cultures of the future. Once, in still more ancient times, the best of Lemuria's achievements had been saved from the fire storms of a doomed world by the westward Adam migrations.

Now, the eastward migrations of Manu saved the quintessence of Atlantean achievements. Through millennia, Manu dispatched colonists — either while he himself was incarnated, or through disciples whom he guided from the spiritual world — who bore within themselves the impulse for inaugurating a definite cultural stream.

The first emissaries, his seven best disciples, were sent into ancient India. Each one of them carried within himself the fruits of initiation from one of the planetary oracles and thus they were custodians of the Atlantean inheritance in an all-embracing way. They have lived on in the memory of the Orient — for example also in the flood saga of Manu's ship — as the seven holy rishis, the founders of the ancient holy culture of India. The primeval Zarathustra, who later founded the Persian culture, was the next great messenger of the sun initiate. In a similar way, the impulse for founding the Egyptian-Babylonian and Greco-Roman cultures also issued forth from the great Manu.

These are the historical processes involving humanity that can become visible through the imaginative transparency of the biblical myth of Noah's ark. Noah is the biblical name for the great Manu. Noah means 'the bringer of stillness'. Along with the seed of the power of thinking, Noah implanted into human souls the faculty to bring about inner calm and balance in the midst of stormy natural forces, which man's inner being was exposed to until Atlantean times. Into the midst of cosmic tempests that tore apart the countenance of the earth, he brought the seed of inner tranquillity. Thus, the dove at first 'found no place to set her foot' (Gen.8:9), literally *manoach*, a place of rest, a word resembling Noah's own name. In the biblical imagination, this site was the mountain peak, the first to appear above receding flood waters, from the olive trees of which the dove plucked the branch of peace.

The power of creating calmness, which Noah implanted in men's souls, had its cosmic correspondence in the completely changed condition of nature after the great Flood subsided. The whole earth seemed transformed into a great *manoach*. Everything formerly engaged in incalculable surging and movement, in violent formation and transformation, now took on permanent form. The supersensory powers of elemental life let go of their creation, in the many kingdoms of which they had been mightily active until then. They withdrew behind the veil of the sense world with its

73

clear forms and colours. The world of natural law developed; measure, number, and weight became operative. The life of nature was ordered according to regular rhythms. It was as if thought, which calls forth order, had been sown in the earth's soul as well as in the soul of man. The very moment that man acquired the faculty of comprehension, nature began to be comprehensible. Today, the only remnant left of the ancient unpredictability of the elements — aside from the occasional flare-ups of volcanic fire — are the phenomena of the weather.

Just as the clear division between solid and fluid substances came about at the end of the Lemurian age, so, now, after the end of the Atlantean epoch, that of the elements of water and air. The dense mists that enveloped the Atlantean world were scattered. The sun broke through and filled the atmosphere, which had only now become transparent, with its light. Astonishment must have stirred human hearts, when, all of a sudden, the colourful sky became visible to the physical eye with the sun, moon and stars. As a sign of the new cosmic life, the coloured rainbow appeared in the sky. The instruction of Manu-Noah that taught men to behold the divine-invisible realm behind the visible finds its most beautiful, sublime pledge in the rainbow. Noah makes it the sign of the new covenant with God. The circle of the seasons with their 'seedtime and harvest, cold and heat, summer and winter, day and night' are now clearly recognizable. Man learns from it to sense the laws of both the divine and human life, and gradually to comprehend them by thinking (Gen.8:22; 9:13ff).

The Bible indicates an important secret of human development in representing Noah as the first to plant grape vines. But as the imaginative quality of biblical descriptions ceased to be understood and the images were held to be direct accounts of external events, the figure of Noah was misunderstood and dragged down to an all-too-human level with the story of his partaking of wine. It even reached into song books and became popular in a manner that stood directly in the way of comprehension.

The image of the first cultivation of a vineyard by Noah must be seen in the light of the radical transformation that occurred in connection with the Atlantean catastrophe in the realm of the ethereal formative forces. Everywhere, the forces of reproduction and growth relinquished their dynamic abruptness and momentum

74

and began to weave more quietly and regularly into the physical world.

Though coarsened, definite memories have been retained in legends concerning the titanic power active in the processes of growth during the Atlantean era:

> Women were pregnant only three days . . . then they gave birth. Indeed, some say that after one day the children were carried to maturity, and they hopped around in front of their mothers . . . At the time of the Flood, the ears of wheat were like the cedars of Lebanon; men did not have to sow or harvest, for the wind blew out the kernels so men had merely to gather them.[56]

After the great Flood, the world of ethereal forces turned inward and henceforth followed calmer, more regular rhythms. Within the fundamentally changed plant kingdom a condensed recollection of the former condition of nature developed in the symbol of the grapevine. In the vine, mighty power of the elements had been captured and turned inward. The earlier uncontrollable outward proliferation became intensity of fragrance and fiery strength. In the grapes, the plant world learned the secret of strong, calm ripening. The legends even sought to indicate that a kind of quintessence of the garden paradise continued on in the grapevine:

> Noah found a grapevine, which the flood waters had carried away from the Garden of Eden . . . He ate of the fruits and the desire arose in his heart to have them always, and so he planted a vineyard from the grapevine. The same day he had planted it, the grapes ripened . . . and Noah drank the wine.[57]

The effect of wine is that it draws man's ego more deeply into his corporeality. In those early ages of human evolution, this brought a powerful new impulse into human nature which was still far from egohood. Man discovered his own inner being; the intoxication of the first self-discovery came over him. This was brought about by the very substance which in later times, when man had become an ego being, was to lead again to self-estrangement and loss of self. The intoxication of the elements was transferred into man's inner being. The Greeks experienced this transition as the supersession of the primeval chthonic gods by the hierarchy of gods related more closely to the human being. And just as there was the grapevine in the new plant kingdom, so, amidst the new Olympian heaven of gods, there was Dionysus, the young god crowned with grape leaves, the leader towards an inwardness sparkling with life. The Titans are superseded by Dionysus. The divine forces in nature become silent, the 'god in man' is to awaken. The dawn of enthusiasm arises and allows man to gain from within a new radiance. One could call Noah the Dionysus of Genesis. He is the leader on the path to the twofold inwardness taking place outside in the elements of nature as well as within the human being.

One of the three branches of humanity deriving from Noah wants to hold fast to the old forces of nature. Ham, together with his son Canaan, scorns Noah his father who has drunk the wine. There are those who go their separate ways. The Old Testament shows us later, where it describes the national destinies of the Israelites — who consider themselves the pure followers of Noah's mission — how they war everywhere with the Hamitic nations: Nimrod in Babylonia, the adversary of Abraham; the Egyptian Pharaoh whom Moses has to fight; the Canaanites with whom, beginning with Joshua, conflicts continue for centuries. All these are sons of Ham, who did not want to leave the world of the Titans, the old laws of nature of the antediluvian age.

With the bloodless offering of the fruits of the field, Cain presented a first, premature prophecy of a future process of turning the sun forces in earth and man into inward intensification. The secret of bread and wine lit up on the distant horizon of evolution.

Through Noah, mankind is led closer to this secret. When the Bible says: 'Noah was the first tiller of the soil. He planted a vineyard' (Gen.9:20), it traces a picture, delicately veiled, of how the great sun initiate is sowing the seeds of a future time, when the spirit of the sun can reanimate itself in earth existence.

Traditions other than those of the Bible add the glory of a supersensory being to Noah's human form. The *Book of Enoch* describes the miracles that surround his birth. It is as if Christ-mysteries are glimpsed here in subtle indications; for it is said of Noah that he was already able to talk when he was born — which is what apocryphal gospels report of the Jesus child:

> And his body was white as snow and red as the blooming of a rose, and the hair of his head and his long locks were white as wool, and his eyes beautiful. And when he opened his eyes, he lighted up the whole house like the sun, and the whole house was very bright. And thereupon he arose in the hands of the midwife, opened his mouth, and conversed with the Lord of righteousness. (106:2–3).

5 NOAH – JOB

According to the Bible, Noah was the first to be born after Adam's and Seth's death. In him, we are to recognize the bringer of the new impulse. The deficiencies of the paling moonlight are once again compensated for by the sun itself, who, in Manu-Noah, has sent forth its messenger. Something of the mystery of the second Adam lingers like a hint around Noah as it does around Enoch according to the Talmudists. They point out that Noah was the tenth after Adam, as Enoch was the seventh, and that in the three sons, Shem, Ham and Japhet, born to him by Naema, Enoch's daughter, the triad of the Adam sons, Cain, Abel and Seth, are reflected.

The most profound reference to the secret of the Noah figure is, however, the name given him by all traditions, 'Menahem', usually translated as 'comforter'. This name also becomes apparent in the interpretation the Old Testament gives of the word Noah: 'He [Lamech] became the father of a son and called his name Noah, saying, "Out of the ground which the LORD has cursed this one shall bring us relief [comfort] from our work and from the toil of our hands" ' (Gen.5:29). Menahem is the Hebrew word for the Greek παράκλητος, 'the Paraclete'. The words of Christ, according to St John, which promise the coming of the Paraclete (John 14:26; 15:26) have been translated as the 'Counsellor'. But Menahem or Paraclete is more than a comforter or counsellor. He is the higher intercessor, the bestower and bringer of the Holy Spirit through the name Menahem. Like the dove, which spiritually appeared at the Baptism in the Jordan as the image of the being overshadowing Jesus of Nazareth, the dove that brought the olive branch was the image of an actual spiritual figure hovering over Noah. For this reason, the dove over the receding waters of the Flood was always perceived by ancient imaginative theology as an analogy and prophecy of the dove over the waters of the Jordan.

From Seth and Enoch, the Book of Adam goes to Noah. He was the figure of continuation of the primal revelation. One thing becomes clear through all the traditions: Noah was to guide the stream of revelation in a certain direction. The first point that is depicted as an essential part of the teaching which Noah imparted to humanity from the holy book arose from the new condition of the cosmos, since now the clearly observable rhythms of the stars and of time emerged: it was the start of a knowledge of numbers, proportions and measures.

Noah learned from Adam . . . the true art of counting and took over from him the book of the signs, the book of knowledge of the stars . . . This book was written on a sapphire stone, clearly and distinctly, and from it Noah learned to know the work of the miracles as well as the secrets and treasures of reason . . . so that he was now capable of fathoming the stages of the upper regions, to roam through all seven spheres and circle all the planets. He could observe their paths and explore the course of the moon, as well as the paths of Aldebaran, Orion and Sirius. Noah knew the name of each heaven and what its function consisted of.[58]

The second part of Noah's teaching was related to the new condition of human nature:

The ancient sages copied a book about the art of healing from a book . . . which had been transmitted to Noah after the Flood . . . God sent one of his angels by the name of Raphael . . . and the angel revealed to Noah the remedies that heal sickness, and showed him the medicines to be taken from trees, herbs and roots . . . From this book, the first sages gathered their knowledge and then wrote many books on healing, each in his own tongue. Thus the art of healing spread to all peoples of the earth; the sages from India, from Macedonia and from Egypt all made use of it.[59]

The origin of medical art presupposes the spread of disease. Noah could become the inaugurator of the art of healing, the Asclepius of mankind, for, after death had become a reality, illness also invaded mankind. The cosmos cleared, and human consciousness also filled with clarity and wakefulness, but man lost his cosmic powers. He became weak in order to be able to become free. The yet unfree man of sleep-filled ancient times required healing no more than does the plant kingdom. But the freer he became, the more man was in need of help and healing, the more he required the helping healer. Through the primeval wisdom that permeated him and the healing spirit hovering over him, Noah was the first healer of humanity.

By saving the chosen part of humanity from the great flood catastrophe at the end of Atlantis, Manu-Noah, the great sun initiate, led man over a significant threshold of humanness. Heading towards freedom, man underwent a transition similar to that which took place in the succession of the kings of the Holy Grail, between the first and the second guardian of the sanctuary. Titurel, the aged father of the Grail lineage, was the great teacher, the king of wisdom. His son Amfortas could not remain at rest in the pure light world of nearness to the gods as did his father. He was driven by unrest into confusion; in the labyrinth of life he received the wound that brought him untold affliction and suffering and filled him with longing for the Redeemer. He was the king of suffering. As humanity proceeded from the Atlantean to the post-Atlantean era, it passed from Titurel to Amfortas. In the exalted early teachers, above all in the figure of Enoch, it had in its midst Titurel, the king of wisdom. Now mankind itself assumed the features of Amfortas, his affliction and longing. As a summation of the Amfortas-like post-Atlantean human being, the figure of Job was placed within the books of the Old Testament. A short study of the secret of Job is intended to make more comprehensible this important turning-point, which divides cosmic-mythological history from the mythological history of pre-historic ages.

The Talmud raises the question: 'When did Job live?' The resulting answers place him in each successive age after the Flood. The conclusion drawn from this is that he never lived at all, or, he lived in all these times. Traditions such as that which equates Job with Terah, Abraham's father, seems to point to a condition of human character, surpassing history, which Job represents for the entire post-Atlantean era. Job means 'the tried one, haunted by destiny'. He is a sort of Faust of post-Atlantean humanity; indeed, even Goethe formulated his poetic work, *Faust*, addressed to the modern age, on the biblical drama of Job.

All negations and trials which have invaded mankind since the end of the Lemurian time along with the solidification of the human body struck Job one blow after another. He faced the loss of his wealth; death confronted him, when his seven sons and three daughters became victims of the elements; he himself was stricken with illness. According to the apocryphal text of the *Testament of Job*, for forty-eight years his body was covered over and over with horrible boils. In Job, a balance of disaster was struck.

To Job's outer misfortunes were added the inner anguish, his isolation, his finally being able to rely on none but himself. From two different sides temptations urged Job to let go of his intense, severely tried ego-will. In the image of his wife, the earthly aspect of his soul advised him to allow the earth and death to gain power over him. In the image of his three friends, other voices of his own self rose up against him: through endless reproaches they

urged him to humble himself before God and to acknowledge his
sufferings as just punishments for his sinfulness. Man stands alone
between heaven and earth in his egohood. His fellow men only
make him more aware of his total isolation. Can the ego-will
assert itself, or will it yield to one or the other side?

The earthly aspect of temptation is easier to resist. The inner
tortures of struggling to find a meaning for the trials are worse
than external sufferings. The three friends caused him greater
anguish than the sores on his body. In the figures of Enoch and
the other patriarchs and ancient teachers, the Old Testament
reaches back far before the development of the people of Israel,
into the womb of humanity — still close to the gods — common
to all races and peoples. In the figure of Job it reached far beyond
the Israelite-Jewish element into a future, all-embracing human
element, to which nations and races relate as do rivers and streams
to the ocean into which they flow.

The three friends with their moralizing sermons represent a
standpoint for which religion and morals are synonymous, and
which had its classical expression in the Old Testament's religion
of law. There, no other answer can be found to the question
concerning the meaning of suffering except the one that it is
punishment for wrong-doing. There is a readily solved equation
between sin and misfortune. But through his religious awareness,
Job rises far above the level of merely human morality. For him
religion is more than morality. He senses something of the cosmic
origin and nature of suffering and from this — from embodying
the longing for redemption contained in all great post-Atlantean
religions — he gathers his confidence and steadfastness. He
accepts the risk of holding the conviction that he himself is not
guilty of his misfortune: 'And even if it be true that I have erred,
my error remains with myself ' (Job 19:4). The friends' concept
of God and his intentions must be insufficient. If the moral balance
sheet were the correct concept, wouldn't obvious evil-doers fare
badly? But the godless grow old and rich (Job 21:7). Yet why
does God punish man who cannot really exist without sin; why
does he pursue the dry chaff (Job 13:25)? If torment derives from
causes and intentions higher than those of the human realm, then
in that same higher realm of divine will, redemption must also be
in preparation.

Job faintly sensed something of the true cause of suffering in
the world. Earth with all its wealth of creation has become com-

pletely earthly. A man can dig into its depths, discover veins of silver and gold, and, from their dark concealment, bring to light precious stones. *One* treasure, however, has been lost; not to be found even by penetrating all the depths of the earth: this is *wisdom*. Ores can be found, but, 'Whence then comes wisdom?' (Job 28:20). Man remembers the time when he was not yet abandoned by the light of divine wisdom: 'Oh, that I were as in the months of old, as in the days when God watched over me; when his lamp shone upon my head, and by his light I walked through darkness; as I was in my autumn days, when the friendship of God was upon my tent . . .' (Job 29:2–4). 'And now my soul is poured out within me' (Job 30:16). Is there a way to the lost sphere of wisdom? Indeed, for 'God understands the way to it and he knows its place' (Job 28:23). But how can man find this way?

As Job touched upon the cosmic secrets of humanity's path, a new figure appeared against him in the dramatic course of events. A young man joined the three old men. It is as if Job's spiritual presentiment itself wanted to turn against him now in the figure of Elihu. With stormy temperament, Elihu urged Job no longer to reckon with God, whose almightiness in ruling the elements is invincible and throws man back on his minuteness and unimportance. And — as if Elihu had summoned it forth with his words — what the youth spoke of ensued: thunder rumbled, lightning flashed, and the voice of God manifested in the tempest.

Now speaking about himself, God puts weighty, soul-shattering questions to Job:

Where were you when I laid the foundation of the earth
. . .

when the morning stars sang together,
    and all the sons of God shouted for joy?
. . .

Have you entered into the springs of the sea,
    or walked in the recesses of the deep?
Have the gates of death been revealed to you?
. . .

Where is the way to the dwelling of light,
    and where is the place of darkness?
. . .

Have you entered the storehouses of the snow,
    or have you seen the storehouses of the hail?
. . .

Can you bind the chains of the Pleiades,
   or loose the cords of Orion?
   . . .
Who has put wisdom in the clouds [that which is hidden – *B*]?
   . . .
Is it by your wisdom that the hawk soars?
   . . .
Is it at your command that the eagle mounts up
   and makes his nest on high?
      (Job 38:4,7,16f,19,22,31,36; 39:26f)

What is the meaning of these questions? Have they no purpose other than to refer man back to his nothingness, to force him into silence and the admission of his insignificance in the face of God's majesty? Is a judgment to be pronounced on the nature of man? Man was not always forced to answer these questions as Job must: 'I lay my hand on my mouth' (Job 40:4). In primeval times there were human entities who would have had the right to hold their own ground against the divine questions. For could not a personage like Enoch have truly said that he had traversed all the depths of existence, and that the gates of death had opened unto him? Did he not bring tidings of the revelations of his ascension through the spheres of heaven?

   And there mine eyes saw the secrets of the lightning and of thunder, and the secrets of the clouds and dew, and there I saw from whence they proceed in that place and from whence they saturate the dusty earth. And there I saw closed chambers out of which the winds are divided, the chamber of the mist, and of the clouds, and the cloud thereof hovers over the earth from the beginning of the world. And I saw the chambers of the sun and the moon, whence they proceed and whither they come again, and their glorious return . . .[60]

If there was once a time when men were worthy to share in divine greatness and wisdom, then man is not condemned for all time to the poverty of Job. It must be possible to rediscover what has been lost. The shattering questions of God speaking out of the whirlwind make man aware of the loss of primeval revelation and wisdom, and at the same time awaken in him the longing and confidence that he will be able to reattain them. Once upon a time, man possessed the Book of Adam granted him in paradise. Where will he find the lost book again? A presentiment of the meaning of suffering flashes through Job's soul. Man suffers because he fell from the radiant light world of divine wisdom. But is suffering at the same time perhaps an impetus for reascent? Maybe it transforms the soul in such a way that it can rediscover what has been lost?

The tempestuous questions of God take on a different sound. They cease to expose the lack of revelation as they themselves become revealing interpretations. But they unveil gruesome apparitions to Job's soul:

> Behold, Behemoth,
>
> . . .
>
> > his limbs like bars of iron.
>
> . . .
>
> Can you draw out Leviathan
>
> . . .
>
> His sneezings flash forth light,
> > and his eyes are like the eyelids of the dawn.
> Out of his mouth go flaming torches;
> > sparks of fire leap forth
>
> . . .
>
> His breath kindles coals.
> > (Job 40:15,18; 41:1,18f, 21)

Is this to frighten Job anew and more deeply than before? A profound secret is involved here. What can be the meaning of the saying which states of Behemoth, the first of the two monsters: 'He is the first of the ways of God'? (Job 40:19*B*).

Enoch is still familiar with this secret. Where his descriptions apocalyptically point to the coming of the Messiah, he — like John in the Revelation (Chapter 13) — shows us the two beasts who rise up from the abyss and must be overcome:

> On that day two monsters will be apportioned, a female one by the name of Leviathan, to dwell in the depths of the ocean above the springs of the water; the male, however, is called Behemoth, and with its breast it takes up a tremendous wasteland.[61]

The cosmic secret that lies open before Enoch and is now also revealed to Job through the divine questions is that of the threshold. Here, two beasts seek to frighten man away and lead him astray. On one side stands the monster of Ahrimanic hardening. Like a machine crushing everything with 'iron bars', the figure of Behemoth rises. On the other side, the flame of Luciferic volatization and arrogance flares up. 'His heart is as hard as a stone' — yet Leviathan sparks forth hot fire. The twofold countenance of evil, which was known to the Greeks as Scylla and

Charybdis, and familiar to Germanic mythology as the Fenris-wolf and the Midgard-serpent, forces man to do battle on two fronts when he approaches the threshold of the spiritual realm. Because they denote the threshold, Behemoth and Leviathan are truly 'the beginning of the ways of God'. Beyond their sphere of chaos the way is open to the lost sphere of primeval revelation. Job beheld the beasts shown him by the divine word, and lo, he was able to endure their sight. The fearsome guardians of the threshold could not block his way. What else but his great suffering gave Job the strength to cross the threshold? At the close of the drama, Job does not appear as the humbled, repentant sinner, which is what ordinary interpretation assumes. He, the 'tried one', had passed the test of suffering by means of the strength gained through it. He himself could now say that he had attained the goal and that his eye for the world of the spirit was open: 'I had heard of thee by the hearing of the ear, but now my eye sees thee' (Job 42:5).

Beholding God is the fruit of the ordeals of suffering. The imaginative descriptions at the end of the Book of Job, elaborated in the *Testament of Job*, show that in Job man regains his lost divinity and hierarchical totality of being. Once again, Job was given seven sons and three daughters. The ten sephiroth of the members of man's being[62] resound harmoniously together once again. The higher triad of daughters, one of which is called 'the dove', are adorned with golden girdles. The first girdle imparts the ability to understand the language of the angels. The second teaches the language of the mights and the secrets of creation. The third bestows the speech of the cherubim and the mysteries of divine glory. A golden zither, a silver incense burner, and a copper kettle-drum are finally given to the three daughters to greet the charioteer upon Job's ascension.

Post-Atlantean humanity has to reckon and live with the suffering that has come into the world. But suffering is not punishment for wrong-doing. It is the driving force of inner progress. It drives man forward on the path on which the blessings of the beginning are to be reattained in freedom.

Atlantean humanity managed to cope with its ominous guest, death, by associating it with its counterpart, the sacrificial death of the mysteries, which won from it a higher life. Post-Atlantean humanity must do the same in regard to suffering. Because of the destinies of human beings, there is suffering everywhere. It tortures and depresses, embitters and shatters, but it can also lead him who bears it forward inwardly. But so that the poisonous sting could actually be increasingly removed from suffering, a form of suffering was quietly added behind the scenes of ordinary life which possessed more than personal significance. In the mystery temples the pupils of initiation were guided through suffering and trials which did not result from their personal destinies but which they took upon themselves, to rise through purification to the point of becoming leaders of mankind. Surrogate sufferings were endured voluntarily in the passion stages of initiation. The aspirant was led through them to the threshold of the spiritual worlds, to the 'beginning of God's ways'. And when he could say, 'I had heard of thee . . . but now my eye sees thee', he reaped the fruit of suffering for all humanity. Beholding God, revelation, was this fruit. Again and again, through the spiritual fruits of suffering the loss of primeval revelation was made good. The great inspirations and impulses for the lofty temple cultures of the post-Atlantean era arose through them. The suffering of Job is an image of what was endured over and over again in the quiet background of human evolution in the millennia after the time of Noah, and it bestows something of this secret upon the suffering of individual man as well. Through the fruits that matured in the soul, personal suffering could now be felt and perceived everywhere as meaningful. All suffering became a prophecy and presentiment of future redemption. The great surrogate suffering on Golgotha, which unlocks the gates of the lost paradise again for mankind, throws an advance shadow in the Job-suffering of post-Atlantean, Amfortas-like humanity.

The Age of the Patriarchs

6 Gilgamesh – Nimrod – Abraham: Between Babylonia and Egypt

From the sensational results of his excavations in Ur, the Chaldean city of Abraham, the English scholar Woolley draws the conclusion: 'We must revise considerably our ideas of the Hebrew patriarch when we learn that his earlier years were spent in such sophisticated surroundings; he was a citizen of a great city and inherited the traditions of an ancient and highly organised civilisation.'[63] The remains of mighty temples and amazing golden treasures of refined artistic quality from royal graves of still earlier times show Ur to be a world displaying the splendour of kings and priests. From the age of Abraham itself, buildings with evidence of great 'comfort and luxury' were unearthed, which present a picture of the cultural environment enjoyed by the citizenry of Ur. Life in these houses was by no means culturally primitive. Tablets were found with inscriptions of temple hymns, and mathematical tables which proceeded from simple problems of addition to formulae of extracting square and cubic roots. Private chapels were built into the homes in which the owners worshipped the house gods above the graves of their dead. From the same age, countless tablets with business data and receipts bear witness to the worldly industry which radiated from the royal palace throughout the whole city. There were, after all, regular factories on the temple grounds, where taxes in the form of raw materials were delivered for processing, and women were employed for spinning wool and weaving cloth.

Through misunderstanding the imaginative descriptions contained in the Old Testament, which were held to be direct recapitulations of external historical reality, people formed a picture of a devout, patriarchal life of shepherds and nomads. One imagines reverent old men in tents surrounded by their families and servants, their flocks kept on great expanses of lonely meadows and pastures. The journeys of an Abraham and Jacob are pictured in no other way than as migrations, which nomadic bedouin tribes were regularly forced to take in order to find new pasture lands for their herds.

Such ideas support the arrogance which believes that all civilization has developed from primitive beginnings to its present-day high level and splendour. It is conceded only gradually that in the same age, when the skyscraper of modern cultural undertakings began to crack, the shovels of archaeologists conjured forth from the ground an undreamed-of world of admirable temple cultures, that were still inspired by the twilight of primal revelation.

The shepherd-tales, in which the Bible speaks of the age of patriarchs, still possess the character of mythological imagination; and as with the descriptions of the time of primordial creation, these must become transparencies for us through which we gradually envision the historic form of ancient time. *Names* which formerly stood for whole generations of mankind and initiates, now actually begin to designate single individuals. The *events*, however, that are narrated are as yet not identical with actual physical occurrences of the era. Instead, they are picture-forms of what was happening in the souls of men, between the lines of external life. The imagination of shepherd life, though indeed present in outer existence, did not solely determine the cultural physiognomy of the age; it mainly indicates the state of soul and consciousness of the persons described. It is not without spiritual reason that the imaginative designation of the shepherd's office (the Latin word for shepherd is 'pastor') has been in use up until our own time for the priests's ministry. By speaking of the patriarchs as shepherds, the Old Testament describes the priestly atmosphere and feeling which was the fundamental soul feature of their culture. We must envisage Abraham as a priest-king, equal in rank to the mighty figures of rulers of ancient Babylon and Egypt emerging from the obscurity of history.

It was around 2000 BC that Abraham of Ur in Chaldea was growing up to meet his destined task. What did the play of forces of nations and cultures look like in the region between the Euphrates and Tigris rivers into which he was placed? An abundant, spiritually vibrant civilization had flourished there for thousands of years. The German excavations of the 1920s in Uruk, the biblical Erech, not far from Ur in southern Mesopotamia, demonstrate this especially clearly. While no sensational findings of gold artefacts comparable to those of the Anglo-American excavations in Ur were made here, the ground yielded a sequence of strata that were extraordinarily clear and informative; they go back as far as 4000 BC and even in the oldest sections contain evidence of advanced cultures.

The young civilization of Mesopotamia must have been in constant flux. It is believed that traces of many migrations and transformations can be deciphered. A particularly decisive time however, was around 3000 BC, a thousand years before Abraham. A long since petrified layer of mud deep in the ground is evidence of tremendous floods that afflicted the region of the Euphrates and Tigris at that time and altered it completely. Directly after this, the clearly-grouped royal lineages of the Babylonian kingdoms commence with the first dynasty of Ur. In ever more grandiose architectural and sculptural forms, the cultures that now arise finally take on the appearance which they exhibited in the days of Abraham.

The traces of flood disaster in Mesopotamia are evaluated by Woolley as outer proof of the biblical myth's historical veracity. Indeed, supporting this assertion, many of the flood sagas, shared by all ancient nations, point by reason of certain suggestions of dates to the same time, namely 3000 BC. This is the case with the Greek myth of Deucalion, the Chinese traditions dating from the age of Yan, and a number of other ancient reports. Simultaneously with the Babylonian flood, catastrophes of similar importance must have been experienced in many different locations of the world.

What happened a thousand years before Abraham's time all over the world were not just coincidental outer events. They were signals and symptoms of a turning point, which, according to the law of repetition and reflection of the greater rounds in smaller ones, represents an exact analogy to the Atlantean Flood. This time, instead of the sinking of a continent, the end of a certain soul condition took place in humanity. This is how the seers, from whose retrospective vision the flood sagas have originated, have looked through the window of the closer, smaller flood back to the great original Flood.

Anthroposophical research gives us a significant explanation concerning the events that occurred around 3000 BC everywhere, but with particular vehemence in Babylonia. Referring to the ancient oriental tradition of Kali Yuga, the Dark Age, lasting

5000 years, Rudolf Steiner relates[64] that its beginning (exactly 3101 BC) coincides with the events indicated by the flood sagas. An ancient clairvoyant faculty was extinguished in human souls all over the whole world at that time. The light of the supersensory world disappeared to man, and in the darkness that now surrounded him, he had to learn to turn his gaze into the physical world. Until then, the auric veil of the ethereal and astral world, woven of flowing colourful images, had concealed rather than revealed the physical-earthly world of objects. The transition must have been of catastrophic intensity, and must have caused an actual faintness of consciousness, which, in a period of weeks, intensified to the utmost. An extremely frightening and oppressive condition of sleep came over people, filling souls with a sense as of drowning. What took place was initially an occurrence in the state of consciousness of humanity. Kali Yuga's oncoming flood of darkness washed away the ancient vision. In many places, ominous external catastrophes must have accompanied this faintness; either, not being themselves, human beings brought about incalculable disaster or, as in Babylonia, where tremendous storms and floods raged, so that large numbers of people actually perished. The imaginations of a great flood, which arise in the recollections of nations, refer primarily to soul events, inasmuch as they point to the beginning of the Kali Yuga, and only to a minor extent to outer happenings. With the figures corresponding to the biblical Noah, spiritual leaders are referred to who in the sudden darkness were able to maintain the light of consciousness and could therefore lead men over to the new form of consciousness.

The great Flood of Noah's time also represented a mighty change of consciousness accompanied by natural catastrophes. The world of Atlantean consciousness was washed away by the flood waters, along with the Atlantean continent. Only those human beings, who already carried the new seed thought within themselves, could make a fruitful transition into new realms of the world and of consciousness under the guidance of the great Manu.

The transformation of consciousness connected with the setting-in of Kali Yuga was nowhere of greater significance and force than in Babylonia, to where the scene of cultural human progress had just shifted. The third pre-Christian millennium, which prepared the way for Abraham's era, abounds with creative action in this particular area. The Kali Yuga produces its first great culture.

After the Atlantean flood, two great cultures had been inaugurated successfully by messengers of the great Manu in the continuing course of human evolution, still receiving their characteristics entirely from ancient clairvoyance: the ancient holy Indian and the primeval Persian culture. Around the turn of the fourth to the third pre-Christian millennium, the Persian epoch had come to an end.* The third epoch, the first culture of Kali Yuga, the beginning of which already falls within the Dark Age, was the Babylonian-Egyptian civilization, a twin-culture divided between the region of the two streams — the Euphrates and Tigris — and the land of the one stream — the Nile.

In the second post-Atlantean era, simultaneously with the advanced culture of ancient Persia, Babylonia was the setting of the exceedingly spiritual, noble life of the *Sumerians*. The ceremonial mild light of ancient vision and wisdom shone on everything that pre-Babylonians produced. Rudolf Steiner relates[65] that the early culture of the Sumerians was characterized in particular by the fact that there was no discrepancy between thinking and speaking. He says that by virtue of its spirit-near purity, the Sumerian language expressed in its sounds the spiritual set of facts referred to. It was, therefore, comprehended by all peoples like a 'kind of primeval language of all humanity', although differentiated languages already existed everywhere. The Sumerians have become the originators of alphabetical scripts through their cuneiform writing, which had been perfected in preceding stages of pictographic writing.[66] The sound-ether harmonies of the starry heaven were the soul of external Sumerian cultural creations. Celestial measurements were mirrored in the measurements in use on earth. Only a faint reminiscence of the highly spiritual Sumerian life was preserved in the language and star-wisdom of the Babylonians.

When, accompanied by great catastrophes, the Dark Age set in, it was as if the radiant vision-beholding soul had vanished from the noble body of Sumerian culture. At just this point in time, Babylonia together with Egypt had to undertake the cultural guidance of mankind. What happened was as if a person were crowned

* The duration of each cultural epoch is about 2160 years; this is the time it takes for the vernal equinox to move through one-twelfth of the zodiac. The end of the second epoch falls in the year 2907 BC.

90

king at the very moment he became blind. In one stroke the appearance of Mesopotamia is changed. The tranquillity of Sumerian time is gone. Sumerian, Akkadian, Assyrian, Aramean, Hittite and Scythian-Nordic tribes mingle together in confusion. With ceaseless dynamic tension and feverish movement, they build a culture in darkness of soul as if to defend themselves against it and rise above it.

One begins to understand the image of the construction of the tower of Babel as a symbolic expression of the cultural drive of will which rose up in Mesopotamia after the great turning point and branched out everywhere. Everywhere human fear pours over souls along with the darkness. As if under an oppressive soul-spiritual shortness of breath, man wants to rush upwards out of the dark depth to the vanished light of the heights. Fear makes him selfish and violent. Until then, culture had been bestowed and inspired from above to below. Out of a form of universal panic a titanic urge is now born which causes abandoned human beings to erect a towering culture of their own upward from below. But darkness can only give birth to the dark, however grandiose the latter may be. The consequence of building the tower of Babel is described by the biblical myth as the confusion of tongues. This indication is all the more revealing the more one becomes familiar with the spirit-near language element of Sumerian prehistoric time. The last remnant of God's Word, which united human beings, is silenced in human language. No longer does speech come from above, there is only speaking from below. As speech becomes devoid of God, it splits up into the many languages that have no linking bridge between them; men no longer understand each other. 'Humanity' pales into abstraction. The age of isolated nations fighting against each other commences. The name Babel changes its meaning. It no longer signifies the 'portal of God', but the 'chaotic mixture' of nations and languages: 'Therefore its name was called Babel, because there the LORD confused the language of all the earth; and from there the LORD scattered them abroad over the face of all the earth' (Gen.11:9). Babylonian history with its impossible tangle of peoples and ruling dynasties is a true symbol of the confusion of consciousness in which humanity now of necessity became caught up.

In comparison with the Babylonian, Egyptian history of the early ages has something much more lineal and uniform about it in spite of the tension that soon existed between lower and upper

Egypt. An extraordinarily important difference of inner character
was concealed behind that of the external course of history of the
twin cultures. Rudolf Steiner presented the former in connection
with the figures of the two inaugurators, Hermes and Gilgamesh.[67]
Hermes belonged to the age before the onset of the Kali Yuga.
He himself represented nothing but the peace and wisdom-filled
repetition of Hermes Trismegistos — synonymous with Enoch
— of the distant primordial past. He was 'a personality who saw
deeply into the holiest secrets of initiation and could therefore
become the great inaugurator of Egyptian culture'. Gilgamesh, on
the other hand, the developer of external Babylonian culture, was
a man of the first millennium of the Dark Age, who had struggled
to make his way to the spirit by means of a destiny already formed
along personal lines to an extraordinary degree. The great Babylonian *Epic of Gilgamesh* shows how the hero, struggling with
his destiny, only penetrated to the threshold of initiation. Tragically, he was no longer capable of passing the final trials. Hence,
'the external Babylonian culture . . . was prepared by a leading
personality, who in his soul had all the qualities that develop when
one does not penetrate into the innermost essence of the holy
secrets.' Egypt and Babylonia both had their mysteries, but the
culture that originated alongside the Nile was a more genuine and
adequate expression of Egyptian mystery wisdom; whereas the
characteristic of the Mesopotamian culture with its powerful development was that its inner and outer life no longer coincided
and were not in keeping with each other. Externalization of culture had its origin in Babylonia. So 'we have . . . in ancient
Babylonia an external cultural development and an esoteric inner
one clearly proceeding side by side. While there is more interplay
between these two in Egyptian life, in the Babylonian culture
. . . they definitely diverge.' Here we have gained an important
key for understanding the world and time into which Abraham is
placed. In Babylonia, Abraham finds himself surrounded by a
magnificent culture, but one already succumbing to externalization
and marked by the spirit of the Dark Age.

The imaginative traditions relating to the Old Testament do not
confront Abraham with the warrior Gilgamesh but with the powerful King Nimrod, of whom Genesis says that he 'was a mighty
hunter before the LORD'. Gilgamesh and Nimrod have often been
equated with each other. On searching among the great Babylonian rulers of Abraham's age for the historical name of the figure,

who is called only by his mythical name in the Babylonian epic and the Old Testament, repeatedly the great lawgiver of Babylonia, the Amorite prince Hammurabi,* who can probably be pictured as a younger contemporary of Abraham, was thought of. But names like Nimrod and Gilgamesh do not designate human individualities in the same way as do the names Abraham and Hammurabi. Though Gilgamesh was indeed the mystery name for a definite historical personality, it points more to the spiritual forces that worked through him; after all, the epic itself states that Gilgamesh was two-thirds god and one-third man. The individual indicated with the name Gilgamesh was not necessarily identical with one of the figures of the great rulers of whom outer tradition speaks. In view of the lively blending of myth and history in those early ages, we must try to arrive at clear images without definite fixation points and sharp contours. The assumption, however, may be justified that Gilgamesh was an older contemporary of Abraham.

The name Nimrod has still quite other dimensions. This, the Talmudists were also aware of; in many old legends they present Abraham and Nimrod as antagonists, for they themselves often point out that Genesis includes Nimrod in the third and Abraham in the tenth generation among the sons of Noah. By virtue of his own nature, a mythological man confronts us in Nimrod. As yet, he had none of the contours of an ego-being; he therefore still reached up into a giant dimension spanning generations. Abraham on the other hand was already the clearly defined figure of the historical human being. Here, two eras overlap. 'Nimrod' was a Babylonian term for Mars, the god of war. This agrees with the old characterizations which state that Nimrod was the first to have waged wars. The fallacies of Kali Yuga assumed tangible form. Hence, the name Nimrod referred more to the spirit that imbued a person than to the person himself. Nimrod meant 'the rebel'.†️ If this word can still suggest the original spatial and pictorial conception of stretching upward, then once again we have the image of the Babylonian tower, graduated upward in steps, in the

---

* He is also taken to be the Babylonian king Amraphel, mentioned in Genesis (14:1). The name 'Amraphel' means 'the obscured word'; hence, like the myth of the tower of Babel, refers to the loss of the primeval language.

† *Translators note*. The German word, translated here as 'rebel', is *Empörer*. The word *Empörer*, as Emil Bock points out, could literally mean 'the one who stretches upward'.

form of a word. Indeed, legend shows us the great tyrannical ruler as the builder of the tower. The designation of 'hunter' must be taken imaginatively just like that of 'shepherd'. The hunter, turned completely to the outside, is concerned with putting into service and mastering the life forces contained in nature — not out of love for the creatures but in ruthless striving for power. In Nimrod and Abraham, hunter and shepherd confronted each other; the tyrannical potentate and one who ministers like a priest. In mythological intensification Nimrod, like Gilgamesh, was the embodiment of cultural externalization.

Abraham's birth is surrounded by especially significant and impressive legendary stories. Their value not only lies in the many parallels reminiscent of the Christmas stories of the Gospel, but above all in the key they offer to the imagery of the concrete difference between Abraham's mission and that of the Babylonian culture. We are told that Terah, Abraham's father, was the supreme commander at the court of King Nimrod. The birth of the boy was announced by the appearance of a new, brilliant star; the astrologers, questioned by Nimrod, said that he who would then be born would overthrow many kings. Nimrod then instigated an infanticide of immense proportion. The later infanticides, the one by Pharaoh at the birth of Moses and Herod's at the birth of Jesus, were far surpassed by Nimrod's action. It is told that an enormous temple was specially constructed, and in it were placed all young mothers with their infant boys and all pregnant women; and 70 000 young lives were destroyed. Terah was able to hide his wife in an underground rock cavern. When she gave birth to her son, 'the whole cave suddenly became light as if by sunshine, for thus shone the face of the infant'.[68] The boy Abraham spent the next ten years growing up in the cave; many miracles surrounded his childhood in concealment. There followed a puzzling period in his life, which the legends judge to be a very long time, and of whose significance we shall speak later.

> He went to Noah and his son Shem and dwelt with them, and learned from them the disciplines of God and his ways. No one knew where he was; and he served Noah and his son a long time; thirty-nine years did he spend in Noah's house.[66]

Following this, he returned to hhis ather at the court of Nimrod; and with great force of spirit he opposed the idol worship in Ur and particularly Nimrod's construction of the tower of Babel.

Tower and cave: Nothing can express the contrast of the streams personified in Nimrod and Abraham more graphically than this image. The Babylonian tower symbolizes an unrestrained urge to expand; Abraham's cave is the image of concealed introspection.[70]

In this contrast we have an exact pictorial formula for the transformation of consciousness and of the soul organism, which took place at that time in the human being. The ancient clairvoyance of mankind had come about, while man's ethereal body, woven of growth and formative forces, possessed a certain independence of the physical body and extended beyond the latter. The part of the ethereal body belonging in particular to the head did not coincide with man's physical head. In his supersensory organism, man had preserved something of the Atlantean possibility of being a giant, although the physical body was already of a density and hardness, which confined it within certain limits of growth. When the Dark Age set in, the light of ancient clairvoyance was extinguished, because a shrinking of the ethereal body commenced. The ethereal body began to adjust itself to the form of the physical body, and the ethereal head also increasingly coincided with the physical head.

Along with a completely new form of consciousness, there had to come a totally changed bodily awareness. Man suddenly felt constricted, as if he were in too small a house. Two attitudes of soul were possible: man either resisted the shrinking with utmost exertion of his faculties and stubbornly sought to perpetuate the old world condition; or he adapted himself to it and tried to wrest a new life-purpose from the new mode of functioning of the formative forces.

The first attitude was that of Nimrod-humanity: it wanted to continue outwardly the ethereal body's working, and now, denied the accommodation of the physical body, built the larger body outside: the larger house, the tower. A mighty will of architecture was born. Since man himself could no longer be a giant, he erected giant buildings; yet, what he accomplished was nothing other than the building of enormous monuments to his past relationship with the ethereal and growth forces. The more violent his struggle against the new laws of life became, the more it led, undeterred, into the black magical degenerations which had already arisen in the Atlantean age. The legend of Nimrod's infanticide is an indication that black magic had early on interfused the external culture of the Babylonians and Assyrians. The forces that built the corporeal sheath within the maternal womb and in the child's infancy fell victim to sinister misuse in the service of greed for power. The far-reaching abuse of the forces of reproduction and growth, which marked a part of Atlantean life, now found its feasible continuation. Setting in at an early date, the decadence in the utilization of the sexual and birth mysteries was the reason why the Apocalypse of John later designated Babylon as the great whore and used it as a symbol of an impure relationship with the supersensory.

The stream of humanity that was able to adjust to the new world condition was personified in Abraham. Actively building within the physical body, the ethereal body formed organs of a new consciousness. The image of man being reared inside a cave became reality. Especially through the ethereal head's coming to coincide with the physical head in the cranial cavity, the brain was perfected into the organ and instrument of thinking. For this was the historic mission of the Abraham figure: 'the shaping and crystallizing of a physical organ' for the intellectual comprehension of the world.[71]

> Thinking can only arise, when the brain and the ethereal body of the brain coincide. The ethereal body then works in the most elaborate way on the brain; exhausts its forces in doing so, and therefore can no longer develop clairvoyance along with it. It was, however, necessary that just this faculty, which is tied to brain-thinking, penetrated humanity. For this purpose, an individuality had to be chosen in whom there remained the least of what can be called old clairvoyance; but in whom, on the other hand, the physical instrument of the brain was perfected to the highest possible degree. This individuality was especially able to command a view of all the phenomena of the physical world as to measure, number, order and harmony, and to seek the common denominator in all the phenomena spread out around him . . . This individuality was Abraham.[72]

It was not only the organ of the brain that was developed into the bearer of a new soul capacity at this turning point of time in the evolution of consciousness. Simultaneously, the sense organs received their clear physical determination and became capable of distinct sense perceptions, which then increasingly took the place of the remains of ancient clairvoyance. Everywhere, the ethereal body relinquished its extension beyond the physical corporeality and thus imbued the latter with a contoured distinctiveness as it flowed into its form. Clear physical seeing and hearing set in as the ethereal parts of eye and ear completely gave up their predominance over the physical part and identified with it. Brain and sense organs now worked together; through the instrument of his senses man received the abundance of phenomena offered by the outer world; through the instrument of the brain he was able to grasp the order and unity of phenomena with his thinking. Brain-thinking and clear sense perception of the physical world were simultaneously acquired by humanity as the first essential fruits of the Kali Yuga. They found their first great representative, in whom they became reality, in Abraham.

In his allegorical study 'On Abraham', Philo of Alexandria offered us an example of the fact that the imaginative cave motif, which surrounded the figure of Abraham, had always been connected with the new organ-development in the interior of the physical body. He compared Abraham's viewpoint with that of the Chaldeans. The Chaldeans remained within a hazy diversity of existence, blind to the unity within this manifoldness. In Abraham, the thinking spirit awakened, coherently guiding the senses and therefore perceiving the homogeneity of the Creator in the multiplicity of creations. Philo connected this with the name of the city of Haran, which Abraham first went to from Ur:

> [Abraham] who had been bred up in this doctrine, and who for a long time had studied the philosophy of the Chaldeans, as if suddenly awakening from a deep slumber and opening the eye of his soul, and beginning to perceive a pure ray of light instead of profound darkness, followed the light, and saw what he had never seen before, a certain governor and director of the world standing above it . . .
>
> It is for this reason that Abraham is said to have made his first migration from the country of the Chaldeans into the land of Charran.
>
> But Charran, in the Greek language, means 'holes', which is a figurative emblem of the regions of our outward senses; by means of which, as by holes, each of these senses is able to look out . . .[73]

Gradually, the image of Abraham's human and historical mission became fully clear. He was a contemporary of Babylonia's division into an esoteric and exoteric culture. Though being himself a product of the Chaldean mysteries, which had preserved the purity of the spiritual heritage of Sumerian prehistory in the quiet background of the increasingly louder cultural activity, Abraham did not merely proceed against the fact of externalization.* He did not want to save or play off the esoteric world of the mysteries against all outer culture. He only had to convert the mysteries in a different manner from Nimrod-Gilgamesh into an external cultural stream. The Nimrod-Gilgamesh culture signified a gigantic personalization of the spirit, a bringing-down of the spiritual context into the realm of personality, ruled to begin with by chaotic will, and its isolation and separateness.[74] The Abraham stream inaugurated a transformation of the spiritual into the impersonal element of thought, of the calculating intellect, which in turn changed human consciousness through and through. Both Gilgamesh and Abraham were traditionally shown as proceeding from Ur, the name of which denotes primal light. But their paths diverged already at the common starting point; Gilgamesh moved from Ur to Uruk and Babylon into the country of powerful development. Abraham proceeded from Ur to Haran and Palestine into the land of the quiet intellectual maturing.

Abraham's spiritual character is indicated, when he is designated as the founder of arithmetic, of calculation, and when the cabbala reaches back to Abraham in its most important section, the holy *Sepher Yetzirah*, the 'Book of Numbers'. The Book of Adam reached Abraham on its many paths of destiny in a very special form. The script of divine images was now transformed into numbers of all kinds.

Along with the brain-thinking, the soul acquired a first ego-point, a centralizing and unifying force. By means of the inner unity, man beheld the divine oneness in the universe. Monotheistic thought was born of the structure that human consciousness now assumed. It had been the mission of Noah to direct human beings to the *invisible* divinity behind all natural phenomena, and

* Today, the opinion is often voiced that in Babylonia's great multitude of races, the Chaldeans were but one tribe making a relatively late appearance. But the reason their name was mentioned relatively late in outer history could well be that it denoted not merely a physical tribal group, but the community of those who guarded the mysteries and therefore remained for a longer time more in the background. Just as the Levites were bearers of the temple service in the national context of the Israelites, so, in Babylonia, the Chaldeans may well have had a specific mission in regard to the mysteries. In any event, their name (Chaldean = Hasid) has remained in use until late for the representatives of a world concept oriented upon the stars; and the members of the mystical direction of Orthodox Judaism, which related itself to Baal Shem, call themselves Hasidim to this day.

thereby to implant in them the first presentiment of the power of thought. In Abraham, humanity began to seek the *one* divinity, the creator of all creatures.

In their way, ancient Jewish legends bring to expression that Abraham was a 'first one'. An interrogation is related which Nimrod conducted with Abraham, when the latter had been thrown into a dungeon because of his protest against the construction of the tower.

> *Nimrod*: Why do you refuse to pay homage to the fire, to my god?
> *Abraham*: Water puts out fire.
> *Nimrod*: We pray to the water also.
> *Abraham*: The clouds carry the water.
> *Nimrod*: We revere the clouds also.
> *Abraham*: The winds scatter the clouds.
> *Nimrod:* The winds too are our gods.
> *Abraham*: But the earth is stronger than the wind.
> *Nimrod*: How long will you blaspheme the gods?
> If you will not do homage to the fire, then it shall consume you.[75]

Abraham wanted to penetrate through the manifoldness of the elements and creatures to the oneness of the creator. Nimrod, however, did not relinquish elementary life.

The story continues that Nimrod actually threw Abraham into a fiery furnace. The fire was tended for three days, but when Abraham was thrown into it, he did not burn. He felt as if he were among blossoming, fragrant trees. 'He moved around in the fire three days and three nights.'[76] The archangel Gabriel had beseeched the Lord to permit him to cool the fire and save Abraham, and he was given the reply: 'I am the only one in my world, and he is the only one in his world. It is fitting that an only one save an only one.'[77] This legend may be an indication that Abraham had to undergo certain decadent initiation ceremonies — the legends themselves follow up the story of the fiery furnace with the explanation that unlike other people the Chaldeans did not baptize with water but with fire[78] — but that his consciousness did not succumb to the trials. It now penetrated even more to the perception of the one divine ego, which proved helpful to him, the first human ego.

It is said that Abraham was the first who called the divine his 'Lord'. He was also supposed to have been the first who became grey and bore the sign of old age. The crown of white hair was placed on him.[79] Man became 'I'-bearing man and found the

'I'-oneness of the Godhead. But he only attained this goal by renouncing his old relationship to the forces of life and youth. The number of dark guests increase on earth. Old age was added to death and sickness. But man could also bear with dignity what was difficult about destiny. With the trials of Job began Job's standing the test of the trials: 'Before Abraham came, the Lord judged the world with harshness. Only to Abraham was it given to atone through suffering. Since then, suffering moves through the world.'[80]

Abraham's journeys were the first events on the stage of historical development that we no longer need to divine through the picture-veils of mythology. Openly and clearly, they appear to our view in their own historical dynamics. Through them, a most important figure was inscribed into the book of history: a figure of self-discovery within a strange environment. Throughout the entire Old Testament, this figure is repeated and retraced again and again. The movement is like the swinging of a pendulum, which swings in opposite directions until it comes to rest in the middle. Abraham left Babylonia, the land of the two streams, and arrived in the region of Palestine. But he did not remain, and instead continued farther into the land of the one stream, Egypt. But the world of Pharaoh could not hold him any more than could the world of Nimrod. Although the Jordan had nothing of the majestic greatness of the rivers in the midst of which it is located, the Euphrates and Tigris in the north-east and the Nile in the southwest, it was the one that finally offered Abraham a new home and the Promised Land. In the middle between Babylonia and Egypt, the pendulum of Abraham's journeys came to rest in the land of the Jordan. Later, with the migrations of Jacob, Joseph's journey, and the two great exiles of the Israelites (the Egyptian and Babylonian captivities) the pendulum again left its position of rest, swinging out again to each side. But finally, after 'the flight into Egypt' had awakened a faint memory of the pendulum-swing of the Old Testament, the figure found its stability in the central events of the Gospel.

What set the pendulum in motion? Genesis says that the divine call sounded forth to Abraham to leave his home in Chaldea. If, however, we want to feel our way towards the concrete historical facts, we must further ask: What kind of destinies gave rise to the call that came to Abraham?

100

6 GILGAMESH – NIMROD – ABRAHAM

There can be no doubt, after all that has been discussed so far, that as time went by Abraham had to place himself more and more consciously in opposition to the Gilgamesh culture arising around him. If he not only wanted to protect himself against this world of externalization and will for power, but also wanted to discover a way of fulfilling his own mission, he had to cut himself loose from the connections with Chaldean-Babylonian life. Did the great, older sister-culture on the Nile perhaps offer him the basis for his mission? Egypt must have appeared to him in many respects as the opposite of Babylonia. On account of the chasm between the contents of its esoteric and exoteric cultures, Babylonia had fallen into decadence sooner than Egypt. There, in Abraham's time, the accord between external culture and the mysteries was still maintained. Whereas Abraham left behind in Babylonia the scene of a great human Fall into sin, in Egypt he entered a land which had received its imprint from a great cosmic Fall into sin. Mesopotamia, the land of the two streams, was rich, abundant, fertile land. A last trace of the times when the sun garden of paradise spread out over these regions could be sensed here and there. Egypt, on the other hand, was a regal, grandiose desert into which only the majestic river Nile with its narrow band of fertility traced the possibility of civilized life. Something of the nether world, something tomblike, has always hung over the land with cosmic solemnity. This is why Egypt was great through the mysteries of death and its sepulchral temples, as was Babylon through the mysteries of birth and life forces. From the land of decadent birth mysteries, Abraham came into the world of the still genuine mysteries of death. He could learn from both cultures, but neither offered him a foundation for the unobtrusive seeds of thoughtful inwardness and egoity he had to sow.

The polarity between Babylonia and Egypt must have been a broader although less intense development of the contrast to be seen in the region of Palestine between Galilee and Judea. As in a larger, hence less intense Galilee, the very last vestiges of the Hyperborean paradisal sun existence and sun separation may have been noticeable in Babylonia, whereas Egypt, like a widely spread-out Judean desert, exhibited moon quality and traces of the moon separation. The fact that Babylonia was experienced as a terrestrial reflection of paradise and Egypt as a land of the nether world, seems to date back to far-distant ages. Even in the Psalms and books of prophecy of the Old Testament, Egypt is designated as Rahab, the 'gaping opening' (of the abyss) and compared with a Leviathan-like monster.[81]

Legendary tradition relates Abraham's exodus from Ur with Nimrod's Babylonian tower-construction. The image of forty-eight-year-old Abraham, who refused to work on the tower and called down a curse on the construction work, does not only contain imaginative but also concrete external historical truth.

The excavations of the last decade have shown us that the age of Abraham was indeed the construction epoch of a great number of tower-like temple pyramids in Mesopotamia called ziggurats, or 'mountains of the gods'. A will to build skyward not only inspired Babylonian life in general, it created a direct expression in architectural achievements of the mightiest proportion. In Ur and Uruk as well as in the temple district of E Sag Ila in the city of Babylon, remnants of the great pyramidal structures have been unearthed, whose huge outside staircases led to successive stepped-back levels, on the highest of which as on a platform, the shrines of the theophany were frequently erected. Throughout the whole of Babylonia, these structures must have existed, which for that time were unprecedented and revealed a completely new feeling towards the world.

Cave-born Abraham departed the land of tower-building. He had to leave in order to find himself and a more inward will to build. The pendulum swing of his journey, however, led him past the middle. He arrived in Egypt. What did he find here? We take part in a dramatic, most exciting and decisive moment of ancient history, if we picture the scene of how Abraham ran into the grandiose Egyptian pyramid structures south of the Nile Delta around the ancient royal city of Memphis. The great pyramids of Cheops and Chephren in Giza, the pyramids of Saqqara and others, had already been erected by that time. The world Abraham intended to escape from on one side approached him again from the other side.

There was in fact a difference between the ziggurats of Babylonia and Egypt's pyramids, which is of considerable spiritual-historical importance, although it appears to be only a technical one. The oldest of the Egyptian pyramids are built of colossal stones; and concerning their manner of construction they present seemingly insoluble riddles to us. In the case of the structures in Babylonia, a land without rock formations, the invention of brick-making was put to use from the beginning; a fact which biblical myth already refers to (Gen.11:3). Egyptian construction technique represents an end. For the last time, forces had been utilized which were quite common in Atlantean prehistory and had been retained in the bodily constitution of the slaves. These were the forces of the ethereal body — as yet not absorbed by the physical corporeality — which made physical accomplishments feasible that today no longer seem believable. Babylonian construction technique, on the other hand, signified a most successful new beginning. By means of the invention of brick construction, Babylonia originated the whole grandiose development of technology. In the presence of the pyramidal towers made of brick, it is understandable that the members of the Abraham-humanity experienced shivers of an eerie presentiment of incalculable effects, a premonition of limitless estrangement from God. Today, we have by far surpassed Babylonian towers in regard to their height as well as the inventions employed then. But only through the set-backs of cultural materialism will a feeling slowly be regained for the ominous inscrutability of this development.

The construction technique utilized on the great pyramids of Giza was something that could not be repeated any more. So it came about that for the time being Egypt's giant structures remained purely concerns of the gods, preserving the close accord with the intentions of the mysteries. The Babylonian style of construction was like the unleashing of a tremendous avalanche. A flood of inventions began, which man's egoism and greed for power immediately put to use. Construction is torn from the domain of the sanctuary. The way is open to the profane utilitarian culture.

Thus, in the presence of the Egyptian pyramids, Abraham was indeed touched by a spirit differing from that of the ziggurats of his homeland; but he could no more fulfil his non-magical, purely human mission in the atmosphere of Egypt's divine magic than in the human magic of Babylonia. He therefore made the inconspicuous land of the Jordan his new home; a region that in all ages has been without architecture, and which, instead of external temples, probably already possessed a hidden world of grotto and cave-mysteries in those early times. Abundant traces of these can still be detected in Jerusalem today. The image of the cave, not the tower, can symbolize the mission of Abraham. The considerations of the next chapter will show that it is possible to feel our way even more concretely and closely into the impulses that motivated Abraham to make his journeys.

It would be quite wrong to assume that Abraham turned away from 'Babylonian-Egyptian paganism' in nothing but total disgust. To arrive at such conclusions is to take the legendary and fairy-tale-like imaginations, which personify everything, as a direct account of the historical course of events. For not only personal but also great cultural controversies came to pass. The civilizations of Babylonia and Egypt were too abundant and worthy of admiration for anyone to have turned his back on them without learning from them. And Abraham, himself emerging from Chaldean life, retained both Babylonia and Egypt in his nature in a variety of ways. It required all the destinies and efforts of the spiritual stream descending from him to transform and deepen the foreign heritage bit by bit. The people with whom Abraham surrounded himself illustrate the fact that he carried with him something of the soul of both great cultures which he left behind, into the land of his own destiny.

Particularly the separation from Babylonia was by no means easy and smooth. The first major move came into Abraham's destiny, when his father Terah and he were driven to leave their home in Ur and make Haran, in the north of the country, the centre of actual Babylonian life, their place of residence. But here, the peremptory voice of the Godhead issued forth to Abraham to leave the country. His mission did not rest within the old; something new was to proceed from him. After he had come to Palestine, he was drawn back, as it says, to Haran once again for a number of years, until he finally departed from Babylonia for good.

One of the most ancient cities of mankind, since primeval times the converging point of the most important trade and travel routes, Haran was interesting from the religious-historical standpoint. Until the Middle Ages, the Sabians residing there claimed to be in possession of special wisdom traditions and astronomical secrets; therefore, they joined none of the great religious faiths. In all ages, Haran was considered the home of the moon mysteries and the site of the main temple of the lunar god.

The moon cult spread over the whole of Babylonia; after all, the word 'Shinar', the biblical name of the land, contains the Babylonian designation of the moon god 'Sin'. But everywhere, the moon service was mixed with other cults and led into ecstatic directions. In very ancient times, as the seat of the pure moon mysteries, Haran must have been filled by a wisdom stream which possessed something of the serene radiance of moonlight. It was, therefore, suitable in aiding Abraham to find his own self. For the brain is a microcosmic mirror-instrument for the spirit in the same sense that the moon is the reflector for sunlight in the macrocosm. Abraham's relationship with the spiritual stream of the city of Haran became personified in Abraham's oldest brother, who was himself named Haran. The traditions outside the Bible describe Terah, the Semitic chief commander of the Babylonian army, as a member of Babylonian cultic and spiritual life in every respect: The same held true for his son Haran, who, as the first-born, was mainly the bearer of the paternal heritage. The synonymity of the name no doubt expressed a soul-spirit affinity on Haran's part with the mysteries of the city of Haran. Nahor and Abraham, the younger sons of Terah, were more independent of the Babylonian spirit from the beginning. The legend therefore lists them as the first of the twelve who refused to work on Nimrod's construction of the tower.[82]

It is said that Haran died while Abraham and Terah still lived in Ur. Haran's death is veiled in secrets. Some legends state that Haran fell victim to the flames of the same fire-baptism from which Abraham was so miraculously saved. Thus, Haran's death again signified a new step on the path, which removed humanity from the old laws of life. 'From the day the world was created until the time Haran appeared, no son had died during his father's lifetime. Thus, with Haran, the first breach had come into the world.'[83] Death tears away one old condition of life after another in its progressive advance.

The conclusion can be drawn from a number of ominous traditions that the sacrifice of the first-born played a ghastly role from early on in Babylonian decadence. On occasion, the misuse of birth and childhood forces must have led to a first-born son being buried alive in the foundations of a house immediately after his birth in order to bestow supersensory powers on the whole family. Terah did not lose his first-born through such a black magical undertaking, but through destiny, which became increasingly harsh. But as indicated by the legend of the fire-baptism, Haran's early death might be connected with his involvement in the decadent Babylonian mysteries. Much of the future development of the Abraham stream, which was supposed to turn Babylonian nature inward, was already suggested. Terah still had to make an actual sacrifice, while Abraham only had to make it spiritually with his offering of Isaac. In Abraham's case, the law now set in which later so often became effective: that it is not the first-born son who becomes the pronounced bearer of the paternal heritage, but a younger brother, who is chosen to continue the mission into the future.

It was after Haran's death that Terah and Abraham moved to Haran. What could no longer continue as a physical heritage was to be received as a spiritual Babylonian gift. Abraham became the bearer of the future in place of Haran. But he became spiritually endowed with Haran's power through the instructions he received in the moon mysteries of the city of Haran. And when Terah sent him forth on his further journeys, he gave him two people as companions, who were to remain with him as embodiments of the Haran-share of Babylonia: Haran's son Lot and Haran's daughter Sarai, whom Terah gave to Abraham as his wife.* Later, Abraham's separation from Lot became a further step in the detachment from Babylonia. But through Sarai, whose name means 'the brilliant one, the one who rules', and whom we probably have to picture as a bearer of Babylonian cultural and governing functions, Abraham remained related with the Babylonian heritage. Aside from Lot and Sarai, it was the servant Eliezer who embodied the world of Babylonia in Abraham's surroundings. This wise servant, who later returned to the Babylonian homeland as bridal suitor for Isaac, is represented in legendary traditions as one who was deeply initiated into the Babylonian mysteries, and whom Nimrod himself sent along with Abraham on the journey.[84] The fact that Eliezer was not a Babylonian by birth, but a Syrian from Damascus (Gen.15:2) is no contradiction of the above.

The Bible describes Abraham's involvement in the spiritual play of forces in Egypt by means of an imaginative, seemingly quite personal scene. Abraham passed Sarai off as his sister to the

---

* In a disguised way, the Bible expresses the fact that Sarai was Haran's daughter. It names two daughters of Haran, Milcah and Iscah, in the same verse where it says that Abraham and Nahor take wives (Gen.11:29). Then, Nahor's wife is indeed called Milcah, but Abraham's wife is suddenly called Sarai. Traditions outside the Bible (for example, Gorion, *Sagen der Juden*, II, 98) equate Iscah and Sarai. Following Genesis 20:12, other legends state that Sarai was Terah's daughter and Haran's and Abraham's stepsister.

Egyptian Pharaoh so that he would not be killed on her account. When the Pharaoh, smitten with her beauty, as were all the Egyptians, wanted to take her as his wife, he met with the resistance of spiritual powers. Plagues afflicted him and his land; they sound to us like a prophecy of the ten plagues, which Moses later conjured up over Egypt. Thereupon, the Pharaoh desisted from his intentions after having showered rich gifts upon Abraham and Sarai.

This scene is all the more puzzling because it is later repeated at the court of the Phoenician king Abimelech at Gerar, first with Abraham and Sarai, and then in a similar way once more with Isaac and Rebekah. To leave this scene standing the way it is told without interpreting it makes no sense. Not only because Sarai was indeed closely related to Abraham, not just allegedly; but also because, from early on, Egypt had nurtured consanguineous marriage among the princes and kings; at first as a mystery procedure and later, in decadence, as a means of power.*

Most likely, the images of this puzzling scene indicate reciprocity between the cultic and wisdom streams embodied in Abraham, Sarai and the Pharaoh. Abraham and Sarai did not come to Egypt's initiate-ruler as nomadic bedouin, but with the splendour of a royal priestly cult-stream. Abraham himself wanted to avoid the task of revealing his spiritual goals to the initiates of Egypt, knowing that an irreconcilable contrast would thereby become evident. The Egyptians addressed themselves to what Sarai radiated of the Babylonian Ishtar-Venus mysteries. But here too they came upon spiritual contrasts. Invisible powers seemed to want to repulse them. Suddenly, they felt poorer instead of richer and desisted from their intention.

As yet, Egypt was not to learn from Abraham, but Abraham was to learn from Egypt. He absorbed into his being what the Egyptian mysteries could give him in the way of help for the fulfilment of his mission. Just as his share in Babylonia became visible in the personalities of his surroundings, so it was now with his share in Egypt. The Pharaoh gave one of his daughters to Sarai as her servant;[85] it was the 'Egyptian maid Hagar', who bore Abraham's first son, Ishmael. The legends point to the inner connections, which now tied Abraham to Egypt still further, when

---

* This is particularly evident in the story of the Lagides, the Ptolemaic dynasty of rulers.

they related that among Pharaoh's gifts to Sarai was also the Land of Goshen, in which the Israelites later spent their Egyptian exile. Now it was not only Babylonia that had to be inwardly transformed and intensified in the sense of Abraham's mission, but Egypt as well. The whole history of the Old Covenant was needed to carry out this task completely.

In its terse imaginative style, the Old Testament says that when Abraham departed from Egypt again, he 'was very rich in cattle, in silver, and in gold' (Gen.13:2). And the legend translates this imaginative description in such a way that the true historical set of facts come through: 'Abraham came away from Egypt rich in cattle, in gold and silver; but he was also enriched by much knowledge, for he had learned the arts of arithmetic and astronomy from the sages and the fortune tellers so that he was wiser than all men before him.'[86] Only when he had made the world of Egypt his own, could the pendulum-swing of his journeys come to rest in the region of the middle and the balance.

7 Melchizedek: The Hidden Sun Mystery

For a moment, the curtain is withdrawn from the deepest mystery of the Abraham-figure and the whole Old Covenant with the terse words that relate Abraham's meeting with Melchizedek: 'And Melchizedek king of Salem brought out bread and wine; he was priest of God Most High. And he blessed him . . . And Abraham gave him a tenth of everything' (Gen.14:18–20).

Abraham was returning from battle. In the King's Valley which tradition equates with the Valley of Jehoshaphat, today's Kidron Valley between Jerusalem and the Mount of Olives, this majestic figure came toward Abraham and blessed him as he bowed before Melchizedek in reverence.

Today, from the city high above, a road lined with dark cypress trees runs down into the valley, whose slopes are covered with countless tombs. A faint sacred radiance hovers over the road, as if it were the memory of that hour when Christ, after inaugurating the sacrament of bread and wine, descended here at night with the disciples on his way to Gethsemane. One could call it the Road of the Last Supper. The solemn recollection of the figure of the priest-king who, bestowing bread and wine, walked down here to bless Abraham, also pervades this path. An important spiritual relationship lights up spanning two millennia, and connects the two scenes, both permeated with the breath of the sacrament.

Who was Melchizedek? Hardly anywhere is the Old Testament so sparing of words. It does not betray its secret. And yet we sense that in the few words, it contains and is to arouse the feeling of a whole world transcending the human plane. The Epistle to the Hebrews in the New Testament lifts this figure to the holiest of heights, revealing him as a being of eternity, transparent for sublime cosmic secrets; yet this too leaves the riddle unsolved:

> For this Melchizedek, king of Salem, priest of the Most High God, met Abraham returning from the slaughter of the kings and blessed him; and to him Abraham apportioned a tenth part of everything. He is first, by translation of his name, king of righteousness, and then he is also king of Salem, that is, king of peace. He is without father or mother or genealogy, and has neither beginning of days nor end of life, but resembling the Son of God he continues a priest for ever.
>
> See how great he is! Abraham the patriarch gave him a tithe of the spoils. (Heb.7:1–4).

Abraham belonged to the great figures of leaders who precede humanity in the formulation of its destiny and mission on earth. In Melchizedek, however, a world of still higher leading beings, who otherwise remained hidden in the background, for once made an appearance. The Bible does not describe the locations of these mysteries. But since, in a few passages, it names and presents the exalted emissaries of the mysteries, its silence is not born of ignorance; behind the lofty figures it hints at the world from which they come.

Melchizedek is described as the eternal priest of the highest god. Who is this highest god, the El-elyon, whose solemn name occurs only in this one passage of the Bible? Is Yahweh, to the perception of whom Abraham has penetrated, not the *one* god, the divine unity of all being? How can a *highest* god be above the *one* god?

Abraham's perception of God was a specific one. It was the fruit of a special transformation of the human organism and consciousness, which Abraham, blazing the trail for all mankind, experienced for the first time. By virtue of the now clearly sculptured instrument of the brain, the human spirit in Abraham became capable of perceiving the world and the spirit ruling therein through mirror images of thoughts. In this manner, he also confronted the divine unity, which his thinking sought and found in the multitude of phenomena. The one divine, creative, central being of the universe could not itself live in his awareness. It could only dwell in his soul through the spirit that had formed the human organism into a wondrous reflective instrument for cosmic spirit. To this spirit belonged the holy name Yahweh. He related to the divine power which bore in itself the fullness of creator-being, as the moon to the sun. Yahweh was the moonlike mirror of the 'highest god', who was the spiritual sun of the universe itself. Thus, Abraham, the priest of Yahweh, and Melchizedek, the priest of El-elyon, confronted each other as do moon and sun. Abraham embodied the spiritualized moon-stream through which mankind now had to pass in its evolution. In Melchizedek, the sun mysteries significantly emerged for a moment from their seclusion; they had to withdraw from humanity so that in a future time they would once again belong anew to mankind.

Here, to the riddle of Melchizedek, spiritual research gives the solution. It is none other than the great Manu, whom the Bible calls Noah, who confronted Abraham in the figure of the priest-king Melchizedek;[87] the leader of the Atlantean sun mysteries, the highest sun-initiate, who saved humanity from the catastrophe of the great flood. Through millennia, Manu-Noah had guided the spiritual destinies of post-Atlantean humanity from the secluded mystery centres of Inner Asia. He had become the founder of the first post-Atlantean culture in ancient India with the sending forth of the seven holy Rishis. Directing humanity to the divine spiritual being of the sun, his great disciple Zarathustra endowed the ancient Persian culture, the second post-Atlantean epoch, with its soul. And in the third epoch, through disciples of Manu, the twin cultures of Egypt and Babylonia were formed. The great Hermes had been his emissary in Egypt; and the ancient epic relates how Gilgamesh also went to Noah or Manu, who there is called Utnapishtim, to undergo the initiation tasks assigned him by Utnapishtim.

Until now, Abraham had learned from Babylonia and Egypt. Through the picture of his encounter with Melchizedek the Bible indicates how he advanced from Noah's pupils to Noah himself. Abraham became spiritually a direct subject by bowing before the great Manu as his higher guide and teacher. He himself became a disciple and messenger of Noah; henceforth, he stood on an equal level with Zarathustra, Hermes and Gilgamesh. The çultural stream that he had to inaugurate flowed silently yet independently into the mainstream of evolution.

The legendary traditions of the Talmud seem to be in obvious contradiction to the solution found by spiritual research for the Melchizedek riddle. They equate Melchizedek not with Noah but with his son Shem. 'The Lord took Shem, the son of Noah, and made him his high priest and servant and let his spirit dwell upon him. He named him Melchizedek, king of Salem.'[88] Particularly in the wording of the meeting between Abraham and Melchizedek, we meet this equation. 'Shem, the son of Noah, went to meet Abraham. . .'[89] 'Adoni-Sedek, also the king of Jerusalem — this was Shem, the son of Noah — came out towards him and brought forth bread and wine . . . in the Valley of the Kings. And Adoni-Sedek blessed Abraham and Abraham gave him a tenth of the spoils; for Adoni-Sedek was priest before the Lord.'[90] (Instead of Melchizedek, king of righteousness, it says here Adoni-Sedek, lord of righteousness.)

To resolve this contradiction we must turn our attention to the figure of Shem.

The three sons of Noah, Shem, Ham and Japheth, are usually exclusively viewed as mythological progenitors of three main races. Without doubt they are represented as such in the Bible. But one would fail to grasp the real significance they possess in the Bible and its related texts if one limited oneself to the physical and genealogical aspect. The names of Noah's sons applied to a point of time in evolution in which the division of mankind into races — fully applicable to Atlantean humanity — slowly began to lose its validity. The names Shem, Ham and Japheth mainly designate three different spiritual streams of mankind. 'Ham' means 'dark one'. What this signifies is not only that the Hamites are dark skinned; they are the bearers of the obscure, hidden spiritual stream which was nurtured particularly in the mystery temples of Egypt, Babylonia and Assyria. 'Japheth' means 'beautiful'. Through his name we are directed to those branches of humanity which, like the Greeks and the tribes of the Celtic-Germanic north, turned their attention towards the beautiful sphere of nature and sustained their spiritual life from it. Only the name 'Shem' is not an adjective. It means 'name' and points to a secret of man's inner being. The name is the spiritual form of a being. All beings in creation have their names, but they cannot name themselves. Only man is invested with the power of giving names. He is not only the bearer but also the sculptor of the spiritual form and can name all beings including himself. By virtue of the capacity to coin thoughts and words, man retraces in his own spirit the spiritual forms woven into all creation. The principle of the name thus rules as an indwelling element in all beings; in man, it is moreover an element of action. The reason is that man bears within him a more far-reaching secret than that of the name. Not only can he name himself, he can also say 'I'. The spiritual form of his name is indwelt by a creative 'I'-being. The name 'Shem,' however, does not include this secret; it does not denote the egos of individual men, but the ego-form common to all men, the 'name-ness', the imprint of uniformity, which, besides the human realm, orders all beings of creation into species. With this, we have touched on the mission of Shem and the Semitic race named after him, mainly the Israelite-Jewish people. The spiritual power to form and to imprint that underlines name-giving, linked to the individual ego-form and ego-imprint, was to be cultivated and nurtured in the stream issuing from Shem. The people of the name and name-giving are the people of the Old Testament. 'Name' is its name through its progenitor Shem.

From Shem, a twofold stream of power had to flow into future humanity. As an essence, the power of the name had by means of inheritance to enter the generations descending physically from Shem. As a creative faculty of spirit, it had to be acquired and perfected ever and anew as a teaching by the leaders of the Shem stream. Both the continuing branches of the Shem-element can be clearly discerned in the course of history. In no other ethnic stream do we find such careful observance of keeping the blood of the fathers, the formative legacy, so pure and sanctified as among the Semites, especially the Israelite-Jewish folk. On the other hand, the traditions outside the Bible represent Shem particularly as the source of especially significant tenets and teaching. The 'School of Shem' surrounded by mysterious importance, is referred to like a central mystery place of humanity. Shem is heir to the Book of Adam; in him, the succession of primal revelations continues:

Japheth, Shem's brother, studied in the latter's school . . . But as Japheth was the older, why did the priesthood pass over to Shem?

Because he searched continually in the scripture and sought to explain the ways of God. From whence did he get the scripture? Already Adam, the first man, knew this scripture; he bequeathed it to his son Seth. From Seth it passed to Enoch, and so on, until it came to Shem; and he occupied himself with it constantly.[91]

Especially where the Talmudic legends equate Shem with the high priest Melchizedek, they refer to him as the great teacher.

Rudolf Steiner makes it comprehensible how this twofold name and form stream could proceed from Shem.[92] It is by no means the purpose of that lecture to solve riddles of the Old Testament. Much less is Jewish legendary tradition a focal point of the considerations. Rather, the laws of great spiritual, supersensory activities are described; and, among others, illustrated by means of the Shem figure. Rudolf Steiner describes how the ethereal body of Shem became a special source of spiritual formative forces through certain influences of supersensory beings: 'A particularly valuable ethereal body was present in Shem, an archetypal ethereal body . . . it was prepared and woven into Shem in such a way that henceforth it could descend in many duplicate likenesses to all those who were to be related by blood to this ancestor'. Through inheritance and propagation of this ethereal body, all those who looked to Shem as their progenitor received a uniform spiritual nature and form.

To the above-mentioned genealogical line was added that of teaching by virtue of the fact that in a certain mystery place Shem's spiritual form remained as an inspirational presence even after his death. Those who came from this School of Shem and had to be active as leaders among men, could therefore assume the spiritual form of Shem; and 'in Shem's name', functioned out of his name-giving wisdom and power.

Aside from the fact that countless replicas came into being from the ethereal body of Shem . . . Shem's own ethereal body was preserved in the spiritual world, because this ethereal body could later on be put to very good use for the mission of the Hebrew people. In this ethereal body, all the characteristics of the Hebrew people had originally come to expression. If something of particular importance was to take place for these people, if a special task, a special mission was to be conferred upon somebody, this was best accomplished by an individuality, who bore within himself this ethereal body of the progenitor. Later on, an inviduality, who intervened in the history of the Hebrews, did in fact possess this progenitor's ethereal body.[92]

Only now have we gained the basis for really comprehending the Melchizedek figure and his meeting with Abraham. The contradiction that seemed to arise between present-day spiritual research and the ancient occult traditions is resolved. In Melchizedek dwelt the 'I', the ego of Noah, the great Manu, and the ethereal body, the spiritual form, of Shem. Noah assumed the 'name' of his son Shem; he arrayed himself with it so as to implant a new spiritual impulse in the humanity descending from Shem. In Abraham lived a copy of that archetypal ethereal body; through this replica, which coincided completely with the physical body, his brain had been formed into a crystal-clear mirror instrument for the spirit, into a special organ for 'name-bestowing'. Now, the archetypal ethereal body, the primordial name, itself confronts Abraham in a figure, out of which a mighty leader of mankind, the messenger of the sun, speaks to him. Rudolf Steiner describes the background facts of this meeting in the following way:

> It is not possible for a Being of such lofty rank as the great Atlantean Sun-Initiate to speak without more ado in words that are intelligible to those who live at some particular time and have a special mission. An Individuality as exalted as the great Sun-Initiate is one who leads an eternal existence, of whom it was truly said — indicating the hallmark of eternity — that he was without name or age, 'without father, without mother . . .' A figure of this eminence in the evolution of humanity is only able to manifest by assuming a form whereby he can establish relationship with those to whom he is to reveal himself. Thus in order to impart the necessary enlightenment to Abraham, the great Teacher of the Rishis and of Zarathustra assumed a form in which he bore the etheric body of Abraham's original forefather; it was the etheric body of *Shem* the son of Noah . . . This meeting between Abraham and the great Sun-Initiate is referred to in the Old Testament as the meeting of Abraham with Melchizedek . . . the 'king and priest of the most high God'.[93]

As we learn to comprehend that Melchizedek is the figure which the great Manu assumes in order to become the concealed inspirer of the stream of humanity specifically descending from Shem, we discover that we have many more traditions concerning the King of Salem than was apparent at first. Actually, in many passages of the apocryphal traditions, where mention is made of Shem, Melchizedek is meant. The name Shem appears because of the identification of Shem with Melchizedek which the legends arrive at by merely beholding the form and figure.

7 MELCHIZEDEK

What the Old Testament relates in its imaginative style as the human scene of a momentary meeting, may have taken place in the course of history as a mystery process lasting for a whole period of time. Abraham encountered not a man but a world. He came to a mystery centre, whose guiding spirit was Melchizedek, and through Melchizedek to the great Manu himself; and he gained a decisive share of the mysteries alive there.

The early Christian text by Ephraem of Syrus, the *Treasure Cave*, which is also designated as the Christian Book of Adam, touches in all its sections on the secret of this mystery centre of Melchizedek and its location. A framework of soulful imaginations permits in some passages a glimpse of the historical reality. Where it follows the Bible in narrating the meeting of Melchizedek and Abraham it indicates through a subtle nuance the mystery process behind it: 'After Melchizedek had blessed Abraham, Abraham gave him a tenth of all that he had in order to allow him to partake of the holy mysteries, the bread of sacrifice and the wine of redemption. After Melchizedek had blessed him and had let him share in the holy mysteries, God spoke with Abraham . . .'[94]

The *Treasure Cave* observes humanity's past with true fairy-tale vision. It particularly turns its loving glance upon a few light centres where it sees a golden, warm aura shine forth. These are Sun Mysteries that rise above the whole of earth existence as do individual bright lights of a landscape observed at night from a mountain. Just as the fairy tales talk of the 'king's palace with the golden roof,' which radiates far and wide and is the goal of all quests, so this text experiences those holy centres of light. The brightest and most wondrous light emanates from the site of paradise and the location of Adam's creation at the gate of paradise.

But the light goes out; and mankind must search for a new homeland. They find it in a cave; but this cave too, which replaces the garden, shines warmly and brightly though not with the same universal intensity. The whole text is named after this cave:

After Adam and Eve left paradise, the portal of paradise was locked and a Cherub stood before it with a two-edged sword. Adam and Eve descended by way of the mountain of paradise. They discovered a cave on a mountain peak; they entered it and hid themselves there. Adam and Eve were virginal. When Adam wished to know Eve, he took gold, myrrh and frankincense from the borders of Paradise, placed them in the cave and blessed and dedicated it to be the house of prayer for him and his sons, and he called it the Treasure Cave.[95]

According to the descriptions of this book, this treasure cave, the smaller substitute for paradise, was the centre of all that humanity experienced until the great Flood set in. It was humanity's sanctuary between Adam's and Noah's time; in it, all the fathers were buried. It could well be that the great sun oracle of ancient Atlantis stood behind the image of the treasure cave, where under the guidance of the great Manu the substance of paradise, the great holy sun centre of ancient Lemuria, was preserved.

What happened to the treasure cave when the great Flood approached? Noah received the task of building the ark from his father, but a specific directive was tied in with it:

> Descend from this holy mountain and take with you the remains of our father Adam and these three offerings, gold, myrrh, and frankincense. Then place Adam's body in the centre of the ark and put on top of it these offerings . . . Following that, command your first-born, Shem,* to take with him the body of our father Adam after your death and carry it to the middle of the earth. There he is to let one of his descendants dwell . . . so that he may serve there. There, he shall . . . offer God bread and wine and . . . remain secluded, because he is a servant of the highest God.[96]

'Then Noah took the corpse of our father Adam and that of Eve. His first-born, Shem, carried the gold, Ham the myrrh, and Japheth the frankincense. Thus they left the Treasure Cave. When they descended from the holy mountain, they broke into sobs and weeping, because they were being deprived of the sacred place and dwelling of their fathers.'[97] The loss of the treasure cave was like a new expulsion from paradise. Where would the life contained in it be able to shine on?

When the Flood was over, Noah revealed to Shem his last will:

> 'When I have died, go into the ark and bring out the body of our father Adam; but let no one see you. Then take with you as provisions from here bread and wine. And take with you Melchizedek, the son of Malach; for God chose him from among all your descendants to serve him over the remains of our father Adam. Go then and put him down on the centre of the earth and let Melchizedek have his dwelling there' . . . And Shem took Adam's body and together with Melchizedek left his folk by night. And the Angel

---

* In the ancient Jewish traditions it always says that Japheth and Ham were older than Shem.

116

of the Lord appeared to them and went before them. Their path was made easy, because the Angel of the Lord strengthened them . . . When they came to Golgotha, the centre of the earth, the angel showed this place to Shem . . . and the earth opened in the form of a cross. And Shem and Melchizedek laid the body of Adam within it . . . And Shem said to Melchizedek: 'You are the servant of God Most High. Remain here forever . . . Spill no blood at this place and sacrifice no animal, only bread and wine always!'[98]

In this manner, the *Treasure Cave* describes the return of mankind's sanctuary, henceforth reserved and secluded, to the place of primeval beginning, where once the human being was created in his radiant likeness of God and where the portal to paradise was located.

During the Atlantean catastrophe, the great Manu led the germinal group of future humanity into the interior of Asia and sent them forth southward and westward to found colonies. But we must probably assume that an inconspicuous branching-off of the Atlantean sun oracle ran parallel with this, in which Noah's Melchizedek-activity took place and which found its location in a primeval mystery site in the region of the later Jerusalem. It was out of this sanctuary of peace, which the old Jewish narrators called the 'School of Shem', that Melchizedek came to meet Abraham.

When the *Treasure Cave* speaks of the transfer of Adam's body to Golgotha and Melchizedek's ministry by this holy tomb, it refers to the sacramental secret of that mystery centre. The altar of Melchizedek was a coffin in which the sun-corporeality of man in its condition of divine likeness and paradise itself were resting and were guided towards their resurrection.

In childlike metaphorical images, the *Treasure Cave* represents Melchizedek's being to us. We see Shem with the boy Melchizedek following the angel and bearing the body of Adam. What this imaginative description shows side by side intertwines in reality. The Christophorus legend describes the giant who bears the child on his shoulders through the Jordan, though what is meant is the event by which the Christ-being was born into the human being, Jesus, at the Baptism in the Jordan. Praxiteles' statue of Hermes at Olympia bears the boy Dionysus on its arm, although the child refers to the ego which has entered Hermes. In like manner, the *Treasure Cave* pictures the boy Melchizedek who walks side by side with Shem; yet it indicates the higher ego-being with this, which descends inspiringly into Shem's soul and embodies itself in his spirit form. As the pictures of the imagination contract for us into historical conceptions, we also understand the fundamental meaning of the fact that Noah commissions Shem to take unto himself the boy Melchizedek. Noah after all is speaking of himself, and through this mission gives the promise to be his son's companion beyond death.

What is it that Abraham receives through Melchizedek at that concealed site of humanity's spiritual guidance? The imaginative description states that the king of Salem administers bread and wine to Abraham. Herewith, he opens to him the shrine of the sun mysteries now resting in seclusion. He allows him to perceive a secret which points to the past as well as the future and thus bestows deeper meaning on the present.

In Ravenna, in the Church of San Vitale, in a mosaic[99] is an altar to which offerings are brought from both sides. On one side Abel offers a lamb. On the other side, the fruits of the field are offered up, but not by Cain. The priest-king Melchizedek stands in the place of Cain and offers bread and wine. A future redemption of Cain is preparing in the figure of Melchizedek; in bread and wine, the Cain offering will be liberated from its curse.

When Cain offered the fruits of the field — when the son of the sun offered the gifts of the sun — his offering was not accepted; the moon blood-offering of Abel was. The paradise time of the sun had come to an end; the moon already ruled over the world. The mysteries of the sun became homeless and had to withdraw into seclusion until, once again, their hour would return in a new world age. In the sanctuary of Manu and Melchizedek the Cain offering was preserved for the future.

When the Bible says, 'Noah was the first tiller of the soil. He planted a vineyard' (Gen.9:20), it could just as well say: He brought forth bread and wine. But he carried them out into external life, drawing a veil over their spiritual secret. They became nourishment for man. In the outside world it was forgotten that they could also be nourishment of the godhead, holy sacrificial substance. But when Abraham returned from the battle of the kings, Melchizedek, who was none other than Noah, brought forth to him bread and wine as a mystery gift.

Had the time of the sun returned already? No, not so; but Abraham, the executor of the Yahweh moon ministry, had to know that through it he too had to prepare the way for the coming of the sun spirit, the El-elyon. One day, the time of the sun would come for all mankind. The 'highest god' would become man and bestow bread and wine to all humanity. Then, Cain would be redeemed from his homelessness. The lost paradise would again make its entrance into humanity.

The sun future gave the moon present its true meaning. Carrying out his moon service, Abraham had to know of the mysteries of the sun. The moon ministry had not to become an end in itself. Those who dedicated themselves to it had to know of a higher secret in the background. Through the formative power of the moon, which was to be imprinted ever more clearly into human nature in the stream of heredity, the task was to fashion the moon vessel for the coming sun content.

Melchizedek himself appeared before Abraham like an embodiment of Messianic prophecy. Shem's ethereal body was the noblest moon chalice produced by humanity up to this point. Among the guiding individualities of mankind, Noah, the great Manu, was the most exalted and advanced servant of the sun who could assume earthly form. Just as Christ, the spirit-sun itself, would in time appear in a human corporeality formed by the moon stream, so, pointing to Christ and transparent for him, Melchizedek appeared in a body before Abraham. This is what the Epistle to the Hebrews refers to with the solemn, mysterious words: 'He is an image of the Son of God' (7:3B). Through Melchizedek, Abraham learned that the Messiah came from a higher sphere than that of Yahweh. And Abraham's Melchizedek-knowledge, through which the Old Covenant looked beyond itself, came through here and there in the scriptures of the Old Testament; for example in Psalm 110, where it relates that Yahweh says to the Messiah, 'You are a priest for ever after the order of Melchizedek' (110:4).

Aside from its prophetic reference to the Christ-future, the administering of bread and wine by Melchizedek had a specific immediate meaning for the age of Abraham. It pointed the way from the blood-offerings to another sacrificial service. The *Treasure Cave* indicates this by reference to the instruction that on Melchizedek's altar no animals, only bread and wine, were to be sacrificed. As yet, humanity was still not mature enough for the pure sunlike 'divine service in spirit and truth', the symbols of which were bread and wine. But mankind could slowly outgrow the ecstatic blood sacrifice, through which it would remain under the spell of the diminishing world of ancient visionary sight. Humanity could pass from the ecstatic moon service to a spiritualized inward moon service which prepared the way for the pure sun cult. The whole development of the Old Testament was occupied with the renunciation of the blood of animal sacrifice and the attainment of the soul's pure inward service of devotion and sacrifice. The 'offering of the tenth', which Abraham learns to give through Melchizedek, was the bridge from the one to the other. We see Melchizedek's teaching coming into action. The sun taught the moon to behold the sun.*

If an understanding has once been gained concerning the Melchizedek-Abraham encounter, and Abraham is seen as under the guidance of a being greater than himself, veils shrouding the past as well as the future of Abraham's destiny are lifted.

We pursued the question of how the impulse to leave Babylonia actually reached Abraham. After its wide oscillations, the pendulum of his journeys comes to rest in the land of the Melchizedek mystery. Was it perhaps even then Melchizedek who called Abraham to him by divine order and exhorted him to leave his homeland and the house of his fathers?

The legendary reports concerning the birth and youth of Abraham directed us to a connection between him and Melchizedek's mystery centre. It said that after spending the first ten years of his life in the cave where he was born, Abraham 'went to Noah and his son Shem', to be their pupil for thirty-nine years (see p. 94). A story that probably follows the same line states that young Abraham received the Book of Adam from God. But however diligently he studied it, it revealed nothing to him. 'Then Abraham went to his teacher Shem and remained with him for three years.'[100] Is it possible that Abraham actually spent a part of his youth, even if it were only a fraction of the alleged time, studying in the land where he later founded the homeland of his people, the site where later his exalted leader came to meet him? It would throw an entirely new light on his renunciation of Babylonia.

---

* The scope of the Melchizedek-impulse within humanity can be observed as the symbol of bread and wine appeared in a great many places. This always expressed a tendency towards spiritualization of sacrificial service. As an example we can name the great Hittite stone relief of Ivriz in the Taurus, where the taller figure of a priest-king hands ears of corn and grapes to a king.

7 MELCHIZEDEK

Once again, the ancient narrators show us young Abraham at the place of Melchizedek. Nimrod sought Abraham's life. But Eliezer, the wise servant whom Nimrod himself had assigned to Abraham, knew what advice to give him: 'Then, Abraham obeyed the voice of Eliezer and hurriedly arose and rushed to the house of Noah and his son Shem; hid there and escaped . . . He remained hidden in the house of Noah for a month, until the king forgot him.'[101]

Everywhere we see Melchizedek's hand protecting and guiding Abraham. Eliezer also is mentioned in such a way that a connection between him and Melchizedek's guidance must be assumed: 'Even in later times, Shem, the son of Noah, told Eliezer, Abraham's servant, about life in the ark.'[102]

According to the ancient traditions, therefore, Abraham's meeting with the priest of God Most High was the fulfilment of a development, which had originated long before. But, as the same narrators make clear, it was also the start of a series of important impulses, which, proceeding from the secret spiritual guidance, came to realization through Abraham.

An important moment in the development was when Abraham sealed the covenant, which Yahweh made with him, with the introduction of the rite of circumcision. In their own manner the apocryphal accounts bring what the Bible describes as a direct occurrence between Abraham and the Godhead into connection with the Melchizedek-influence. 'Abraham had Shem sent for, the son of Noah, and he circumcised Abraham and his son Ishmael.'[103]

The rite of circumcision placed the Abraham stream into fully conscious contrast with the spirit that clearly predominated increasingly in the world of Babylonia. There man's old relationship was maintained with the ethereal forces of the cosmos pertaining to nature. The world of visionary sight and ecstatic intoxication was not to perish. Therefore, all means by which the human ethereal body was still capable of cosmic intensification, above all the sexual and reproductive forces, were made the object of a religious cult in their natural instinctive driving force. The foundations were laid for what emerged later in the course of progressive decadence as the phallic cult of the Near East.

The rite of circumcision, which originated with Abraham, was a kind of anti-phallic cult. The concentration of the ethereal body on the sphere of the physical body, the turning away from any sort of ecstasy, the renunciation of all ancient clairvoyant experience in favour of the external development and forming of the

physical organization came to expression in this voluntary conse-
cration of the sexual element. The forces of human nature that
strove outward were to receive a specific impetus towards an
inner, organ-forming activity. What streamed out as unconscious
ecstatic will was to benefit the inner secretion of the organism and
to be transformed into conscious forces of thinking. Thus, circumcision expressed the willingness for the final shaping of the human
organism and for a hereditary stream, which, from generation to
generation, would propagate and intensify the physical-ethereal
corporeality's state of form and character. The power of Yahweh
as the highest spirit of form was received into corporeal existence
and heredity. In the most literal sense, the human body becomes
the temple of Yahweh. This is why circumcision was also the
sealing of the covenant with God through which Abraham receives
the promise of a line of descendants having significance for all
mankind and one ordered according to the formation of the stars.
The forces through which other streams of humanity still tended
to be transported into the starry spheres were turned inward by
the Abraham stream so that thereby reflections of the stars' constellations would arise on earth in the organs of the human body
and in the sequence of generations of blood-related human beings.

As a sign that the conclusion of the covenant with Yahweh
signified a kind of new creation of man, a repetition of the primeval creation when Yahweh sculptured and moulded man's form
out of earth substance, the two figures, who in the new creation
take the place of Adam and Eve, received new names; into both
names the 'H' sound is inserted. Abram is changed to Abraham,
Sarai becomes Sarah. Abram meant 'the father of the height';
Abraham means 'the father of nations'. Sarai signified 'the one
wanting to rule'; Sarah means 'the one consecrated to rule'. But
more important than the change of meaning that occurred along
with the name-change was this: As Yahweh once breathed his
divine breath into Adam, now, with the 'H' sound, he breathes
into the 'name' of man a hint of the future. The form received an
intimation of a content which the future would bring. This is the
meaning of the course of generations, now beginning, namely to
build a form and vessel for the divine spirit. Yahweh entered the
human sheath of Abraham. In time to come, the higher one, the
El-elyon, would enter into a human body which was to be formed
through the consecrated heritage of this lineage. By indicating
that Melchizedek was supposed to have performed the priestly act

of circumcision on Abraham, the apocryphal tradition helps us to form concrete historical *aperçus* and conceptions concerning the events of this important turning-point in the Abraham-destiny. Again and again, the curtains part in front of the mystery-guidance from which mankind's destinies are led.

An event that the legendary traditions place with greatest distinctness and accord into the sphere of the Melchizedek mystery is the sacrifice of Isaac, which is usually pictured — following the imaginative biblical description too literally — as a simple human scene in a lonely mountainous region. The sacrificial rock of Moriah, on which Solomon's temple was later erected, must have been the site of a sanctuary in all ages. Abraham brought his son, the embodiment of the covenant with God, into the realm of this sanctuary. Through the son's death, the whole promise for the future that was tied to the generations beginning with him would be sacrificed.

The *Treasure Cave* states outright that Abraham brought his son to Melchizedek:

> 'Isaac was twenty-two years old when his father took him and ascended the Mount of Jebus to Melchizedek, the servant of God Most High. Mount Jebus is the mountain range of the Amorites; on the same place, the cross of the Messiah was later erected. On this very spot, a tree sprouted forth, which bore the lamb that saved Isaac. This place is the central point of the earth; the tomb of Adam; the altar of Melchizedek; Golgotha, the Place of the Skull. There, David also beheld the angel who carried the fiery sword. There, Abraham offered up his son as a burnt offering.'[104]

We will have more to say later on regarding the more specific meaning and the course of events surrounding the sacrifice of Isaac. The *Treasure Cave* places the founding of the city of Jerusalem into the time of this occurrence. The city was built around the mystery centre of Melchizedek, which must not have been torn thereby from its seclusion:

> In the same year that Abraham offered up his son as a sacrifice, Jerusalem was built. The beginning of construction occurred in the following way: After Melchizedek had appeared and had shown himself to the people, twelve kings came to him. When they beheld his form and heard his words, they begged him to go with them. He said to them, 'I may not leave here to go to another place.' Then they took counsel among themselves whether they should not

build a city for him; and they said to one another: 'He is in truth the king of the whole earth, the father of all kings.' So they built him a city and made Melchizedek the king within it. Melchizedek bestowed on it the name Jerusalem.[105]

All traditions are in accord on the point of relating the name Jerusalem back in some way to the king of Salem, Melchizedek. Abraham is supposed to have called the place Yare, 'Yahweh appears,' in connection with Moriah, 'the place of beholding Yahweh.' Shem (Melchizedek), on the other hand, is reported to have given it the name Salem, 'the peace'. From these two designations, the name Jerusalem is supposed to have been put together.[106]

The Melchizedek-guidance, under which Abraham placed himself at the most important turning-points of his work, continued through the coming generations for a time as we can learn from the apocryphal descriptions: 'Rabbi Berachya says . . . that immediately after the sacrifice Abraham sent Isaac to Shem, the son of Noah, to have him instructed in the scriptures by him'.[107] And in another place it says: 'Isaac went into the house of Shem in order to learn the ways of God and his discipline, and remained there three years'.[108]

The legends show Melchizedek among Abraham's guests at the burial of Sarah and also earlier at the celebration of Isaac's birth.[109] The greater one stood at the side of those he was guiding, helping them in all their destinies. When Isaac and Rebekah were saddened over their unfruitfulness, they went up to the Mount of Moriah and beseeched Shem-Melchizedek to pray for them.[110] Then, when Rebekah was pregnant with Esau and Jacob and became greatly troubled, she went 'to Melchizedek. And he prayed over her and said to her: "Two nations are in your womb." . . .'[111] Finally, the Talmudic narrators report also of Jacob that for a long time he was thought to have been a disciple of Melchizedek: 'After that, Isaac sent his younger son Jacob to the house of Shem . . . to be instructed in the disciplines of God and his teaching. And so Jacob went to Shem . . . and learned from him the ways of God, and remained with him thirty-two years'.[112]

In the exoteric foreground, the Abraham stream proceeds on its moon-way. But it was guided on this way by the sun-mystery which remained in the background. The name Melchizedek encompassed the esoteric stream, which time and again gave the great origins of Hebrew history their direction.

8 Lot – Abraham – Isaac:
Between Legacy and Promise

At the time when Abraham's journeys came to an end in the land between Babylonia and Egypt, the southern Jordan valley must have been a region of the most abundant fertility and wealth. The Bible says that 'the Jordan valley was well watered everywhere like the garden of the LORD,' (Gen.13:10). And according to the old narrators, the inhabitants of this region, the people of Sodom, were the richest nation on earth.[113] An old world-condition of an overwhelming activity of growth forces, which in other areas had long since been replaced by a moderate activity of nature, must have survived there and developed to an overripe state. But all traditions lead to the conclusion that people there were no longer able to put this superabundance of ethereal forces to beneficial use, but had been led astray thereby into building up a culture of extreme, magical decadence.

When he parted from Abraham, Lot was lured by the riches of this region and established his home there. If the imaginative descriptions of the Bible are taken for outer historical fact as is usually done, the separation of Abraham and Lot appears to be caused by differences between two nomadic tribes over pasture ground. But the descriptions of the Bible still require translation, although their externally valid historical character grows progressively. First, the individual *figures* become historical as the names cease to refer to whole series of generations and begin exclusively to designate definite persons. The *events* that are depicted must continue to be understood imaginatively. Then, more and more clearly, the *dynamics and structure* of the story become an expression of the actual historical event, whereas the substance filling the individual scenes is still composed not of physical but of soul images. The biblical picture sequences are then in a way similar to certain dreams, which glean their pictorial material in varied and ever-changing manner without strict order from the most diverse provinces of memory and soul life, whereas the dynamics of the dream, the manner and intensity in which the images follow one another, reveal the truth inherent in the dream.

The dynamics of biblical representation are of direct historical applicability, beginning with the journeys of Abraham. The great geographical movements which we can trace there are already real history in the physical sense. But, as we showed in the example of the events in Egypt, the individual pictures are still wholly submerged in the soul language of imagination. This is also the case with the stories that describe the parting of Abraham and Lot. We witness the increasingly distinct emergence of irreconcilable contrasts. But this is a matter of more than outer conflicts. Behind the image of quarrelling shepherds there arise spiritual and religious dissents. Abraham and Lot, whom we must actually regard as bearers of high priestly functions, can remain in accord with each other despite the difference of the cultic streams that manifest in them. But among the leaders under their authority and the people following them, the widening breach in feeling and life-style soon becomes irreconcilable. Finally, it is Abraham who suggests a peaceful separation and leaves it to Lot to choose the region that he and his people want to join.

The pronounced after-effect of the Babylonian legacy in the soul of the Haran-son Lot is the cause of his choosing the region of Sodom. He belongs to those human beings who do not want to be poor. He does not comprehend the necessity for the humility and poverty of soul that are part of the mission of the Abraham stream. He wants to hold on to the former world condition and the earlier relationship of man to the cosmic forces. Magical abundance is a greater ideal to him than inner freedom and clarity. The physical-ethereal organization of Lot was probably dominated more by the preponderance of cosmic ether forces than was Abraham's nature, which was already determined by pronounced inward intensification and distinctly formed organs. Something in Lot is magnetically attracted to the nature and culture of the Sodom area. The old wealth draws him into its bonds and he is unable to discern that he has chosen a world doomed both inwardly and outwardly to destruction.

This does not mean that Lot has allowed himself to be drawn into the far advanced black magical decadence of the Sodom culture. Despite Lot's kinship with the existing soul attitude which is turned toward the past, a seed of good will and pure humanness enters through him into the realm of the demonic depravity. Legend has it that Lot soon assumed the position of a supreme judge in Sodom.[114] We can perhaps picture his role like that of Joseph in Egypt and Daniel in Babylonia, who, although they were foreigners, were enlisted for the duties of high leadership so that a new impulse could be injected through them into a stagnating cultural condition. Lot may even have thought that he could work in Sodom as a reformer, and did in fact appear there as such. But an uneven struggle ensued. Lot could pit only his human power against the might of the demons, which had long since grown to superhuman proportions.

His name indicates that he was still the bearer of certain super-sensory powers. It means 'the magician', but clearly contains the nuance of casting magic spells. Lot was not in a position to disenchant anything. An old decrepit force pervaded him too deeply for him to work in a healing, progressive way. He was related not only to the wealth of Sodom but to its doom. Only in his case the doom did not flow from the source of evil, as was the case with the Sodomites; in him it was born of tragedy.

The nature of enchantment consists of the fact that a being is thereby banished backwards to a lower level of existence. Through sodomite decadence the being of man was thrust down to the animalistic level. All traditions, including today's use of the word 'sodomy', permit the conclusion that not only were animal passions released in the region of Sodom, but that an actual physical interbreeding of human beings with animals and the cultivation of an animal-human race was customary. A cosmic enchantment of man was to be attained. An ominous insatiability was in effect. To be able to look only upon man's lower nature and not upon his true being, was to increase the animal tendency within man and brought about the opposite of enhancement — namely enchantment.

From Babylonia, Lot bore in his nature a residue of the magical forces of growth. To work with these would have meant that physical intensification would be brought about in a magical manner within the realm of animate substance; be it in the plant, animal or human kingdom. But the physical, material world has now become too dense and hard to obey the magically employed life forces. Instead of expanding the physical substance its life was driven out. The life-bearing plant element was turned to petrified mineralization. Only the degree of deadness was increased and enchantment of the animate into the inanimate state was brought about. On a different level of existence, something corresponding to the sodomite enchantment took place. Lot could not bring about the disenchantment of Sodom. By his activity there, the fate of Sodom could only be more quickly and completely sealed.

Where once the luxurious wealth of Sodom abounded, the nether world of the Judean Desert and the glistening expanse of the Dead Sea, 400 metres (1300 feet) below the surface of the Mediterranean Sea, spread far and wide today. This is truly a world, which, despite the glorious colours that the setting sun can pour upon it, is weighted down by the dark spell of enchantment. Everything breathes death in majestic greatness and other-world-liness. After descending through the sharply cleft, canyon-like valleys of the desert into the depths and, in the increasingly sub-terranean heat, looking upon the glimmering waters of the great lake, one may seem to be approaching the most living refresh-ment. At the edge of the mountains below, where the wide Jordan steppe begins to spread out, in the region of ancient Jericho, is a narrow strip of tropical growth which is perhaps the very last remnant of Sodom's lushness. But today it is not able to arouse even an inkling of the famous 'Gardens of Jericho' that still existed there a few decades before the turn of time and were the delight of the Egyptian Queen Cleopatra. Sultry stifling heat broods over everything. And finally, by the shore of the lake into which the Jordan pours its weary, muddy waters, comes the realization that here even the water, otherwise the element and bestower of life, assumes dead, mineral character. It is brine that takes the appear-ance of living water. No fish, no snail can exist in it; and a noxious odour creeps up the rocks on the shore from the lake and would destroy any plant life that might be there, if it were not already the great desert in which the lake is embedded. It is indeed the dead sea and as such the emanation-centre of a dead world. What was once abounding life has been banished down and enchanted on the mineral level in the broadest possible scope. Jebel Usdum, the mountain of Sodom southwest of the Sea, is an enormous block of salt. In bright daylight, without descending into the in-terior of the earth, one can break off pure salt crystals from large sections of the rock walls. The once living Mother Earth has rigidified into a pillar of salt here. The seemingly human scene of the enchantment of Lot's wife, who could not part from the world of Sodom, has become reality in superhuman dimensions through-out the whole of the landscape. A greater 'enchanter' than Lot has poured the meaning of Lot's name over a whole world.

All of Judea receives its character from the Judean Desert and the Dead Sea. But proceeding from Jerusalem, if, instead of heading eastward over Bethany down into the desert, one turns south, it is to find, no further than Bethlehem, a world which seems to have remained entirely free of the rigid Judaic severity. Rather, it bears something of the ethereally blessed brightness and cosmic youthfulness of Galilee. This Galilean island in Judea extends to the region of the ancient Abraham-city of Hebron; and in two places, the murmurs of a paradise-sphere that was not completely drawn into the Fall can be especially clearly detected: in Bethlehem in the Field of the Shepherds and on the site of the grove of Mamre near Hebron. All around, the rigid moon world of the desert, the scenery of the Fall, draws near. Perhaps the name 'Beth-lehem', 'the house of bread', has something to do with the town's location in an island of fertility amidst the desert. It is not as if one could see or experience the wonder of nature there in an external tangible way. A delightful, uplifting, hidden loveliness weaves in everything. In Bethlehem, it comes to expression even today in a special beauty and childlike joyousness of the people. Not quantitatively but qualitatively one thinks that ethereal forces can be sensed, which have asserted themselves against the catastrophes of world destruction by which life all around was bewitched into death. Here, nature takes us back more directly into ancient times than the most admirable man-made monuments. In the shepherds' valleys around Bethlehem, its beauty has something soulful and loving and awakens the feeling that here there may have been a primeval holy place of the goddess Natura, a special site of Mother Earth's generosity. In the grove of Mamre also blows a pure breeze of primordial time, and the rustling of the wind in the tree-tops of the stone-pines and cypresses, which Greek monks cultivate here, tells of holy primal beginnings. But the spirit of this place is graver and more masculine, pointing more inwardly and stimulating the force of the ego.

It was to this region, which even today stands out so clearly above Judea's countenance of death, that Abraham turned when Lot decided on Sodom. Lot felt drawn to an opulence which had no future. Abraham turned to a plain, unpretentious region, because he perceived spiritual forces there which would be able to survive great crises. Mamre means 'place of strength', and even before Abraham's time must have been a holy site. But the spirit-contact that was bestowed there on the reverent soul could not have had anything of the ecstatic, intoxicating rapture of consciousness that we must picture as being nurtured in Sodom. The spiritual experience of Mamre must have been a quiet seeing-through the veil of nature combined with a thoughtful awareness, a listening to the spirit-voices in nature's whispers. Abraham felt related to the inward, weaving power of the spirit of Mamre. And so he erected an altar there to the divine power that he had to serve.

In the grove of Mamre, Abraham had an encounter that equalled the meeting with Melchizedek. At high noon, the curtain was torn away from the world of the senses for him and three divine beings revealed themselves to his vision. Legend calls the 'three men', who visited Abraham in the holy grove, by name and shows their wonderfully shining threefoldness of colours: 'As the rainbow rises above in three hues, so the three messengers appeared in colours of white, red and green. White was Michael's colour; red in colour was Gabriel; and green in colour was Raphael'.[115]

Spiritual greatness holds sway in the image of Abraham's meeting with Melchizedek; heartfelt soulfulness fills the image of the three archangels' visit in Mamre. Here, Abraham was not the royal pupil of a still more exalted leader, but the friend of God, whom the angels visit as his guests. It is not without reason that the tender piety of the Eastern Church, which has still retained a hint of a primordial closeness with nature, recognized this image of the three angels in Mamre repeatedly as the most beautiful expression of its own nature, and reproduced it on many icons with the touch of a blessed spirit-nearness.

The secret of this place streamed into the angel-visitation of Abraham just as it did into the appearance of the angels, who revealed themselves to the shepherds on the field of Bethlehem. Where nature had preserved something of the sphere of paradise, reminiscences of God's nearness in paradisal time were bestowed on man.

When Abraham beheld the angels, Mamre was not yet an island of life in the midst of the desert. At that time, the world of Sodom and Gomorrah still existed in all the abundance of its wealth. But the preview of the cosmic storms soon to break over its surroundings were a part of the revelation Abraham received from his heavenly visitors. Legend relates that Gabriel announced the destruction of Sodom and Gomorrah to Abraham, while Michael brought Sarah the message that despite her age she would bear a son.[116] And after they had revealed themselves to Abraham in the sacred grove, the archangels approached Lot dwelling in Sodom, filling his soul with a preview of the cosmic judgment threatening the ancient wealth.

Then, the catastrophes set in. It was as if a remnant of the fiery conflagration of Lemuria had continued to glow in a seemingly long-extinct volcano, which now erupted and transformed the luxuriant land all around into a desert of the nether world and the brine of the Dead Sea. Just as the fiery catastrophes, which destroyed the Lemurian continent, cannot be taken as volcanic eruptions in the sense of a lava-spewing crater, the cataclysms of Sodom and Gomorrah's destruction cannot simply be grasped as ordinary volcanic processes. The earth's countenance, into which the Jordan Valley had already cut a deep gash — perhaps a trace of the tremendous cosmic chasms of Lemurian time — must have received breaks and tears. Out of these fissures, burning gases, steams of sulphur and boiling water hissed forth. The earth itself was on fire; after all, in this region, where the salt lake later appeared, there were at first, according to the Old Testament, pitch and asphalt pits (Gen.14:10), after which the Dead Sea was called Asphalt Sea. The Valley of Arnon which adjoins it on the eastern side, is a mighty inferno-like rock canyon, which geologists do not believe was washed out by flowing water. It is assumed that owing to inner volcanic processes the earth burst apart here so that gases and steam, which caught fire, issued forth and gave the rock formation its fantastic forms and colours. This is an example of the far-reaching fire-storms to which Sodom and Gomorrah fell victim, and which transformed almost the whole of Judea into the field of slag and ashes of a gigantic world conflagration.

The people of Sodom had wanted to unleash hidden forces of the depths; now, the infernal flames of Tartarus leaped up in overwhelming cosmic proportion. Thus, the enchantment of petrified death covered the site of overabundant life.

We again encounter the law of the greater and smaller rounds in the fate of Sodom and Gomorrah. What happened is a smaller repetition and reflection of Lemuria's destruction at a later stage of evolution. A concentrated replica is formed of paradise, the

Fall into sin, and the expulsion from paradise. It was this that surrounded the figure of Abraham in the grove of Mamre with the magic of a primeval homeland; something like a spiritual reflection of Adam's image in the garden of paradise enveloped him. The grove of Mamre and the whole island of life in Judea extending all the way to Bethlehem was one of the centres of emanation of life-ether forces that could be called a small earthly paradise. The so-called Oak of Abraham, which is still held sacred in Mamre today, points to a paradise-related side of Abraham's being; it always comes to the fore where we behold Abraham as the planter of holy trees.[117]

What surges towards the grove, all around, of Sodomite decadence, corresponds to the cosmic temptation, symbolized in the dragon-animal forms in Lemurian time. An animal kingdom that had become by then completely materialized surrounded the as yet not completely physical humanity and bore towards it the danger of premature hardening. The Fall was connected with an inclusion of animalistic hardening in human nature. In Sodom, this Fall found a grotesque and ominous culmination through the unrestrained mixing of human and animal elements. Again, the result could only be an infinite further hardening of human nature. If the race of animal-humans, cultivated in Sodom, had not perished in the fire storms of cosmic judgment that set in there, it would have created a dangerous materialization process into man's corporeality. And even despite the great cataclysm, a wave of hardening tendencies must have proceeded from there. The myth of the enchantment of one person, unable to free herself from Sodom, into a pillar of salt, was not only realized cosmically through the geographical transformations, but also inwardly in human nature through the gradual increase of sclerotic and calcific phenomena, building a column of dead mineral substance into man. When it is said that Abraham was the first human being on whom external signs of old age became visible, this is an indication that the shadow of the pillar of salt fell on everyone, even Abraham. From the time it originated, the Dead Sea has been a great natural symbol of the ever increasing penetration of death forces into the living human being.

During the later smaller reflection of the primeval Fall, the element of unity represented in the Adam figure was divided into the two figures of Abraham and Lot. Abraham corresponded to the part of the Adam nature that was not drawn into the Fall.

And Abraham struggled for Lot and his world. Just as Abraham had gone into the battle of the kings for Lot and Sodom, he made himself the intercessor between Sodom and the spiritual world in the face of the approaching catastrophe (Gen.18). Just as a hint of the paradisal Adam-being hovered over Noah, the spirit-power by reason of which he was designated Menahem, the Paraclete and higher intercessor, seems reflected in Abraham. Light rays of humanity's spiritual guidance fall into Abraham's soul.

While the fires of the earth's interior raged over a wide area surrounding the grove of Mamre, there formed on a smaller scale a protected area like that of Adam within the volcanically roaring Lemuria. An image arises: out of the fire, God spoke to Abraham in the sacred grove. This image is the intermediate link in an important chain of developments. The biblical image of the cherubim with the flaming swords is not the only one telling us that after the Fall, God spoke to Adam out of the Lemurian fire surging near from all sides. Some legends relate that Adam received the Book of primal revelation out of the fire: 'At the hour when Adam received the Book, a fire arose on the shore of the river, and the angel ascended to heaven in its flames'.[118] Later, another important fire-revelation followed at the same great earth rift, only further south: the Sinai revelation to Moses. The volcanic fire forces, which offered this great spirit event its basis in nature, were a smaller afterglow of the Sodom conflagration, just as the fire of Sodom had been an afterglow of the great Lemurian fire catastrophes. The stages of planetary evolution run parallel with the stations of the spiritual path of mankind. Finally, when Elijah beheld the roaring fire at the foot of Mount Horeb in the realm of the Sinai-revelation, the Godhead no longer spoke out of fire but in a purely inward manner (1Kings 19:12).

The name Hebron has often been interpreted as 'site of fire' and as the seat of the Hebers, the servants of fire.[119] A confirmation of this interpretation was seen in the fact that the Bible surrounds Hebron with a number of names that seem to point to the region of ancient fire cults.

The Hittite prince who ruled over Hebron and from whom Abraham acquired a major portion of his territory, was called Ephron, 'man of ashes' (from *epher*, ashes); he was the son of Zohar, 'the fiery glow'. The wife of Caleb, who later became ruler of Hebron, was called Ephrath, 'woman of ashes', and she was the mother of Hur, 'the burning one'. The word 'Hebrew' is related to the name of the Hebers contained in the word Hebron as well as to the name of the Habiri of Samothrace, as has frequently been pointed out. When Abraham settled in Hebron and created the site of the source of Hebrew spiritual life, perhaps he did in fact join with mystery streams already present there, in which an inward view of the Saturn-spirituality revealed in fire was cultivated. In that case, when Sodom was destroyed, a fire of judgment would have confronted a 'fire that does not consume'; the place where the spiritual secrets of fire and ashes were known would have been spared from the consuming fire and the rain of ashes.

After the Sodom catastrophe, Abraham was led by his destiny out of Mamre, the realm of peace. The soulful apocryphal scripture, *The Testament of Abraham*, reveals the whole paradise-magic of the grove of Mamre and the friendship with God, when it is describing the end of Abraham's life. A short résumé of the content of this text can round out our account.

The archangel Michael was told to inform Abraham of his impending death. He found him in the grove of Mamre and walked with him under the trees, but could not bring himself to carry out his task. Then, a breeze moved the top of a tamarisk tree and Abraham felt that its rustling was supposed to tell him a secret. When back in his house he was washing the feet of his guest this feeling was intensified into a premonition of his death. Abraham began to weep and Isaac and the guest wept with him. In the basin used for the washing of the feet, the archangel's tears turned into precious stones. When the sun was setting, Michael, who as the highest angel had to intone the hymns of praise of the hierarchies, returned to the spiritual world without having accomplished his task. He beseeched the Lord to tell Abraham of his death himself. Once again, Michael was Abraham's guest. This time he had leave to eat and sleep in Abraham's house and the assurance that Isaac would receive the weighty message in a dream.

During the night, Isaac came weeping to Abraham. Again, the archangel wept with the human beings. A bright radiance came over all of them. Sarah recognized their guest as the angel who, as one of the three messengers of heaven, once prophesied the birth of her son. Abraham found assurance in the premonition that dawned in him when he washed the feet of the angel. Isaac related his dream: He wore sun and moon as wreaths upon his head, but the Father of Light came and removed the wreath of the sun amid the lamentations of all the stars.

Abraham asked for a bodily ascension so that he could behold all creatures before his death. Michael carried Abraham through all the spheres. Then, death was deprived of its power and Abraham could blissfully die.

In an important sense, Abraham's mission was one related to the body. He had to inaugurate a specific line of heredity and through it a patterning and forming process, which, from generation to generation, would produce a human figure freed of all atavistic residues. The divine promise that went forth to him had been summed up in the new form of his name: Father of Nations; and it placed before his soul the image of descendants comparable in number and order to the stars.

But what about the fulfilment of the promise and the mission, since Sarah proved to be unfruitful?

Hagar, the Egyptian maid, had borne Abraham a son, Ishmael. He, too, shared in the promise that predicted an imprinting of the order of the stars in the descendants who were to follow: '. . . behold, I will bless him and make him fruitful and multiply him exceedingly; he shall be the father of twelve princes, and I will make him a great nation' (Gen.17:20). This word of God concerning Ishmael was fulfilled. As Jacob, later on, Ishmael became the progenitor of twelve tribes. But Ishmael was not suited for the fulfilment of Abraham's task, the propagation of pure form and character. In his blood lived and seethed Babylonia and Egypt. Hagar's Hamite blood worked powerfully within him. A quality that relates him to Nimrod, 'the great hunter', is referred to by the Bible, when it calls Ishmael 'a good archer' (Gen.21:20 B). Ishmael was endowed with the intellectual power, which had been attained in Abraham through the clear formation of the brain. But his thoughts were not clear reflections of the universe. Unrefined passions and will forces intruded and made of them something injurious. Ishmael was not a thinker but a 'mocker' (Gen.21:9B).

The nations who later accepted the Islamic religion, in particular the Arabian tribes, descend from Ishmael. In Ishmael's soul, Islam's nature was preformed; and the symbol of Islam, the moonsickle with the star of Venus, could also serve as an expression of the forces active in him. The moon forces dwelt in him;

however, not in a pure but in an ecstatic way. The soul forces of
the Babylonian Ishtar and the Egyptian Hathor-Isis, which still
belonged to the ancient world order and were subject to decadence, mingled with the form and thought-power of the moon. If
Ishmael had had to be the heir to the Abraham mission, then
Abraham's detachment from Babylonia and Egypt would have
been in vain. Hagar and Ishmael were cast out of the incipient
folk-community.

The future of Abraham's mission was saved by the birth of
Isaac. This birth was a miracle; it was a violation of the laws in
force everywhere, which prescribed the limits and rhythms of the
life forces. For Abraham was a hundred and Sarah ninety years
old when the divine promise was finally fulfilled. This entry of a
higher world order, which had already withdrawn from the earth,
affected the surroundings of the birth of Isaac as well. A miracle
attracted miracles. The legends relate that at that time, many
barren women conceived; many deaf regained their hearing, and
the blind their sight; the number of lights in heaven was increased.
On the day Isaac was born, the Lord caused the light of the sun
to become forty-eight times brighter.[120] But was Isaac not more
a son of the spirit than a scion and bearer of heredity, by virtue
of the miraculousness of his birth? We touch upon the deepest
secret of Isaac's destiny with this question. Isaac was less a Yahweh man than Abraham. Whereas Ishmael was a moon-nature
too deeply involved with foreign impulses, Isaac was too much of
a sun-nature simply to carry on the pure Yahweh moon stream.
In Ishmael lived an obsolete past; in Isaac, on the other hand,
humanity already reached too far beyond itself into the future.
What could happen?

Abraham received the command to sacrifice Isaac. What is the
meaning of this severe order by the Godhead? Why did the divine
world give the promised son to Abraham with such an obvious
outpouring of its forces of grace only to demand him back immediately? And did it not appear as if the whole horrible decadence of Babylonian human sacrifice and slaughter of the first-born
now is about to flare up in Abraham's surroundings?

We have groped our way toward a comprehension of the mystery centre of Melchizedek on the site of the later Jerusalem. It
is here that Abraham brought his son to execute the grave command of the sacrifice (see p. 123). As we recognize this, we come
closer to the complex of historical facts likely to be concealed

behind the mysterious image of Isaac's sacrifice; and at the same time we also see more deeply into the secret of Isaac's nature.

Abraham, devoted with all the powers of his soul to the pure moon service of Yahweh, knew of the hidden sun mystery and acknowledged him who led it as his own higher leader. He was willing to offer up his promised son to the Melchizedek mysteries. He felt that they had a right to him, whose being radiated sun qualities.

We can imagine that Abraham, who himself had not undergone initiation in the way it was conducted in the mystery centres, did not know in what sense he would have to make the sacrifice. In his soul lived the heroism of obedience and an unreserved spirit of sacrifice.

Among the ancient legendary traditions there are some that point in an imaginative way to an important spiritual process that occurred during the scene of the sacrifice:

> When the sword touched Isaac's neck, his soul flew from him. But because the Lord let his voice resound from the sphere of the cherubim, calling, 'Lay not thy hand upon the boy,' the soul returned into Isaac's body. Abraham untied him and Isaac stood up on his feet. Thus, Isaac experienced that there is a resurrection of the dead . . . In this hour he opened his mouth and said, 'Praised be the Lord who awakens the dead.'[121]

It is not as if nothing had happened to Isaac's soul because the spiritual powers put a stop to what was going on. Isaac actually had undergone a death. It was, however, not the death that permanently separates the soul from its body, but the initiation-death that leads to resurrection and intensification of life. The sunlike son of Abraham passed through an initiation at the site of the secluded sun mystery and became a pupil of Melchizedek. Apocryphal reports indicate this by saying that after the sacrifice, Isaac remained on Mount Moriah for three years in the School of Shem (see p. 124).

What will Isaac do now? Will he begin to work out of the element in his nature which is akin to the sun? He would have done so, if he had been left to his natural development. Through a premature fulfilment and at the same time insufficient anticipation of the Messianic future, he would have allowed the Abraham mission to become exhausted. Just because of the transformation that his soul went through in the sacred realm of the sun initiation, he became aware of his true nature and the tasks of the present resulting from it. He gained insight into the necessity of the sun renunciation in favour of the Yahweh mission, which, for the time being, had to be carried out by those human beings suited for it. The 'sacrifice of Isaac' in which Isaac was to be offered up became the sacrifice of Isaac which he himself had to bring.

Where the Bible in its imaginative description speaks of the ram, sacrificed in place of Isaac, soul-spirit processes of perception and sacrifice are concealed that occur in Abraham and above all in Isaac. Ancient paintings representing Isaac's sacrifice still frequently show traditions of wisdom at work — at least in artistic creativity — which sensed that the image of the ram is not meant in an earthly-material sense, but must be grasped as a vision that appeared to Abraham's and Isaac's souls. The ram, appearing not on the ground but above in the branches of a tree, is surrounded by a radiant sunlike light-aura. It is as if the sun itself were beheld, and sketched into it the image of a ram. One could say: Abraham and Isaac behold 'the sun in the sign of the Ram (Aries)'. During that cosmic age, the sun's vernal equinox* was still in the sign of the Bull (Taurus). Only in a future evolutionary cycle, would the sign of the Ram be the spring image of the sun.† It was therefore a vision of the future that filled the souls of Abraham and Isaac. They were directed to a future in which the sun faculties of Isaac's nature could and had to be fulfilled. For the sake of this future, a renunciation had to be made in the present and a sacrifice offered up. In Isaac's soul, forces of the future were active which were ahead of humanity's development.The sun of the Ram had implanted them in him; of these he had to divest himself.

They were the same forces that later lived in Moses and are shown in artistic representations of Moses with the horns of a ram or with two beams of light proceeding from his forehead. In Moses' time they necessitate the sacrifice of the lamb. In conformity with ancient world concepts, Anthroposophy calls these forces

---

* The sacrifice of Isaac, as is assumed by all ancient traditions, falls in the time of the vernal equinox, in the beginning of the spring, hence in the time of the Feast of Passover; in turn, both the lamb-offering of Moses during the exodus from Egypt, and Christ's sacrificial death on Golgotha fall during this time.

† During the third post-Atlantean epoch, the Egyptian-Babylonian culture, the equinox stood in the constellation of the Bull. This was from 2907 to 747 BC. In the fourth post-Atlantean cultural epoch, from 747 BC to AD 1413, thus also at the time of the mystery of Golgotha, the sun stood in the constellation of the Ram.

the two-petalled lotus flower. Rudolf Steiner indicates the following in regard to the meaning of the ram that is sacrificed in place of Isaac:

> The human corporeality which was to propagate itself through the generations and which possessed the faculties necessary for comprehending the world according to number and measure, by mathematical logic — this human corporeality was to be preserved intact and received back as the gift of Jahve. But in order that the intrinsic nature of this bodily constitution should remain pure and unalloyed, it was necessary that all old, shadowy clairvoyance . . . all inflowing revelations such as had poured into the ancient religions, including those of Chaldea and Egypt, should be renounced. Every gift from the spiritual world must be renounced. The last gift from the spiritual world, the one gift remaining after all the others have been dimmed, is denoted in mystical symbolism by the *Ram*. The two horns of the ram symbolise the sacrifice of the two-petalled lotus-flower . . . In order that this bodily constitution might be preserved in Isaac, the last clairvoyant gift, the gift of the ram, the two-petalled lotus-flower is sacrificed.[122]

> The individual clairvoyant faculties can be related to one of the constellations . . . the last of the gifts of clairvoyance which was sacrificed voluntarily was connected with the constellation of the Ram. This is why we see the ram at the [scene of] sacrifice of Isaac.[123]

The vision of the sacrificial animal in the thicket of the tree showed Isaac what he had to sacrifice and the kind of future for which he thus prepared the way. In their attempts to demonstrate the spiritual origin of the ram, the apocryphal traditions constantly touch upon these secrets with their images. They state that an angel brought the ram out of the Garden of Eden, where it was grazing underneath the Tree of Life;[124] that Elijah led it to Abraham[125]; mainly, however, by explaining that 'the departing soul of Isaac embodied itself in the ram'.[126]

What had taken place in Abraham's case when, through the encounter with Melchizedek, the sun messenger, he had been directed to the proper service of the moon, took place with Isaac, the bearer of the sun forces, in an intensified and deeper manner, gripping his whole being during his initiation at the site of the Melchizedek sanctuary. The sun directed Isaac to the moon path. For the fulfilment of the Abraham mission, Ishmael brought with him too little and was cast out. Isaac brought too much; and in order to be the bearer of the legacy, he had to make the great sacrifice. Henceforth, the whole Isaac destiny was veiled by the secret of great restraint and taciturnity. The sacrificial scene on Mount Moriah dominated Isaac's whole being and life. And his turning blind appeared like a physical manifestation of the sun renunciation that had become reality in him. 'When Isaac became old, his eyes were beclouded. For in that hour when he was to be sacrificed on the altar, the heavenly hosts wept and their tears fell from their eyes into the eyes of Isaac and left traces therein.'[127]

Just as Melchizedek, the great sun messenger, completely withdrew into the seclusion of the mysteries in this era, and from there only occasionally helped humanity to tread the path necessary for the present age, so, as a soul with sun nature, Isaac had to withdraw into seclusion and be effective more through his existence than his actions. But what had been sacrificed returned inwardly intensified on a higher level of existence. The sun element which Isaac personally surrendered dawned like a golden gleam of the future over the beginning community. The individual bearers of the legacy had to be moonlike so that the whole of the tribe could be guided by the spiritual sun. This secret, which took on increasingly discernible form in the succeeding generations of the development, overspread the life of Isaac like a glorious dawn. Just as reflections of the paradisal Adam-past played into Abraham's destiny, so lights flashed through Isaac's destiny which were like advance sun reflections of the Christ-future. The promise was no abstract affirmation. It had its obvious signals. The future lit up through the events themselves.

The most obvious and significant image of the promise is Isaac's passing through a death and resurrection during his sacrifice on Moriah. The Christ-destiny, which in time was to find its earthly fulfilment in death and resurrection on this same site, found a first realization in a prophetic reflection.The legends bring the Messianic emanation of the Isaac offering to expression in their way. 'Abraham took his son Isaac and saddled the donkey. This was the donkey . . . on which Moses later rode when he came to Egypt, and on which the Messiah, the son of David, will one day make his entrance.'[128] 'Abraham took the wood of the burnt offering and carried it like a person who bears his cross upon his shoulders.'[129]

Above all, by showing how Isaac sojourned at a well and how he dug wells of living water, the Bible weaves images that point to the Christ-future. The role that trees played in Abraham's life is taken over by wells in the life of Isaac.[130] Where Isaac stayed, new life was won from what was dead. Beer-sheba, the city of 'seven wells', south of Hebron in the already devastated region of Sodom, was the true city of Isaac. In the land of the Philistines, Isaac restored the dried-up wells of the paternal past (Gen.26:18) and added new ones. During special events of his destiny, for instance, when the bridal suitor Eliezer brought him his wife from the ancient Babylonian homeland; and after Abraham's death, when we find Isaac at the 'well of the living and seeing ones'. (Gen.25:11; 24:62). Such prophetic images of a re-quickening of dying earth life, of a re-attainment of lost paradise, shine forth like hidden veins of gold from the quiet stories about Isaac.

Of the trinity of the patriarchs, only Abraham and Jacob, drawn into the great swing of the pendulum of evolution between Babylonia and Egypt, emerged in mighty actions in the foreground of history. The figure in the middle remained at work in quiet seclusion; his destiny ran its course without great outward movements. Isaac never ventured into the great countries of the past. He remained within the Promised Land. If the trinity of Abraham, Isaac and Jacob is taken — as has been the case in all ages — to be a human reflection of the divine Trinity, in Isaac, the image of the Son is beheld, who remained hidden as yet. The time for the Son had not yet come. The Son remained veiled in the sphere of sacrifice. Later on, in Saul, David and Solomon, the first three kings, another reflection of the Trinity was placed in the Old Testament development. This time it was the figure in the middle, David, who stepped actively into the foreground. The time of the Son was drawing nearer. Especially if the figures of the Old Testament are considered in their continued development, one may sense the magic, fraught with significance, pervading the origins of those who are symbols of a spiritual sunrise.

9 Jacob: The Babylonian Legacy

In his *Poetry and Truth* (*Dichtung und Wahrheit*), where he relates his early preoccupation with the story of Joseph, Goethe once put in words the nature of the first two patriarchs. He speaks of Abraham's 'tranquillity and grandeur', and of the 'stillness and submission' of Isaac. To designate the new element that entered the development through Jacob, the third of the patriarchs, in the same way, one would have to seek an expression for mastery of a dramatic, combative destiny. In the Talmudic texts we come across the sentence: 'Abraham is the root of Israel's *life*; Isaac is the root of its *spirit*; Jacob is the root of its *soul*.'[131] With Jacob, a strong struggling element of personal soul is in fact added to the holy primal life embodied in Abraham and to Isaac's spirit-creator existence that remained in humble self-effacement. Evolving humanity leaves the primeval womb of the Godhead and enters the stage of its own soul existence and personality.

After the figure in the middle, Isaac, had remained in mysterious silence, the journeys of Jacob led with as wide a movement into the same regions as did the journeys of Abraham. The impulse, however, for Jacob's expeditions was not the call of the spirit to seek the promised land, but the necessity of destiny, which entailed privation, persecution and homelessness. His flight from Esau took Jacob to Babylonia and when, toward the end of his life, he travelled to Egypt, it was in the course of the fateful events resulting from the loss of the favourite son and the famine and impoverishment of the country. Everywhere, Jacob had to struggle. The Bible depicts him struggling with the twin brother while still in the mother's womb. He had to compete for his birthright; he had to fight for Rachel; he had even to fight with beings of the spiritual world. And the name Israel, 'warrior of God', finally transfigures his battle-filled destiny.

The promise of descendants reflecting the order of the stars did not immediately attain visible fulfilment in Isaac's case as it did in that of Ishmael through the birth of twelve sons. It had to be preceded by a test and a differentiation. Rebekah bore Isaac the twins, Esau and Jacob. Which of the two sons would become the bearer of the promise?

Esau was the first to be born. In his mother's womb, Jacob had held on to Esau's heel and did not let go until after he too was born. This image already contains the decision in veiled form. Jacob came into the world later; but he carried with himself faculties that had progress and the future on their side. Esau belonged to an ancient world order, which, though it commanded powerful forces, was no longer in keeping with the times and had to lose its position of leadership over a humanity pressing ever more impetuously and aggressively into the future. His heel was weak. He could proceed forward, but limped behind.

9 JACOB

Esau and Jacob are related to one another as Achilles and Odysseus of Greek mythology. Achilles was the hero, powerful bearer of the ancient divine forces; but his heel was vulnerable; he lacked power to cross the threshold of the dawning age. He had to give way to the man of the future, Odysseus, who could avail himself of the ferment of human progress, namely cleverness. Esau too had an 'Achilles heel', and was outflanked by the bearer of intelligence, who could substitute cleverness and cunning for what he lacked of the old forces.

Beginning with the story of Jacob, a fairy-tale element entwines the mythological imaginations of Genesis. The more pronounced the historical dynamism of the imaginative descriptions becomes, the more compressed in scope are the individual images. But the pictorial content of the individual scenes does not gain in historical accuracy in the external historical sense of the facts. On the contrary, it is as if by the shrinking of the pictorial dimension in the transition from myth to fairy tale there occurred a concentration and intensification of the imaginative element. Therefore, the pictures within the increasingly tense, dramatic force injected particularly by the aggressive element of Jacob's destiny require more than ever to be made transparent for the historical facts. The possibility of misinterpretation of the processes described by taking them at face value increases. The figure of Esau has fallen victim extensively to such misinterpretation. Through the usual manner of reading, the biblical descriptions have had to arouse a strong emotional bias for Jacob, although the same form of comprehension must necessarily perceive his behaviour as morally objectionable. Legends outside the Bible do the figure of Esau more justice. They show that ancient sun forces were alive in Esau, whereas Jacob was the bearer of the moon element: 'Already at the time of the creation of the world, the Lord determined that the sun would be Esau's realm and the moon the realm of Jacob'.[132] The sun component that was spiritually present in Isaac's nature but had to be sacrificed, manifested corporeally in Esau. In this form it could and had to be eliminated from the stream of inheritance, which was increasingly to absorb the form forces of the moon into itself. If Isaac had not had to undergo the sun renunciation, the solar aspect of his nature would have been effective in a much nobler, more spiritual and promising way than Esau's. In Esau lives the sun-nature of the human corporeal being, which — while abandoned by mankind as a whole — still

143

decadently recurred now and then. The growth forces of the ether body had not yet been brought to coincidence with the organic forms of the physical body, and still extended into the cosmically gigantic dimension of outer nature. This is why Esau is described as a man of large physical stature and strength; a hunter, like Nimrod. While Jacob, in conformity with the constitution of his physical organism, prefers life within his house, Esau lives outside and roams the fields as a hunter. The ancient legends, which for this period of evolution also adopt, and intensify, the fairy-tale element of the biblical descriptions, relate how the two hunters, Nimrod and Esau, met each other time and again on a hunt, and how in mutual envy over the game each had killed, their ancient natures of fury clashed, until finally one day Esau cut off Nimrod's head with his sword. A prelude of the Goliath tale takes place, but this time it remains, as it were, still within the sphere of giants. Jacob is not yet David and therefore not superior to Nimrod-Esau as David is later in regard to Goliath.

It follows from this juxtaposition of Esau with Nimrod that his historical figure does not coincide with the imaginative picture the Bible gives him. Only in soul-imagery does Nimrod appear as a savage hunter, while in historical reality he was one of the great and powerful kings and creators of Babylonia's culture. Likewise, Esau must also be pictured historically as a high-ranking tribal leader in surroundings that are by no means primitive but in accord with his noble office.

Esau means 'the hairy one'. The description that his body was hairy all over, as if he had been covered with a hairy mantle (Gen. 25:25), contributed in no small measure to his being regarded as a primitive savage, since the pictorial language of the fairy tale was not translated. Again, the ancient solar effect of the ethereal forces is indicated by means of the image of hairiness. The ancient narrators touch upon this secret in their way. They say that not only the Book of Adam but also the Garment of Adam was inherited from Adam through the generations. With these two images, they distinguish between the two ways of propagating the old solar forces: one relating to the nature of consciousness, the other to that of physical being.

It says that when Adam had to leave the Garden of Eden, God gave him a garment to wear on the way, which, like the robe of Allerleirauh in the Grimm's fairy tale, was put together out of every kind of animal skin. This Garment of Adam was supposed to have passed on to Enoch and finally to Noah. But while the Book of Adam then passed to Shem, Adam's furry Garment came into Ham's possession, for he stole it from his father in the ark and concealed it from his brothers. Among the sons of Ham, Nimrod became its heir; and it is said that through this garment he became the mighty hunter, for when he wore it, all the animals came to him and took him to be their king, since he was clothed like them. When Esau returned home after slaying the great hunter, 'he had first seized the precious garment of Nimrod for himself, which the latter's father had left to him and through which Nimrod had become victorious over the whole earth'.[133] Other legends state that Adam's furry Garment had been handed down as a holy priest's robe from generation to generation — always in possession of the first-born son — and that this was how it came into Esau's hands.[134]

Such imaginative traditions indicate that remnants of the paradisal sun corporeality of man remained alive until the threshold of historical times — although not among the progressive branches of humanity. Within it, the images of all creatures were archetypally concentrated together. What was still left of the sun forces during the age of the patriarchs, about 2000 BC, was antiquated and decadent, while the moon forces cultivated in the Shem-Abraham stream were the bearers of progress by producing the intellectual thinking of the brain.

Jacob confronted Esau similarly to the little tailor who faced the giant in the delightful fairy tale. Through his still cosmic will, which contained nature's greatness, Esau was larger than his body. In him dwelt forces more powerful than those of his separate individual personality, but the light of consciousness could not yet penetrate his being. Jacob was completely enclosed within the abode of his physical corporeality; but for this very reason he possessed intellectual cleverness. Just as in the fairy tale, the brave little tailor brought about the downfall of the clumsy giant through his cunning, Jacob gained the advantage over Esau.

The customary interpretation of the biblical description cannot see anything but the story of a deception in what took place between Jacob and Esau. Everything indicates that the real meaning of the story has hereby not been grasped. First of all, the advantage Esau had over Jacob as the first-born could not be of such decisive importance, since they were twins. Moreover, keeping within the imaginative logic of the story, one might ask how it was possible for Isaac to know nothing of Esau's renunciation of his birthright in favour of Jacob. This is all the more puzzling, since, according to the biblical account, the impulse for employing trickery did not actually proceed from Jacob but from his mother, who categorically declared that she was ready to take the curse of wrongdoing upon herself. (Gen.27:13).

The traditions outside the Bible give a whole series of indications that behind the images of Genesis historical facts are concealed that make everything appear within cultic, sacramental connections. It is said that the dish of lentils for which Esau sold Jacob his birthright was a cultic meal of mourning celebrated by Jacob on the occasion of Abraham's death. Esau, who is always described as being filled with pronounced feelings of resignation and death, was said to be attracted in some special way by this death-meal. It always states (as also in Gen.25:32) that Esau said: 'What good is the birthright to me since I am going to die?' Perhaps what is meant to be indicated is that Esau was conscious of the fact that he was the bearer of forces that no longer had a future; and that because of this, while he still possessed an ancient angry nature, he had no creative courage regarding the future. It is quite likely that certain ritualistic customs of the ancient world are indicated with the puzzling dish of lentils. One need only recall that ascetic religious movements of later times, such as the Indian Brahmins and the Greek Pythagoreans, strictly avoided consumption of legumes, because the soul would thereby become too strongly tied with matter. In any case, Esau manifested an attitude of consciousness in which his soul wanted to extend with sensual pleasure into the substance of its own body and nature.

The legends furthermore describe how along with the birthright Esau also gave Jacob its emblems. Hence, from this time forward, Jacob is said to have been in possession of Adam's Garment of furs. This is to indicate that Jacob used rightful, not deceptive, means, when he put on the robe of skins in order to receive the blessing of his blind father.

One could assume that the descriptions outside the Bible tend to cleanse the patriarch of the odium of deceit. But if the imaginative character of the biblical scenes is understood, it is clear that in the Jacob-Esau story we are dealing with none other than the myth of the origin of intellect. It is not Jacob who commits a personal wrong; humanity takes a further step on the path of the Fall into sin. The old world lived in the essence of being; now, semblance is added to the essence of reality. Striving toward egohood, man produces reflected images of reality through head-thinking. But since they are *his* world, he would like to claim for this world of images an essential being of its own. Thus, the world of semblance, of illusion, arises. The intellect conceals within itself a cosmic cunning, a deceit in regard to essential being, an estrangement from God. From its inception, the nature of illusion and deception attaches to the intellect. Man no longer attains to the true essence of the world with the intellect. He believes that he possesses the truth in his thoughts; but what he does possess are only pale images, reflections, and abstractions of being. The cosmic delusion takes on the image of a personal deception in the myth of the intellect related by the Bible. It is a cosmic delusion that mankind had to suffer when, in order to gain the freedom of the individual human being, it ceased to weave within the solar essence of true being, and began to exchange this true reality for lunar semblance.

The problem of the ancient order of the first-born and its suspension does not emerge in the Bible for the first time in the case of Jacob and Esau. We witness an important process of selection that goes back a long way. Cain had had to relinquish his right as the first-born when Seth became the progenitor of the first progress-bearing humanity. Shem also was the bearer of the development represented in the Bible as willed by God, though he was not the first-born among his brothers. The ancient traditions alternate between designating Ham and Japheth as the older. Abraham was preferred over his older brother Haran, and Isaac over Ishmael, who was born before him. Through inheritance, a quite specific mission of humanity was to be carried toward its fulfilment; a eugenic providence was at work. But from the beginning it is clear that the results of the merely hereditary nature force alone do not lead to the goal. An inheritance that merely preserved the forces of the past unchanged, such as was active in the first-born male, had actually to be distilled out from generation to generation. Although its bearers possessed the right of the first-born, they had to be eliminated from the main stream. They became progenitors of collateral lines, in which the different forces of the past were physically preserved so that later on they could be reabsorbed by the main stream in a spiritual way. Thus, Cain, Ham and Japheth, Haran and his son Lot, Ishmael, Esau, and later Reuben, the first-born of Leah, and Joseph, the first son of Rachel, were eliminated from the main stream of inheritance. A continuing historical sacrifice of the first-born is woven into the history of the folk-community of the Old Testament. It was not offered up in the gruesome manner of Babylonia. This law, which also went into effect when Jacob instead of Esau became the bearer of the birthright, can appear like a Babylonian sacrifice of the first-born turned inward.

With each step on the path of the generations, a quite definite spiritual progress had to be attained, which made it necessary to eliminate sole dominance of the natural law to a certain extent. Only an inheritance that became spiritualized was suitable for preparing the way and the vessel for the future of God.

Heredity had to be brought into harmony with the principle of a spiritual selection and choice. All ancient supersensory forces of clairvoyance and magic were distilled out; and thus, the inheritance and selection of the pure form came about. The members of the Israelite folk-community were 'the chosen people', not by virtue of some kind of divine arbitrariness, but through the eugenic providence, which had regulated the course of their inheritance and their generations from the very beginning.

Jacob was the first who consciously undertook the emancipation, the freeing of himself from the sole activity of the natural law. But then he had also to experience the agonies and repercussions that resulted from elimination of the old order of the first-born in his own destiny.

By taking hold of the emancipated intellect, Jacob had made a bold step into the future. Now it was made incumbent on him to catch up on the legacy of the past that he had bypassed in an inner way. The human forces eliminated from the blood line of heredity could not simply be totally abandoned by the branch of humanity arising through the special selection. What was rejected from corporeal development had to be brought back in a soul-spiritual manner. Therefore, Jacob received the instruction to go to Babylonia.

In order to relate the reason for this journey, the imaginative description of the Bible interlaces two motives: the flight from the wrath of Esau and the search for the right wife. Spiritual necessities stood behind both the negative and positive impulse to make the Babylonian expedition. The outward marriage was probably a sign that Jacob had earned the right of domicile in a soul realm that at first was foreign to him. Esau's wrath was a significant imaginative symbol. An outward flare-up of Esau's angry nature may well have played a part in the course of events. But the fact that this time Jacob made no use of his cleverness to calm Esau's wrath shows recognition of a legitimate claim that the world of Esau had to make of that of Jacob. And when we are told that upon his return home, Jacob celebrated his reconciliation with Esau, there is more to it than the length of time that had elapsed. Through his sojourn in Babylonia, Jacob had in an inner sense absorbed the heritage of the ancient world which, in the figure of Esau, he had to begin with passed over as insignificant.

Jacob began on his journey. He retraced the path of Abraham in reverse direction, as though he were returning home into the great Asiatic womb of humanity. Customary interpretation fails to attribute the proper cultural-historical importance to Jacob's migration and his sojourn in the country of his people's roots. Again, the shepherd imagery is taken as historical writing; therefore one does not notice how different the world and the culture was which Jacob now came into and what a pronounced transition he had to undergo.

The goal of Jacob's journey was the ancient temple city of Haran; the first place where Abraham also went, when he left his home in Ur. In order to gain an idea of the life that Jacob found and led in Haran, we must completely discard all conceptions of pastoral life on broad fields with large flocks. If only meadows and shepherds' tents had comprised the scenery of his life, Jacob would have remained in the same world crossing from Palestine to Mesopotamia. In reality, a most grandiose temple and cultic world formed the background of his stay in Babylonia. Especially in that age, the centres of Mesopotamian life, headed by Babylon, had developed into powerful cities; and a life astir with activity, which extended in its effects beyond the borders of great empires, filled these cities. Aside from the cultic life of its temples, Haran in particular, one of the ancient world's most important junctions of military, caravan and trading routes, must have harboured a colourful multinational community of people.

Jacob entered into this world of highly civilized culture. Laban, who as the brother of Jacob's mother Rebekah, was also a descendant of Abraham's brother Nahor, could by no means be imagined in reference to the simple biblical images as a rich nomadic sheikh. The name itself points in the right direction; for

'Laban' is a significant designation of the moon divinity and means 'the one shining in white', the *deus lunus*, the masculine moon.* Haran, the city of Laban, was, as we mentioned before, the moon city of the ancient world. All life of the city centred in an ancient moon temple which, as the true dwelling of the moon divinity on earth, was held sacred above all the other moon sanctuaries of mankind.† One comes closer to the historical facts when Laban is conceived as one of the leading priests of the great moon sanctuary, and the imaginative picture of the flocks in his possession are taken as an expression of his far-reaching priestly authority.

Usually, also, the significance of the long time Jacob spent in the service of Laban is overlooked. Jacob remained for twenty years within the Babylonian life of Haran. These are the most creative years of a man's life. Though it was not the longest, it was the most important chapter of his earthly destiny, which more than any other determined his nature. Almost all his children were born in Haran. Eleven of the twelve sons and his daughter Dinah were Babylonians by birth; and Jacob himself turned into more of a Babylonian than a Palestinian through his long residence there.

Jacob could nevertheless confront the cultic world of Babylonia as a foreigner in Haran and needed only absorb from it what was of importance for the fulfilment of his mission.

The apocryphal traditions relate that when he had to flee from Esau, Jacob first went to the School of Shem. Only after remaining there as a disciple for fourteen years, he moved to Haran. We have seen that the term School of Shem refers to Melchizedek's mystery centre at Jerusalem. Though the tradition concerning the length of time spent by Jacob studying with his progenitor Shem might well not correspond to historical facts, they do point out that after leaving his parental home, Jacob had to undergo a lofty and important period of study under the same exalted guidance that Abraham had been subject to before him. As one who learns, he also served and lived within the circle of Laban.

According to the imaginative description, he served the first

* Up until the Roman era, the moon was worshipped in Haran as an androgynous divinity having both a male and female face. The female moon, Luna, in correspondence to Laban, was named 'Lebanah'.

† Even Clemens Romanus, one of the first great leaders of early Christianity, denotes Haran (Carrhae) as the tomb of the moon in listing the cities in which the ancient gods are buried.

two of his three seven-year periods for his wife, and the last for possession of the flocks. His father too had received his wife from Haran, but Isaac himself had not had to travel to Babylonia and serve there. Abraham had sent the wise servant Eliezer there in his place as a bridal suitor. This was an expression of the fact that in Isaac's soul a spiritual content was alive, which also found recognition among the guardians of the Babylonian mysteries. But in order to win Rachel, Jacob had to serve there for a long time. Comprehended from a historical standpoint, the two seven-year periods in which he served as a suitor were occupied with a development that he personally had to absolve. At their completion, he could finally be declared of age and accepted by the guardians of the mysteries in Haran. The time which it says that he had to serve for the flocks, added a further development, which he himself would no longer have required, but which he completed in order to be able to take back with him something of the treasures of Babylonian life into the Promised Land.

In his desire to win Rachel for his wife, we see Jacob involved in a see-saw battle of dramatic proportion. Was he now only paid back for the cunning that he employed against Esau, when Laban wedded him to Leah instead of to Rachel? Deeper secrets are concealed here. The clever one did not encounter cleverness. Laban's giving him Leah's hand in marriage was not deception but adherence to the ancient holy order. Jacob's unreasonable demand that Laban give Rachel to him for his wife sprang from the same disregard and bypassing of the ancient customs that he previously had exhibited in regard to Esau. Here in Haran, the old world order did not allow a person simply to ignore and pass over it. The past insisted on its rights. When Laban said, 'It is not so done in our country, to give the younger before the first-born,' (Gen.29:26) he permits us to look deeply into the sacramental configuration of Babylonian culture. In Babylonia, a law must have existed in regard to a female first-born, which was held to be especially sacred. The first-born daughters of rulers and leading priests were brought up to be priestesses. We know from subsequent centuries, for example from the rule of the great Sargon, that the eldest daughter always had to assume the office of high priestess in the temple of the moon divinity. And we are probably not wrong in assuming that Leah and Rachel, but above all Leah as Laban's first-born daughter, had to execute definite functions as priestesses in the moon sanctuary there. The sphere of the rights of the first-born demanded the recognition refused it until then by Jacob.

Beholding the impressive statue of Moses by Michelangelo in Rome, and the subordinate figures of Leah and Rachel, the two wives of Jacob, who hold the balance on either side of the Zeus-like enthroned figure, his forehead adorned with the horns of the ram, one becomes aware of the pictorial value that these figures possess and the symbolism that through them pervades the life of Jacob. A part of our soul forces derives from the past. It contains what is merely inherited and tied to the body and what in the end consumes itself. Only with a smaller part of our soul do we thrust forward into the untouched ground of the future: it is the part that struggles upward to the spirit. Leah means 'abatement and self-consumption', and is an image of the inherited soul forces, which are related more to corporeal existence through which the past lays its claim on us. Rachel means 'the ram's lamb', and is a manifestation of the spiritual forces of the future such as were present in Isaac and had to be sacrificed. But from generation to generation, they must be newly acquired; therefore, the love of the future-orientated Jacob belonged to them.*

Jacob serves seven years for Leah, though he means to win Rachel. Only through an additional seven years of his service can Rachel too become his wife. The imaginative descriptions of the Bible show us how Jacob, when he continues to serve for the acquisition of the flocks, once again makes use of his cleverness. By employing a brilliant cunning and a discovery in the area of animal breeding, he acquires a large part of Laban's riches and finally secretly leaves the country with all this wealth. Again we would go wrong if we saw nothing more in these stories than a shepherd's tricks of breeding and a cunning deception. The riches Jacob acquired in Babylonia were treasures of wisdom and temple traditions. But through the power of his intellect that was alive in him as a new faculty and by which he distinguished himself from the Babylonian surroundings, he could shorten the means by which the ancient treasures of wisdom were otherwise acquired. Jacob incorporated the mysteries of Haran into his nature, although in changed form, translated into the wealth of intellectual thought. Transformed into an inward impulse, he brought Babylonia back into the Abraham stream. The imaginative wording of

---

* The names Leah and Rachel have often been interpreted as indicating the last quarter of the waning moon and the first quarter of the waxing moon.

this process may indicate that the Babylonian wisdom imparted deeper insights into the nature and development of animals and could therefore lead to discoveries such as Jacob employed in breeding of the flocks, according to the description of the Bible.

The mystery character of the riches that Jacob took westward comes most clearly to expression where it is said that Rachel stole the images of the gods of her father and carried them along. She was not satisfied with the inner soul content offered to him who penetrated the cultic world of Babylonia. She did not want to cut herself off from the cult itself and its implements and symbols.

Many have puzzled over what was meant by Laban's *teraphim*, which Rachel purloined. There are many gruesome descriptions of *teraphim* from later centuries that were in use in decadent Babylonia. Heads of slain children, mostly first-born males, were set up somewhere with gilded lips, and by a number of sinister invocation-charms were made to speak.[135] In regard to the more ancient times and the cults that had not yet fallen into decadence, the remark of the *Sepher Hayashar* is probably an indication: 'Some make *teraphim* in the form of a man out of gold and silver; and at certain hours this figure receives the forces of the constellations and predicts the future'.[136] The new insights that were obtained by the use of such oracle-images must surely have depended on the soul condition and training of human beings. In any event, through the biblical stories, we see the customs of the Babylonian cultic configuration penetrate into the closest surroundings of Jacob.

Laban followed Jacob's expedition all the way to the borders of the Palestinian region. But there, Jacob was not called to account by Laban. Instead, through inner revelations, Laban was motivated to carry out a reconciliation with Jacob and solemnly to set his seal on it. Jacob had obtained temple secrets of Haran in an unusual and to begin with improper way. Now, belatedly, he received the approval of those who had to guard these secrets. His Babylonian training period was declared to be absolved; Jacob was elevated from the state of being a disciple to that of a fully accredited member in the Haran mysteries. Babylonia acknowledged the form in which Jacob had absorbed these into himself and the humanity he was to lead. And the reconciliation with Laban could be followed by the reconciliation with Esau. The demands of the ancient world order had been satisfied.

But before the Babylonian chapter of Jacob's life fully culminated, another development had to be completed that interwove in a threefold supersensory experience, the great migration by Jacob.

In those early ages of history, each outward journey was at the same time an inner path. When physical man travelled from one country to another, the soul also was led through certain spheres. When Abraham left Ur, the land of primeval light, and travelled westward — following the sun from where it rises to where it sets — he passed in an externalized picture through the whole destiny of mankind that was driven from paradise; and, as it were, anticipated all future cultural developments, which were increasingly to move from east to west. The external journey was an exact expression of the inner process: the gradual separation from the ancient supersensory experience and the striving towards individual consciousness and freedom. But the powers of the spiritual world, who bore and guided man in the beginnings of his earth existence, were not willing to dismiss him sooner than was good for him.

In Jacob, humanity had advanced beyond the organic progress of its destinies through the Fall of the intellect. Now, Jacob was confronted with the task of retracing the Abraham-path in reverse direction. He had to travel east, as was said of Adam in primeval time, when the Godhead had bestowed on him his earthly form (Gen.2:8). The servants of heaven would like to bring the human, who had fallen from them, all the way back to the gates of paradise. Jacob was to go into the land beyond Jordan, which the ancient world perceived as the region of the earthly reflection of the spiritual world. With the Jordan, Jacob would be crossing the border and threshold of two worlds.

It is soon evident that the journey brought about a reimmersion in the sphere of supersensory experience and nearness to God. Jacob, the human being who had become intellectual and estranged from the supersensory was blessed with an important spiritual experience. He was suddenly received back into the fullness of spiritual existence when, in a dream, he beheld the heavenly ladder on which the angels of God ascended and descended. During the day he was spiritually completely on his own in his thinking; but at night he experienced himself as a member of the living stream of being, which flowed up and down between heaven and earth through all the levels of the angelic hierarchies. The prodigal son had returned to his father's house. Upon awakening from his sleep he exclaimed, 'How holy is this place! This is none other than the house of God, and this is the gate of heaven' (Gen.28:17*B*). Jacob called the place Bethel, 'house of the godhead', and erected a stone pillar in memory of his beholding the opened worlds of the spirit. It is far from the usual level of comprehension to see this scene against a religious and cultural-historic background. It is usually pictured quite primitively by assuming that Jacob once spent the night in the open and erected the stone on which he had rested his head as a monument to his dream. The Bible, however, gives the name of the city, Luz, where this experience occurred (Gen.28:19). Can one simply ignore the resulting contradiction of the conception?* Jacob must have found himself within the realm of an ancient sanctuary when he beheld the heavenly ladder; and it was in the tradition of the spirituality there to erect the *maçebhah*, the holy stone pillar.

Here, we touch upon an essential part of that early Palestinian cultural and cultic life, evidence of which we still encounter in stones found in many places throughout the country. On the heights of Samaria, Galilee and the eastern Jordan region, ancient stone-settings abound, like those preserved also in the regions of the old European Druid culture, above all in Ireland and Brittany. But also in northern Germany, for example, in the region southwest of Bremen and in the Lüneburg Moor, we find circles of stone, dolmens (tomb-like stone dwellings with heavy stone covers) and menhirs (stone columns placed singly or in a group). The stone Jacob erected at Bethel was a menhir and undoubtedly belonged, as did the stone circle of Gilgal erected later by Joshua, in the realm of the ancient culture of stone-settings, which probably went back to Atlantis.

The menhirs and dolmens were monuments of an ancient sacred association with the spiritual sun forces of the cosmos. Where the stone blocks the physical sunlight and brings about the area of shadow filled with the deeper ethereal forces of the sun, the Druid sun-priests of prehistoric time penetrated behind the veil of physical nature and beheld 'how heavenly powers ascend and descend

---

* De Wette, a theologian of the last century, says, 'Luz cannot have existed as a city, otherwise Jacob could not have spent the night under the open sky. Also, it would have been odd for a wandering nomad to want to give a city another name'. It would, however, be more correct to say the opposite, namely, that the Bible itself suggests by the means of the seeming contradictions that the imaginative description of a wanderer sleeping under the open sky be translated into historical fact.

and hand on their golden pitchers', receiving their divine inspirations and impulses thereby.[137] The spiritual cosmic forces of the sun were experienced particularly in the vertically effective forces of nature in both the plant kingdom and the upright form of man, in the spiritual passing of forces from below upward and from above downward concealed behind the earthly mask of sleep and death. The erection of menhirs — of which the Egyptian obelisks are but a variation — at sacred sites as well as on graves, was a cultic act of homage and celebration of the cosmic force of comforting uplifting, which the sun bestows everywhere.

In Luz, Jacob had entered the realm of such a cosmic sun sanctuary.* During the night, the sun recalls him, who during the day follows his moonlike intellect, back into its domain. Jacob experiences the vertical elevation by the sun, which, in the ancient world, was designated as 'head elevation'. With the *maçebhah*, the menhir, he later does the same thing that the spiritual sun had done with him; he pours oil 'on the head of the stone' (Gen.28:18 *B*).[138]

Throughout his stay in Babylonia, the experience of Luz-Bethel must have persisted as a question in Jacob. The external countenance of Babylonia was determined by the mighty temple-tower structures, the Nimrod-creations through which Abraham had recognized the necessity of his journey's course. In these ziggurats, the uplifting forces of the sun found gigantic expression. The temple region, in which the great tower of the city of Babylon was erected, was called E Sag Ila, 'the elevation of the head', and, as were the other ziggurats, was probably dedicated to Marduk, the dragon-slaying archangel of the sun, who in the Bible is called Michael. But the Marduk-cult of Babylonia called out into empty space. It echoed a sun and Michael-activity that belonged to the past. The powers of the spiritual sun had withdrawn, dismissing man from their cosmic influence and freeing him for an earthly soul life of conscious being. The cosmic intelligence that once reached into human nature as a force of essential being, had made room for the emergent personal intelligence of moonlike consciousness of thought. And the titanic tower-pyramids of the Babylonians were nothing but an expression of a powerful desire not to let go, but to hold on to the old sun forces. Jacob could agree even less than Abraham with the rebellion and resistance, prevalent in the Babylonian Marduk cult, to destiny's future inten-

* Luz is interpreted as 'the turn'; and Alfred Jeremias, for example, assumes that Jacob's experience in Bethel stands in connection with the summer solstice.

156

tions. Jacob was prepared to struggle free of the ancient solar state of being, and since his experience of 'head elevation' in Bethel, he knew what he was giving up. He therefore turned to that branch of Babylonian spiritual life, which had already exclusively decided in favour of moon worship, and to which his blood ties directed him. Inconspicuously, but in cosmic proportion, a repetition of the Jacob-Esau drama came about. The light of the moon is not the moon's property; it is borrowed, reflected sunlight. The moon purloins the sun's birthright from the sun. He who separated himself from the sun and turned to the moon, became an accomplice in this theft. Jacob dealt with Marduk as he did with Esau; but thereby he fulfilled a necessity of human evolution.

When, after twenty years, Jacob departed from Babylonia and returned home with the treasures of the East, he retraced the path of Abraham's westward journey, and had the second of his three great spiritual experiences as an echo of his reconciliation with Laban at the border of the Palestinian region. The heavenly hierarchies revealed themselves to him: 'And when Jacob saw them he said, "This is God's army!" So he called the name of that place Mahanaim.' (Gen.32:2). What he had perceived at the beginning of his journey in his nocturnal consciousness, he now beheld at the end of his path in bright daylight and fully awake consciousness. The veil of the sense world and of physical light parted before him, and he saw into the sphere of the spirit. This was the fruit of his reimmersion into the world of the heritage, although he had wholly dedicated himself to the service of the moon: the ancient solar gift of spirit vision lived again in him. Invisible hands held him and battled for him.

And now Jacob again approached the Jordan from the opposite direction. This time he wanted to cross it in an external way as the threshold of the great paternal home that he was leaving. Had he attained sufficient independence and maturity to be released into the land of freedom by the spirit powers holding him?

At the Jordan, the third and most decisive spiritual experience came over him, not in the night as in Bethel, nor in the day as in Mahanaim, but where night and day touch at the threshold between sleep and waking, before the sunrise that was to lead him once and for all into the wakefulness and 'this-ness' of the land of the present and future. A mighty spirit-form stepped in his way as he tried to wake up. He had to fight and struggle to earn his way. The first part of the great battle of awakening, permeated immediately with holy import, consisted of Jacob's wanting to struggle free. But it was as if the spiritual power that held him was saying, 'I will not let go of you unless you have withstood the test.' Jacob prevailed in the struggle, but now he was the one who would not let go the other, whose divinity he sensed, 'I will not let you go, unless you bless me.' Jacob won Isaac's blessing through his cleverness. He earned the blessing of the divine power with whom he struggled at the Jabbok ford by courage of soul and inner strength. In a new name that he received he became aware of this blessing. Henceforth, he was called Israel, 'warrior of God'.

Who was it who stepped in Jacob's way? During the struggle, Jacob asks for his name. But his opponent, blessing him, does not answer in words. Inwardly beholding him, Jacob received the answer. He had named the site of his night-experience in the beginning of his journey Bethel, 'house of God'. He named the site of his morning-battle at the end of his path Peniel, 'the countenance of God', because the countenance-being of the spiritual world, the archangel of the sun, Michael, revealed himself to him after the battle.[139] The countenance of God watched him go, when he left the divine paternal home, released into freedom. 'So Jacob called the name of the place Peniel, saying, "For I have seen God face to face, and my soul is restored." The sun rose upon him as he passed Peniel' (Gen.32:30–31B).

The traditions outside the Bible describe Jacob's struggle with Michael in a great variety of ways. But one motif that underlines the character of the experience — dawning of the day and awakening — returns again and again. The rosy dawn calls the archangel back to the sun: 'The angel begged Jacob, "Let me go, the sun is about to rise." Jacob answered, "Are you a thief or robber that you fear the sun?" But then came hosts of serving angels and cried, "Michael, arise; it is time to let the morning hymns resound. If you do not begin the hymn, our prayer is not possible".'[140] During the day, the archangel of the sun could not dwell in the soul of man in those times. The spiritual sun had to conceal itself from the waking human being behind the veil of physical light. Earlier, in the paradisal time, it permeated man also during the day and shone forth from him corporeally. But then, man was but an unfree vessel of cosmic sun-intelligence. In the future, he must once again become capable of being a bearer of the spiritual sun and the Michaelic spirit. In between lies the long path of the moon, on which man participates in the moon's mirror-theft of the sun's light, in order to attain to personal intelligence and freedom in his brain's thinking.

Jacob's struggle by the Jordan was the completion of his wresting himself free from Marduk's realm, the ancient Michael-effects. And the sun did let him go free. It allowed it to happen that man, with personal intelligence acquired in a moonlike manner, slipped away from it. The sun could do this, because the spark of freedom and self-sufficiency now glowed in man and had passed its test. The seed of the militant ego-force was a guarantee to the Michaelic power for its future incorporation into the thinking human soul, the future sun-evolution of man, still in the grip of the moon. It could confidently withdraw from him along with the cosmic equilibrium, which, until then, it had implanted in him. It takes from him the power of the Scales and wrenches his hip.* From now on in the ups and downs of destiny, man himself had to fight for and preserve the power of the scales, the inner balance. The wrenching of the hip is not an act of hostility but one of confidence. The sun trusts in the freedom of man and acknowledges his freedom as well.

The reconciliation with Laban and Esau, from whom Jacob had turned away after acquiring what he needed from them, was followed by the reconciliation with the spiritual power of the sun. The sun recognizes the moon's right to its light just as Esau now acknowledged Jacob's right to Isaac's blessing and as Laban had affirmed his right to the Babylonian treasures.

But the archangel of the sun not only released the human being; in blessing him, he also bestowed on him a certain share of his power. The name he gave Jacob reveals the secret of the Michael-blessing. 'Israel' is not a personal name, but the name of the people, who descended from Jacob. Michael gave himself as reward for the won battle. And while the great angel of the sun could not yet dwell within the individual human ego, he could make himself the protector, guide and genius of the chosen people. In a first step that prepared the way, the sun incorporated in a people before it became man. For himself, Jacob struggled free of the angel into awakening. For the folk-community that was coming into being he attained the angel's presence and union

---

* The figure of the archangel Michael is connected with the image of the Scales, Libra. The day of Michael, September 29, falls in the time of the year when the sun stands in the sign of Libra.

with it. The people themselves became a Messianic fact; a historical development began that outwardly was borne by the people of Israel, but inwardly by its newly attained folk-spirit, the archangel Michael. From now on, what the prophet Daniel said, came into force, namely that 'At that time shall arise Michael, the great Prince who has charge of your people' (Dan.12:1).

The early morning battle of Jacob with the angel is an exact analogy and metamorphosis of Abraham's encounter with Melchizedek. The great sun-initiate came to meet Abraham and, without leaving the mystery site, offered him the help of the sun on the path of the moon. The sun-archangel stepped into Jacob's way, releasing him from his guidance. But at the same time, the mysteries of the sun took an important step forward out of concealment by having made themselves the soul of the people. In the future, the moonlike human being, who felt himself a member of the God-sent people, could go on his way under the shining cloud of his sunlike folk-genius.

10 Joseph and his Brothers: The Egyptian Destinies

When Jacob received the name 'Israel' at the break of dawn by the Jabbok ford, the nation of Israel was spiritually born. It overshadowed the one human being in spiritual form. Together with Jacob, eleven sons and one daughter were in the process of exchanging their native country, Babylonia, with Palestine, the native land of their father. Later, when the birth of Benjamin rounded off the number of sons at twelve, Israel also became a people on earth. The twelve tribes had their beginning and formed a human reflection of the twelve constellations of the zodiac. The promise was fulfilled that a people would arise like the stars of the heavens. Out of the soul realm of Mesopotamian culture, the Chaldean star-wisdom became embodied and 'precipitated' — analogously to chemical processes, in which the solid substances contained in a liquid solution are precipitated and crystallized out — through Israel's thus becoming a people. The people of Israel arose on the earth as an everlasting reminder to themselves of the divine spiritual worlds ruling behind the stars.

10 JOSEPH AND HIS BROTHERS

Among the twelve sons of Jacob there was one who was so totally different from his brothers that one could believe he had been a product of another race, indeed another world. He was the youngest of those born in Babylonia, Joseph. Something unearthly, something of the beyond, hovered over the figure of the youth, who was of an almost feminine beauty. Like an Adonis or Tammuz — the god of youth of the Near East — become flesh, Joseph walked among men.

With Jacob, a militant element entered into the successions of figures of the Old Covenant. Joseph was no warrior, although his destinies appear like the acts of a mystery drama. He seemed to be the favourite and darling of the gods, even when human beings would cast him into misfortune. His destiny seemed to evolve by itself, as if it had already been solved in another world and was now only being repeated on earth. A guest from the beyond carried a starry destiny down among men; and human beings were openly or secretly enchanted by him, even if they expelled him for not fitting in with them.

Jacob clung to Joseph with idolizing love. For, as the first-born of Rachel, he was the reward of Jacob's long years of service in Babylonia and a pure remaining mirror of the soul of Rachel, who had already departed the earth. But the Adonis-magic of the youth probably played into Jacob's feeling for him. Rachel had not only taken along Laban's *teraphim*, hidden under the saddle of the camels, but also the divine youth Tammuz in the soul of her son. In this human form, Jacob was allowed to venerate the gods of Babylonia from whom he had struggled free. He adorned his son with a ceremonious garment normally used only to adorn the images of the gods. It was a garment of veils, elaborately composed of many pieces,* 'the living garment of the deity', which, through its images and colours was meant to form a composite of all the realms of creation. Jacob saw the twelvefoldness of the cosmos that was mirrored in his twelve sons embodied once again in a special way in the one beloved son. He therefore distinguished him with the garment of the gods, emphasizing his unearthly difference in the most striking way. This garment must have been a variation of what in apocryphal traditions is called the furry garment of Adam, and which was represented as the

* The common translation, 'coat of many colours', is completely wrong. The Hebrew word is a cultic expression and means 'garment of pieces'.

161

emblem of the first-born (see p. 144). Perhaps, by way of this garment, Jacob actually wanted to express the fact that he wished to give preference to Rachel's first-born over the first-born of Leah. In the stories of Joseph, the militant element of Jacob's destiny was subdued to some extent. The pictures, compressed into fairy-tale imaginations, gain in volume and substance. An epic element enters, a style of narration that gives the impression that now, finally, the outer historical course of events is described without distortion. The epic imaginations, in which the vision of Genesis is now clothed, are in fact more readily transparent for the physical-historical element. They do, however, require translation, if they are not to be misunderstood. Many an image requires just such religious-historical unveiling.

More than through his nature, Joseph distinguished himself from his brothers through his form of consciousness. A strong and pure echo of the old clairvoyant faculties lived in him. He had visions and dreams and was surrounded and ensheathed by supernatural images that his soul beheld. The garment of veils with the images of all creatures woven into it, which his father had given him, was a true symbol of his soul content and his type of consciousness. He did not look upon the world of objects through wide awake, clear senses, pondering his perceptions in thought. He beheld the outer world only as through a veil of dreams; thus it was no surprise that he came into conflict with the more matter-of-fact world of his brothers.

Joseph related his dreams to his brothers with divine unconcern. The world of dreams was to Joseph the real world. At this stage of his life he was far from wanting to interpret his dreams, that is, to bring them in harmony with the everyday world. He lived in the images and did not consider what kind of conflicts might arise between his dream world and the waking world of the others. Therefore, when he related his dreams, the incompatibility of two worlds had to be tragically revealed.

Joseph's dreams showed him elevated above his brothers and even his parents. First, he dreamt of twelve sheaves of ripe corn, of which one each was given to the twelve sons of Jacob; and the eleven sheaves of his brothers bowed and paid tribute to that of Joseph. Then he beheld the twelve constellations of the zodiac, and the signs of his eleven brothers, together with sun and moon, bowed down before his sign. The resentment of his brothers was bound to arise. But it was not kindled by the content of the dreams by which they felt themselves being humbled, but by the very fact of the dreams. That Joseph had visions and dreams at all created an unbridgeable gap between him and his brothers, and had to arouse in them the will to rid themselves of him.

The awareness of the Abraham mission lived powerfully in the will element of the ten older sons of Jacob. More by instinctive feeling than logical clearness of thinking, they knew that it was important to eliminate all the old clairvoyant forces in order to allow the pure, stern form to prevail in the nature and consciousness of man. Therefore, a basic repugnance to the fact that Joseph had visions and dreams and did not exclusively follow the direction of thought in his soul was added to their obscure, not fully conscious astonishment over his unearthly nature. When Joseph went to them in Shechem in Samaria with a message from their father, and the brothers saw him in his formal, ceremonious robe, they said to one another: 'Behold, there comes the lord of dreams!' (Gen.37:19*B*). And the decision was made for his expulsion. Rudolf Steiner has repeatedly used the destiny of Joseph to illustrate the inner determination of the Abraham stream: 'The last gift of clairvoyance is sacrificed, it must be thrust out . . . and if it still emerges as an inherited quality, it is not tolerated, as it were. In Joseph, a throw-back is evident. He has his dreams, he has the ancient gift of clairvoyance. The brothers expel him from their midst. This shows how tightly this whole mission was controlled.'[141]

At the same location, where Joseph's brothers decided in favour of his expulsion, their will to annihilate completely the atavistic nature of the old world had earlier expressed itself in a violent, dramatic eruption. The mysterious and gruesome Dinah drama had occurred there. The key to this event must be sought in the kinship, which, since primeval times, must have connected the soul nature of Samaria with that of Babylonia. In later centuries, Samaria, the Palestinian province in the middle between Judea and Galilee, was in a direct way integrated with a Babylonian infusion. In place of the Israelite tribes, whom they led eastward into imprisonment, the Mesopotamian rulers settled their own Babylonian subjects in Palestine, specifically in Samaria, thus laying the basis for a mixed population of strongly Babylonian character. From this originated the deeply rooted abhorrence and hatred of post-exile Judaism for the Samaritans. The people sensed the dreamlike, dark, ecstatic world of Babylonia in the Samaritans and believed that any contact with them was contaminating in the worst sense. The similarity and accord of Samaria with Babylonian spiritual life, which must have existed long before the direct Babylonian miscegenation, was probably one of the reasons that caused Jacob to choose Shechem, the capital of Samaria, as the main dwelling place for himself and his family after his return from Haran. Samaria was a bridge for him from Babylonian life into the land of the pure future.

It was not long before relationships ensued between the people living there and the groups of people gathered around Jacob, into which a decadence threatened to enter that was reminiscent of that of Babylonia. A cultic life mingled with sexual elements reached towards the Israelites and drew Dinah, the daughter of Jacob, into its sway. The Bible's imaginative description relates that Shechem, the sovereign of the country, was passionately attracted to Dinah and, without the consent of her father and brothers, made her his wife, and that the people of Shechem proposed general interbreeding to the Israelites. Here, Jacob and his sons encountered the world to which, since Abraham's time, their world had placed itself in irreconcilable opposition by means of the cult of circumcision. The general introduction of circumcision was made a condition to the people of Shechem, before the marriage of Dinah and Shechem could take place. The Samaritans agreed to the stern demand. But among Jacob's sons there were those who were imbued with a radical will and bore within them the impulse for complete rejection and extermination of the Babylonian character of soul. They knew that the external act of circumcision could not as yet effect purification from the twilight of ancient dream-ecstasy and could not prevent contamination of the stern mission of Israel. In bloody pictures, the Bible describes how Simeon and Levi, the ardent fanatics, conjured up destruction over the world of Samaritan corruption.* Only in the Dinah drama, the Babylonian epoch in Jacob's life and with it the Babylonian destiny of Israel came to a final conclusion. Now, the

---

* That Simeon and Levi were supposed to have slain all the males dwelling in the city with their swords is part of the imaginative style of the description, which first requires translation. The text seems to imply a general castration, which they performed in Shechem. The reflection of the event in the New Testament occurs in Luke 9:52–54. Two of the twelve disciples, the sons of thunder, James and John, wanted to call down fire from heaven upon the Samaritans, who refused to accept Christ.

path was cleared for their own pure future in the sense of the instruction issued to Abraham.

Now, it was also in Shechem that the sons of Jacob thrust from among them the one in whose soul the old world lived on in an untimely though fascinating manner. How was the expulsion to take place? The brothers gave up their plan to kill Joseph, when Reuben suggested throwing him in a pit. The word that the Hebrew Bible uses for 'pit' reflects from the physical into the mythological sphere. It also denotes the 'grave' and, further, indicates the nether world. It is not unlikely that one of the dolmen tombs is referred to, which are preserved to this day in Palestine as witnesses of that time and still older epochs. In these grave-like caves, built of great stone blocks, the sun priests of prehistory, similar in attitude to the Druids of the north, had themselves buried alive for a number of days and transported into somnambulistic states in order to receive the dream revelations of the spiritual cosmos. Perhaps the sons of Jacob locked their brother in such an ancient sun-grave, ridding themselves of him and at the same time scorning the whole world of old clairvoyant experience. Then, however, they freed him again from the tomb, when Judah suggested selling him to the Ishmaelite caravan for twenty pieces of silver. The apocryphal text, the *Testament of the Twelve Patriarchs*, relates that Joseph spent three days and three nights in the grave.[142] This suggests that without intending to do so, the brothers contributed to an indirect initiation of Joseph, in which his soul crossed the threshold of the spiritual world and achieved an important intensification and consolidation of his clairvoyant power.

For similar reasons and in a similar way, Joseph was cast out of the arising folk-community as once was Ishmael. From his Egyptian mother, Ishmael had inherited an excess of old soul elements, which made him unfitted to be the progenitor of the chosen ones. It was similar with the young Babylonian Joseph. The connection between the Ishmaelite nature and Egypt, as well as the similarity of Ishmael's and Joseph's destinies, plays imaginatively into the Joseph story. The caravan of Ishmaelite merchants who happened to be on the way to Egypt, the land of their ancestral mother Hagar, brought upon Joseph the Ishmael destiny, when they took him to Egypt. Faintly indicated images of distant future events met images of the past in the mirror of Joseph's being. Ancient destiny was repeated and a future precast its reflection, when, once again, there would be a Judas among a group of twelve: who, for a sum of silver pieces, would betray a being, walking among men and bearing the touch of the supersensory in himself.

Finally, imaginations that belong to the culture of the Near East weave into the tapestry of imagery thus coming about. The brothers took Joseph's ceremonious garment, drenched it with the blood of an animal, and brought it to the deeply shocked father. A conception arises that played an important role in the Adonis-Tammuz cult of Syria and Babylonia: the divine youth had been dismembered by a wild boar. And the lamentation that Jacob raised was coined in ceremonious rhythmical words, as if it had been taken from the cultic mourning dirges, which at certain times of the year resounded in the temples of Adonis: 'Ṭaroph ṭoraph Joseph', it says in the Hebrew wording of Genesis (37:33).

With the three days spent in the grave-like pit, a time of trial began in the destiny of Joseph, corresponding to the sojourn of the mythological Tammuz youth in the nether world. Joseph's trek to Egypt was permeated with an other-worldly element. It was the human incarnation of a myth.

In Egypt, Joseph entered a world of grandiose cultural development. By then Egypt's cultural centre had moved from the ancient royal city of Memphis in the north to the southern residence of Thebes. It must have made a powerful but almost eerie impression to see the gigantic structures of the pyramids and sphinxes around the now abandoned royal city in the south of the Nile Delta. A first inkling arose that in time to come the sandy desert would have dominion over the imposing ruins of ancient developments.

The shift of the Pharaoh's court to the southern residence points to an important turning-point in Egyptian life. The time had now finally expired, when, in an untroubled, natural way, Egypt could be the bearer of a mythical, supersensory stream of revelation. The breakdown of the ancient divine powers became increasingly evident. Visiting the remains of the new capital in southern Egypt today, one is placed within an impressive duality. In Thebes and Karnak, facing each other from the right and left sides of the Nile, stands the divided royal and priestly world of old Egypt. Two functions of the spiritual guidance of culture have split apart, the political and the religious life, which earlier had been united in a still larger totality. This split has probably been germinally present from the time Thebes took over from Memphis. And it is in this that the important turning-point in the decline of the old Hermes mysteries has come to expression.

When Joseph arrived in Egypt, he encountered the beginnings of decadence, which, after the Babylonian civilization, was now also taking hold of the Egyptian culture. In the story of Joseph's temptation in the house of Potiphar, in which he prevailed, but which caused him years of imprisonment, is concealed Joseph's encounter with Egyptian decadence. In Genesis (38 and 39), the Bible impressively contrasts the destinies of the two brothers, Judah and Joseph. While Joseph resisted temptation in a strange land, Judah became deeply entangled in impurity in his own country. Judah was unable to withstand the temptation emerging in the Dinah drama. He took a Canaanite wife, but the three sons she bore him could not become representatives of the Abraham mission. The tragedy of the first-born was played out once again in climactic intensification. Judah's first-born died without leaving descendants. The second son refused to procreate descendants for his dead brother. Before the youngest son had reached manhood, Judah himself had united with his first-born son's wife, whom he did not recognize and considered a harlot. Through the older of the twins, Perez and Zerah, which Tamar bore Judah, the race of the promise continued.

The name Potiphar or Potiphera signifies 'the priest of the holy bull', and occurs twice in the stories of Joseph. Through this name, we twice see Joseph involved in the configuration of Egyptian cultic life; first in his degradation and then in his elevation. Joseph had a star-relationship to the temple world of Egypt. Like all twelve sons of Jacob, Joseph too received his nature and strength from one of the twelve constellations of the zodiac. His sign was that of Taurus, the Bull.* This constellation, which was the position of the vernal equinox in the age of the Egyptian-Babylonian culture (2907 to 747 BC), was at the same time the constellation of Egypt and dominated life in the Egyptian world by means of the cult of the holy Apis Bull. In the primordial beginnings of evolution, shining forth out of the constellation of Taurus, the sun formed the human larynx into the organ of the

---

* The blessing of Moses indicates this, 'His glory is like that of the first-born of a bull' (Deut.33.17*B*), as does the blessing of Jacob, 'Joseph is a fruitful bull' (Gen.49:22*B*). (Current translations are due to a misunderstanding of the meaning.) Joseph's association with the sign of the Bull is based on ancient traditions. See, for example, Nork, and A. Jeremias (p. 390).

resounding word.[143] By virtue of the sun forces of the Bull, the magic word of the priest was the soul of ancient Egyptian culture. Numerous traditions exist concerning Joseph's special connection with the word and with speech, in which his Egyptian nature comes to expression. 'Joseph mastered all languages. When he saw the groups of various nations standing in the market place and heard them speaking in their own tongue, he understood everything they were saying.'[144]

Joseph serves the first Potiphar as overseer of his house. In his service, temptation approaches. The part of the Adonis-Tammuz myth that relates to us how Venus-Aphrodite tries to seduce the beautiful, divine youth is reflected here. The imaginative description of the Bible tells how the temptress takes revenge. Through her lie, she is successful in making Potiphar throw Joseph into prison: Adonis, dismembered by a wild boar, which a jealous goddess dispatched, is banished into the nether world and its shades. After years of service in prison, Joseph is freed by the Pharaoh and promoted to the highest offices in the land. He is thirty years old when his destiny changes in this way. Then, for the second time, a 'priest of the holy bull' enters the mystery drama of his life. Potiphera is the highest sun priest of On-Heliopolis, whose daughter Asenath the Pharaoh marries to Joseph.

Through the style of the biblical narration, one must recognize that in the image of Joseph's marriage, his initiation into the Egyptian mysteries is referred to as well. By giving his daughter in marriage to Joseph, the sun priest of the sun city acknowledges Joseph as a rightful co-guardian of the secrets entrusted to himself. As has always been noted, in the name of Asenath, Joseph's wife, the word Neit is contained, the name of the veiled goddess of Sais, 'the primal mother of the sun', the 'mother of the gods'. At the place of the first Potiphar, Joseph encountered the terrestrially distorted mirror-image of the holy Isis; in On-Heliopolis, the second, greater Potiphera unlocked to him the genuine sanctuary of the great goddess. Freed from the nether world, Adonis finds the bride instead of the seductress.*

Heliopolis, Beth-Shemesh, 'the city of the sun', was situated north of Memphis at the southern end of the Nile Delta and obviously retained the mysteries of ancient Egypt until late ages in a pure form as did Sais, which lay still further north in the

* The novel-like apocryphal text, *Joseph and Asenath*, reflects the initiation experience of Joseph in richly pictorial imaginative descriptions.

delta. For even Plato was a disciple of the Egyptian priests of Heliopolis for thirteen years. Only one lone obelisk remains today of the splendour of the ancient temples; but in the midst of the sands of the desert one feels transported to a lovely island of life. A site of the goddess Natura, the life-bestowing mother, must have existed there in all ages — and doubtless much more noticeably in biblical times than today — conjured forth a paradisal oasis within the world of dying nature. There, the soul of young Joseph, radiant with ancient maturity, achieved complete fulfilment of its nature and life.

Joseph owed the turn in his Egyptian destiny — the liberation from the nether world of the prison and his elevation to co-ruler of a mighty kingdom — to his ability to read the dreams of the Egyptians. He bore within him two elements: the twilight-heritage of ancient clairvoyance and the Abraham-power of brain-thinking. In the circle of the descendants of Abraham, his kinship with the Babylonian-Egyptian past was more pronounced: he was the dreamer. In Egypt he was more a bearer of intelligence: he was the dream-interpreter. Therefore, he was in a position to incorporate a new impulse into Egyptian life. Through Joseph, the Egyptian culture was injected with the fruits of the Abraham stream. Joseph not only interpreted the dreams of his highly placed fellow-prisoners and those of the Pharaoh, but he used the same power, with which he explained the dreams, to bring about a regular reform in Egypt, where he became viceroy. The dreams of the two fellow-prisoners and those of the Pharoah were themselves imaginative premonitions and perceptions of the exhaustion of the Egyptian temple culture. When one of the prisoners in the gaol dreamt that the birds ate up the bread out of the baskets of man, when the Pharoah dreamt that the seven fat cows and plump ears of corn were devoured by the seven gaunt cows and thin ears of corn, this indicated not only an external famine. Egypt felt and beheld the approaching end of the spirit-revelations flowing within its mysteries. The civilization borne until then by the gods would succumb to a process of inwardly running dry. The dark age long since felt in Babylonia would break in over Egypt, which had used up its reserves. Here, as a messenger of the Abraham-culture, which in quiet obscurity progressed on its way, Joseph brought a force through which Egypt could be preserved one more time from the fall into nothingness. He brought the power of the intellect, which could put human organization in place of divine guidance, and through clever preservation could maintain the substance of temple tradition for a while. Through the union of Egyptian and Israelite spiritual substance in the person of Joseph, the art of statesmanship was born. In the same context in which he spoke about the spiritual reasons for Joseph's expulsion, Rudolf Steiner said of Joseph's Egyptian mission: 'Joseph brought about a complete reversal in Egypt, in that he adapted his gift of clairvoyance to correct the declining Egyptian culture. He placed his gift in the service of outer institutions.'[145] And so it was Joseph who possessed both the clairvoyant gift as an atavistic legacy so that he could understand the people of Egypt, and the capacity of mathematical logic, which these people did not have; thus, he could form a natural bridge between the two nations. The Pharaoh was incapable of bringing economic order into his affairs because of this lack of the capacity of calculation. Joseph could bring about this order, for in him the Yahweh doctrine was a concentration of the external mathematical world picture, which received a content of colours from the Egyptian world view.[146]

It has been assumed that a record would have to exist in outer historical documents regarding a personality who was so decisively engaged in the Egyptian destinies. And a number of Semitic names were found, which, it was believed, could be identified with the biblical Joseph. In the El Amarna archives (from the period around 1400 BC), for example, a man by the name of Yanhamu is mentioned, who, invested with the most extensive authorities of the Pharaoh, controlled the corn granaries and storage houses and regulated the grain distribution of Syria. But it could never be established with certainty, whether this was or was not Joseph. Perhaps one obstacle in this search is that the biblical descriptions of the famine and the corn storehouses, which refer to the whole of Egyptian spiritual and political life and must be understood imaginatively, are taken too literally. Attention is thus focused only on powerful administrators of the grain supplies. Also, Joseph is usually placed in too late an age. If we follow the biblical indications, and there is no reason at all not to do so, we must picture Joseph's activity in Egyptian Thebes at the foot of the majestic mountains, which look down upon the broad Nile delta and the temple city of Karnak situated above it, at around the year 1700 BC.

In the historical world-power play revealed to us by the stories of Joseph, Israel first helped Egypt, then Egypt helped Israel. In Egypt, where the ancient power of clairvoyance that people had relied on quickly became extinguished, a stifling chaos threatened to break out; for, in place of the impulses of the gods merely human passions remained. On the other hand, the development of Israel, which quite consciously relinquished the clairvoyant element of revelation, threatened to culminate in cold emptiness of soul. The same period of drought that set in over Egypt brought the Israelites to awareness of the deprivation to which they were exposed and the crisis for which they were heading. They sought contact with Egypt. From the folk-community propagating through the blood-lines, any resemblance to the Egyptian spiritual character had been carefully distilled out by virtue of casting out Ishmael and Joseph. But this did not preclude a search for cultural fecundation from outside through the world of Egypt. Joseph's brothers travelled to the land of the Nile to obtain for their own people a share of the treasures that human beings there still possessed. Finally, the whole folk-community settled within the realm of Egyptian culture, submerging in the world of ancient spirit-revelation. It is not necessary completely to discard the images of famine, Joseph's large granaries, and the brothers' sacks of grain. It is indeed possible that for both the Egyptians and the Israelites an outward time of need was the cause of action. But what did occur outwardly then became an image for far-reaching developments that also encompassed the spiritual life. As Egypt built granaries for the grain that was soon to become scarce, it also brought the temple revelations, which threatened to dry up, into such form that they could be handed on and benefit a future devoid of revelations. And as the sons of Jacob travelled to Egypt to obtain grain, they could not but immerse in a sacramental world and gain a share in the soul of an inspired culture as they beheld the Egyptian temples and Egyptian life.

After Joseph had revealed himself to his brothers, and after all those of his people who had thrust him out had followed him into the sphere of Egyptian rule, a time of learning commenced for Israel, which spanned centuries and was only completed and terminated by Moses. Jacob's sojourn in Babylonia had been an inner education. It had transformed the one who himself was the bearer of inheritance and had thus directly influenced the blood that was to be passed on in the Messianic lineage. The Egyptian period of learning, beginning with Joseph's expulsion and leading on to Moses, was an outer education. Through Joseph, Egyptian culture had been imbued with an Israelite impulse. Now, Israel could learn from an Egypt that had become adapted to Israel. What it had eliminated from its blood, it reabsorbed spiritually. When, through his Egyptian initiation, Moses had completed and ended Israel's immersion in the world of the mysteries, Joseph's spiritual return home was a total one. We shall see later that through Moses in the Sinai revelation, a spiritual restoration of Ishmael also took place. The four centuries between Joseph and Moses, which the Bible passes over, as it does with the periods in the thousands of years between Noah and Abraham, were a time of outward absorption, assimilation and quiet, inward incorporation of Egypt by Israel. Thereby, this time saw a first permeation of the pure form with a supersensory substance, which had not been allowed to flow into the development of the form itself. Concerning the law of the spiritual reabsorption and return of what has been cast out of the stream of inheritance, Rudolf Steiner said:

> The element which the members of the Hebrew nation still needed and which could not flow from their own organism, was to be given them in the roundabout way by Egypt through Moses . . . If the ancient Egyptian wisdom, which originated from the Egyptian initiation, and which left Israel with Joseph and returned again with Moses, had been injected into the Jews, it would have resulted in a cultural miscarriage.
>
> And now we witness a peculiar drama. We see that those who were the missionaries of outer thinking according to number and measure are no longer on the earlier path; through Joseph, they particularly seek the outer relationship, inasmuch as they seek in the reflection of Egypt what they themselves could not produce. So they move there and they absorb . . . what they need . . . What is necessary . . . and cannot be brought forth from within, is given outwardly through . the Egyptian initiation [that Moses underwent].[147]

The whole great union between Egypt and the old Hebrew people was then brought about by Moses. He could lead the people back again so that they could digest what they had received in a way appropriate to their own folk-character, independently and undisturbed by other nations, so that the specific characteristic of the blood of these people could be retained.

10 JOSEPH AND HIS BROTHERS

In the transition from Joseph's degradation to his elevation by the Pharaoh, more than personal destiny was involved. A spiritual guidance and providence, encompassing a whole folk-community, was at work, secretly preparing the way for a reversal of the common inner destiny. Until then, Israel had been increasingly separated from the forces of the supersensory world. The sun of direct spirit-experience was removed into ever greater distances. The expulsion from paradise became more and more complete; and all that was left was the lunar form-world of indirect spirituality in the thoughts of the head. Now, suddenly, the destinies brought the Israelite folk-community once again near the realms of the supersensory in Egypt. The individual human beings remained on the path of the moon, but the totality of the people seemed to be gently led closer again to the sphere of the sun. It was as if the angels at the gates of paradise were already beginning to call back the chosen branch of humanity.

It becomes noticeable that the sun-archangel Michael has become the folk-spirit of Israel. Within the folk-sphere, a sunrise of new supersensory experience was preparing. Christ-secrets hovered over the events, and in the soul of Joseph their images could be indicated. When, upon the advice of his brother Judah, he was sold for twenty pieces of silver, this was an event that referred less to Joseph than to the soul of his people, for in reality, not only Joseph but all his people were thereby led to Egypt. Within the folk-sphere, a prophetic reflection occured of the Judas betrayal, which was later to bring about the full enactment of the mystery of Golgotha. When, at the age of thirty — the same age at which Jesus of Nazareth became the bearer of the Christ-being at the Baptism in the Jordan — Joseph experienced his great elevation, in reality there occurred an approach of the Christ-sun towards the folk-sphere. On that same level, a prophecy of the event of the Jordan Baptism was alluded to.

And now, a truly sacramental sequence of pictures unfolds in a broad development, which already had its quiet beginnings earlier. It is just this that fills the Joseph stories with such soul-substance, makes them so impressive and keeps them alive in everybody who has become acquainted with them in childhood: that the secrets of bread and wine and the atmosphere of communion breathe through them. Not to the individual humans, but in the spiritual realm of the clouds, the sacrament of the sun with bread and wine is administered to the soul of the people.

173

Already in Joseph's two dreams, when he was still at home with his family, the image of bread and wine vibrates in the background. The ripe sheaves bestow the bread of spirit-revelation, and out of the ceremonious moving round of the stars flows the wine of the higher soul force.

In the dreams of Joseph's fellow-prisoners in the Egyptian gaol, the duality of bread and wine is already more clearly discernible. The two, whose dreams Joseph interpreted, should of course not be taken profanely — as the usual translation suggests — as the chief baker and first cup-bearer of Pharaoh. They must have been personalities, who, within the cultic configuration of the Egyptian temple world, which still extended into all realms of everyday life, had charge of the administration of bread and wine. The dream of the bread contains pictures of an approaching end. The dream of wine is of a more comforting nature. Egypt still sustained itself on the communion of the old sun forces. But it was running out of the bread: its spirit revelations died away. The wine remained, but only as a dull, ecstatic soul force, which, if unguarded, would turn into passion and greed for power. As the cup of intoxication, the secret of the wine lived on in Egypt.

The dreams of the Pharaoh were already completely determined by the dying away of the old sun-communion. Again, the duality of bread and wine varied in the images of the ears of corn and the celestial bulls, but the twilight of the sunset was spreading over both.

From now on, the image of bread and wine played from the realm of the dream world into the awake day-world and the world of outer destiny. But now, our glance is directed from the waning ancient sun-gift of Egypt to the dawn of a communion of the future, which would benefit Israel. Joseph's brothers returned from Egypt with their grain for bread, that the great unknown and yet known one had given them. To their horror, they found the money with which they paid for the grain back in the sacks with the corn. From the sphere of earthly things that are subject to calculation and commercial life, their souls were directed to the sphere of the spirit where grace, the sacrament of giving, of the higher beings, rules. They had to seek the path from earthly bread to the bread of spirit-revelation; from the world of numbers to the sacrament. And during the return from their second Egyptian journey, they were led a step further. Again, they not only found the money in the corn, but in Benjamin's grain they were shocked to discover Joseph's cup. In the subtlest hint, to the image of bread that of wine is added.

Israel had renounced the gifts of the ancient sun. From the beginning, Israel had rejected the bread of spirit-revelation now depleted in Egypt. The wine, which Egypt still possessed, was likewise completely lacking in Israel. Indeed, Israel was inviting the danger of coldness of soul and a state of inner death as the result of the one-sided orientation towards the intellect. Israel was now ready to acquire the secret of the bread for itself. But the bread was not given to it separately. Simultaneously, the secret of the wine was incorporated into Israel, though not as a bliss-bestowing gift. Just as Egypt possessed the old wine only in the cup of intoxication, Israel had to drink the wine of the new sun from the cup of suffering, which had to be drained to the dregs. Joseph's cup was the beginning of a chain of destinies of suffering through which the people were to attain their higher soul force. Joseph's expulsion to Egypt brought about the homelessness in Egypt of the whole people, which would then be replaced by one trial of destiny after another. But all hardships and all shocking experiences were stations on the path on which humanity rediscovered in a new form what it once had lost. The shock of the brothers over the money in their sacks and over the cup in Benjamin's grain was but the forerunner of the joys of being able to embrace the one who was believed lost.

The stories of Joseph thus form a mean between Melchizedek and Christ in the story of bread and wine. Melchizedek bestowed bread and wine on Abraham but without yet removing the veil of the mystery from the sacrament of the sun. Now, in the sphere of the folk-soul, bread and wine were administered to the twelve-foldness of the tribes by the archangel Michael as the leader of Israel's destiny. But the veil of the mysteries was lifted only slightly for the world of outer objects, in which the individual human beings live. Bread and wine, secreted in the events, flashed forth only in a concealed form out of the folk-soul into the individual souls. Thus, the way of the future was prepared, in which bread and wine, as gifts from the spiritual sun, would completely emerge from the mystery and would be administered to each human ego. When, in time, the tribal twelvefoldness of Jacob's sons would be replaced by the ego-bearing twelvefoldness of the disciples, the Egyptian cup of intoxication and the cup of suffering of the Israelites would become the Christian cup of freedom.

In the centuries between Joseph and Moses, the world changed. This comes to expression in the fact that at the end of this time Israel no longer stood in the same relation of friendship and unity with Egypt as in the days of Joseph. The surrounding world had become foreign and hostile. Something took place on a large scale that was repeated later in Palestine where, one and a half centuries before Christ, Judas Maccabeus called the Romans into the country as allies, so that by the time of the mystery of Golgotha, the allies had made themselves into tyrannical executors of foreign rule. The world was no longer a great paternal home, it had become an alien land. The homelessness of humanity increased. The legacy of ancient spirit-activity was utterly depleted; the expulsion from paradise was complete. And when the maternal countries of the great temple cultures of Egypt and Babylonia broke out in endless wars against each other, motivated by insatiable greed for power, there arose here and there imposing kingdoms, but the world was devoid of God; the stores of corn had been consumed in spite of Joseph's granaries. The great battle at Megiddo around the middle of the second millennium BC, a hundred years before Moses' time, in which the great Egyptian conqueror Thutmose III forced the entire Near East under his dominion on Palestinian ground, sealed the death of the ancient supersensory world-condition. This is why, for the seer of the Apocalypse, this battle is the past's mirror-image of spiritual events of the future through which the supersensory sphere of the sun-spirit fights its way once again completely into humanity: in the Battle of Armageddon (Rev.16:16).

Joseph's pure Adonis-like adolescent soul was a preserver of ancient wealth, but above it flashed the prophetic light of the Christ future. With masculine will, Moses inaugurated the manhood of the Old Covenant and courageously began the journey through the desert.

References

1 Steiner, *The Gospel of St. Mark*, lecture of September 20, 1912.
2 Gorion, *Sagen der Juden*, I, 286, 291, 35.
3 Gorion, *Sagen der Juden*, I, 31.
4 Gorion, *Sagen der Juden*, I, 37.
5 See particularly Steiner, *Occult Science* and *Cosmic Memory*.
6 More detailed descriptions about the beginning of Genesis are found in Steiner, *Genesis*.
7 Concerning the relationship of mussel, fish, batrachia, and so forth, with these first metamorphoses of human corporeality, see Poppelbaum, 'Menschwerdung und Tiergestalten' in Vol. 5 of *Gäa Sophia*.
8 Steiner, *Genesis*, lecture of August 19, 1910, p. 35f.
9 Concerning the further evolution of the developing earth-planet's warmth organization, details are given in Wachsmuth, *Kosmogonie und Erdgeschichte*, II.
10 Gorion, *Sagen der Juden*, I, 57.
11 Gorion, *Sagen der Juden*, I, 91.
12 Ephraem, *Treasure Cave*, Ch. 12.
13 Gorion, *Sagen der Juden*, I, 100.
14 Kayser, *Geologie*.
15 See Wachsmuth, *The Etheric Formative Forces; Erde und Mensch, ihre Bildekräfte, Rhythmen und Lebensprozesse; Die Entwicklung der Erde*, also various books and essays by Eckstein, Pfeiffer, and Poppelbaum.
16 Wachsmuth, *The Etheric Formative Forces*.
17 Suess, *The Face of the Earth*.
18 Kayser, *Geologie*.
19 Wachsmuth, *The Etheric Formative Forces*.
20 Steiner, *Cosmic Memory*.
21 Bachofen, *Myth, Religion and Mother Right*.
22 Steiner, *Cosmic Memory*, p. 82f.
23 In his spiritual research, Rudolf Steiner has often graphically described the life of these prehistoric animals and the state of the earth at that time. Examples are *Mystery Knowledge and Mystery Centres*, lecture of December 1, 1923, and *Die Erkenntnis des Menschenwesens nach Leib, Seele und Geist — Über frühe Erdenzustände*, lecture of September 20, 1922.
24 Steiner, 'Der Streit Michaels mit dem Drachen', *Das Goetheanum*, III, 8.
25 Suess, *The Face of the Earth*.

26 Translated into German by Herbert Hahn in *Wege und Sterne*.
27 Gorion, *Sagen der Juden*, I, 95.
28 Bengel, *Tischreden*, p. 61.
29 Gorion, *Sagen der Juden*, I, 261.
30 Norberg, *Codex Nasaraeus*.
31 Chvol'son, *Die Ssabier*.
32 Gorion, *Sagen der Juden*, I, 263f.
33 Gorion, *Sagen der Juden*, I, 263.
34 Gorion, *Sagen der Juden*, I, 265.
35 Steiner, *Human Questions*, lecture of July 2, 1922, p. 61.
36 Gorion, *Sagen der Juden*, I, 139.
37 Steiner, *Grundelemente der Esoterik*, lecture of November 4, 1905.
38 Gorion, *Sagen der Juden*, I, 267.
39 Gorion, *Sagen der Juden*, I, 268.
40 Gorion, *Sagen der Juden*, I, 269.
41 Gorion, *Sagen der Juden*, I, 153.
42 Gorion, *Sagen der Juden*, I, 154.
43 Gorion, *Sagen der Juden*, I, 167.
44 Gorion, *Sagen der Juden*, I, 168.
45 Gorion, *Sagen der Juden*, I, 169–173.
46 Augustine, *De civitate Dei*, XV, 23.
47 Gorion, *Sagen der Juden*, I, 271.
48 Gorion, *Sagen der Juden*, I, 290.
49 Steiner, *Christ and the Spiritual World*, lecture of December 30, 1913, also *Pre-Earthly Deeds of Christ*, lecture of March 7, 1914.
50 Gorion, *Sagen der Juden*, I, 270 and 292 etc.
51 See illustrations in Bock, *The Catacombs*.
52 See especially Steiner, 'The Development of World and Man' in *Occult Science*, and 'Our Atlantean Ancestors' in *Cosmic Memory*.
53 Steiner, *Occult Science*, p. 197.
54 Steiner, *Occult Science*, p. 196.
55 Steiner, *Cosmic Memory*, p. 63f.
56 Gorion, *Sagen der Juden*, I, 189f.
57 Gorion, *Sagen der Juden*, I, 230.
58 Gorion, *Sagen der Juden*, I, 234 and 274.
59 Gorion, *Sagen der Juden*, I, 237f.
60 *Enoch, Book of*, (41:3–5).
61 *Enoch, Book of*, Ch. 60.
62 See Bock, *Könige und Propheten*, p. 133, for details about the teachings of the cabbala, about the ten sephirot, which the Book of Job touches upon here, as well as descriptions of the parts of man's being related to them.
63 Woolley, *Ur of the Chaldees*, p. 168f.
64 Steiner, *Earthly and Cosmic Man*, lecture of May 20, 1912.
65 Steiner, *Occult History*, lecture of December 30, 1910.

REFERENCES

66 Noeldecke, *Vierter Bericht über Uruk*.

67 Steiner, *Occult History*, lecture of December 28, 1910.

68 Gorion, *Sagen der Juden*, II, 36.

69 Gorion, *Sagen der Juden*, II, 32.

70 Concerning the legend of Abraham's birth, see Steiner, *The Gospel of St. Matthew*, lecture of September 3, 1910.

71 Steiner, *The Gospel of St. Matthew*, lecture of September 3, 1910.

72 Steiner, *Die tieferen Geheimnisse*, lecture of November 14, 1909.

73 Philo, 'On Abraham' XV–XVI.

74 Steiner, *Occult History*, lecture of December 30, 1910.

75 Gorion, *Sagen der Juden*, II, 94.

76 Gorion, *Sagen der Juden*, II, 118.

77 Gorion, *Sagen der Juden*, II, 88.

78 Gorion, *Sagen der Juden*, II, 98.

79 Gorion, *Sagen der Juden*, II, 325f.

80 Gorion, *Sagen der Juden*, II, 139.

81 See for example, Ps.87:4; 89:10; Isa.51:9. In regard to this polarity see also Jeremias, *Das Alte Testament*, p. 373.

82 Gorion, *Sagen der Juden*, II, 78.

83 Gorion, *Sagen der Juden*, II, 97.

84 Gorion, *Sagen der Juden*, II, 119 and 171.

85 Gorion, *Sagen der Juden*, II, 158.

86 Gorion, *Sagen der Juden*, II, 158.

87 Steiner, *The Gospel of St. Matthew*, lecture of September 4, 1910.

88 Gorion, *Sagen der Juden*, II, 175.

89 Gorion, *Sagen der Juden*, II, 174.

90 Gorion, *Sagen der Juden*, II, 165.

91 Gorion, *Sagen der Juden*, II, 175f.

92 Steiner, *Das Prinzip der spirituellen Ökonomie*, lecture of February 15, 1909.

93 Steiner, *The Gospel of St. Matthew*, lecture of September 4, 1910, p. 75.

94 Ch. 28. Quoted according to Riessler, *Altjüdisches Schrifttum*.

95 Ephraem, *Treasure Cave*, Ch. 5.

96 Ephraem, *Treasure Cave*, Ch. 6.

97 Ephraem, *Treasure Cave*, Ch. 7.

98 Ephraem, *Treasure Cave*, Ch. 22, 23.

99 Reproduced in Bock, *The Catacombs*.

100 Gorion, *Sagen der Juden*, II, 143.

101 Gorion, *Sagen der Juden*, II, 123.

102 Gorion, *Sagen der Juden*, I, 210.

103 Gorion, *Sagen der Juden*, II, 193.

104 Ephraem, *Treasure Cave*, Ch. 29.

105 Ephraem, *Treasure Cave*, Ch. 30.

106 Gorion, *Sagen der Juden*, II, 304.

107 Gorion, *Sagen der Juden*, II, 303.
108 Gorion, *Sagen der Juden*, II, 316.
109 Gorion, *Sagen der Juden*, II, 251 and 316.
110 Gorion, *Sagen der Juden*, II, 349.
111 Ephraem, *Treasure Cave*, Ch. 31. See also Gen.25:22f.
112 Gorion, *Sagen der Juden*, II, 377.
113 Gorion, *Sagen der Juden*, II, 230.
114 Gorion, *Sagen der Juden*, II, 228.
115 Gorion, *Sagen der Juden*, II, 203f.
116 Gorion, *Sagen der Juden*, II, 200.
117 See Frieling, *Von Bäumen, Brunnen und Steinen*.
118 Gorion, *Sagen der Juden*, I, 261.
119 See Nork, *Hebräisch-Chaldäisches Wörterbuch*.
120 Gorion, *Sagen der Juden*, II, 252.
121 Gorion, *Sagen der Juden*, II, 292.
122 Steiner, *Deeper Secrets*, lecture of November 9, 1909.
123 Steiner, *Die tieferen Geheimnisse*, lecture of November 14, 1909.
124 Gorion, *Sagen der Juden*, II, 295.
125 Gorion, *Sagen der Juden*, II, 308.
126 Gorion, *Sagen der Juden*, II, 308
127 Gorion, *Sagen der Juden*, II, 383.
128 Gorion, *Sagen der Juden*, II, 291.
129 Gorion, *Sagen der Juden*, II, 300.
130 Frieling, *Von Bäumen, Brunnen und Steinen*.
131 Gorion, *Sagen der Juden*, II, 417.
132 Gorion, *Sagen der Juden*, II, 354.
133 Gorion, *Sagen der Juden*, II, 20 and 366.
134 Gorion, *Sagen der Juden*, II, 370.
135 Details, for example, in Chvol'son, *Die Ssabier*, Vol. II.
136 Quoted after Chvol'son, *Die Ssabier*.
137 Concerning menhirs and cromlechs, see Steiner, *Das Goetheanum*, III, 6.
138 See Frieling, *Von Bäumen, Brunnen und Steinen*.
139 Concerning Michael as the countenance of the deity, see Steiner, *The Mission of Michael*, lecture of November 22, 1919.
140 Gorion, *Sagen der Juden*, III, 15.
141 Steiner, *Die tieferen Geheimnisse*, lecture of November 14, 1909.
142 *Testament of the Twelve Patriarchs*, Sebulon, Ch. 4.
143 See, for instance, Steiner, *Man in the Light of Occultism*.
144 Gorion, *Sagen der Juden*, III, 69.
145 Steiner, *Die tieferen Geheimnisse*, lecture of November 14, 1909.
146 Steiner, *Deeper Secrets*, lecture of November 9, 1909.
147 Steiner, *Die tieferen Geheimnisse*, lecture of November 14, 1909.

Bibliography

Augustine, St Aurelius, *De Civitate Dei*, (*The City of God*).

Bachofen, Johann Jakob, *Mutterrecht und Urreligion*, Kröner, Leipzig, 1926.

——*Myth, Religion and Mother Right*, Routledge & Kegan Paul, London, 1967.

Bengel, Johann Albrecht, *Tischreden* [Conversations at table].

Bock, Emil, *Könige und Propheten* [Kings and prophets], Urachhaus, Stuttgart, 1977.

Bock, Emil and Robert Goebel, *The Catacombs*, Christian Community, London, 1962.

——*Die Katakomben*, Urachhaus, Stuttgart 1962.

Chvol'son, Daniil Avraamovič, *Die Ssabier und der Ssabismus*, St. Petersburg, 1856.

Enoch, *Book of*, (from the Ethiopic text), Clarendon, Oxford, 1912.

Ephraem of Syrus, St, *Treasure Cave*.

Frieling, Rudolf, *Von Bäumen, Brunnen und Steinen in den Erzvätergeschichten* [Of trees, wells and stones in the stories of the patriarchs], Urachhaus, Stuttgart, 1961.

Gorion, Micha Josef bin, *Sagen der Juden* [Sagas of the Jews], Frankfurt a.M., 1926.

Hahn, Herbert, *Wege und Sterne*, (collected poems), Orient-Occident Verlag, Stuttgart, 1928.

Halliday, Frank Ernest, *The Legend of the Rood*, Duckworth, London, 1955.

Jeremias, Alfred, *Das Alte Testament im Lichte des Alten Orients*, Hinrichs, Leipzig, 1930.

——*The Old Testament in the Light of the Ancient East*, William & Norgate, London, 1911.

Kayser, Emanuel, *Lehrbuch der Geologie*, Enke, Stuttgart, 1923.

——*Textbook of Comparative Geology*, London, 1893.

Noeldeke, A., *Vierter vorläufiger Bericht über die von der Notgemeinschaft der deutschen Wissenschaft in Uruk unternommenen Ausgrabungen*, (Excavation reports of Uruk 1930/31), Abhandlungen der Preussischen Akademie, Berlin, 1932.

Norberg, Matth. (Ed.), *Codex Nasaraeus*, Friedr. Brummer, Hafniae, n.d.

Nork, *Hebräisch-Chaldäisches Wörterbuch*.

Philo (of Alexandria), 'On Abraham' in *The Works of Philo Judaeus*, Bohn, London, 1854.

Poppelbaum, Hermann, 'Menschwerdung und Tiergestalten' [Man's evolving and animal forms], in Vol. 5 of *Gäa Sophia*.

Riessler, Paul, *Altjüdisches Schrifttum außerhalb der Bibel* [Old Jewish writings not in the Bible], Filser, Augsburg, 1928.

Steiner, Rudolf, *Aus der Akasha-Chronik*, *(Cosmic Memory)*, Rudolf Steiner Verlag, Dornach, 1973, (Gesamtausgabe (GA) No. 11).

——*Christ and the Spiritual World and the Search for the Holy Grail*, Rudolf Steiner Press, London, 1963.

——*Christus und die geistige Welt. Von der Suche nach dem heiligen Gral*, (*Christ and the Spiritual World*), Rudolf Steiner Verlag, Dornach, 1977, (GA 149).

——*Cosmic Memory*, Harper & Row, San Francisco, 1981.

——*Deeper Secrets of Human History in the Light of the Gospel of St. Matthew*, Anthroposophical Publishing Co, London, 1957.

——*Earthly and Cosmic Man*, Rudolf Steiner Publishing Co, London, 1948.

——*Die Erkenntnis des Menschenwesens nach Leib, Seele und Geist, Über frühe Erdenzustände* [The knowledge of the being of man as body, soul and spirit. About early conditions of the earth], Rudolf Steiner Verlag, Dornach, 1976, (GA 347).

——*Die Geheimnisse der biblischen Schöpfungsgeschichte. Das Sechstagewerk im 1. Buch Moses*, (*Genesis*), Rudolf Steiner Verlag, Dornach, 1976, (GA 122).

——*Die Geheimwissenschaft im Umriß*, (*Occult Science*), Rudolf Steiner Verlag, Dornach, 1977, (GA 13)

——*Genesis. Secrets of the Bible Story of Creation*, Anthroposophical Publishing Co, London, 1959.

——*Das Goetheanum*. Weekly paper published by Allgemeine Anthroposophische Gesellschaft, Dornach.

——*The Gospel of St. Mark*, Rudolf Steiner Press, London, 1977.

——*The Gospel of St. Matthew*, Rudolf Steiner Press, London, 1965.

——*Grundelemente der Esoterik* [Foundations of esotericism], Rudolf Steiner Verlag, Dornach, 1976, (GA 93a).

——*Human Questions and Cosmic Answers, Man and His Relation to the Planets*, Anthroposophical Publishing Co, London, 1960.

——*Der irdische und der kosmische Mensch*, (*Earthly and Cosmic Man*), Verlag der Rudolf Steiner-Nachlaßverwaltung, Dornach, 1964, (GA 133).

——*Man in the Light of Occultism, Theosophy and Philosophy*, Rudolf Steiner Press, 1964.

——*Das Matthäus-Evangelium*, (*The Gospel of St. Matthew*), Rudolf Steiner Verlag, Dornach, 1978, (GA 123).

—— *Der Mensch im Lichte von Okkultismus, Theosophie und Philosophie*, (*Man in the Light of Occultism*), Rudolf Steiner Verlag, Dornach, 1973, (GA 137).

BIBLIOGRAPHY

——*Menschenfragen und Weltenantworten*, (*Human Questions and Cosmic Answers*), Rudolf Steiner Verlag, Dornach, 1969, (GA 213).

——*The Mission of the Archangel Michael*, Anthroposophic Press, New York, 1961.

——*Mysteriengestaltung*, (*Mystery Knowledge*), Rudolf Steiner Verlag, Dornach, 1974, (GA 232).

——*Mystery Knowledge and Mystery Centres*, Rudolf Steiner Press, London, 1973.

——*Occult History*, Anthroposophical Publishing Co, London, 1957.

——*Occult Science – An Outline*, Rudolf Steiner Press, London, 1979, and Anthroposophic Press, Spring Valley, N.Y.

——*Okkulte Geschichte*, (*Occult History*), Rudolf Steiner Verlag, Dornach, 1975, (GA 126).

——*Pre-Earthly Deeds of Christ*, Steiner Book Centre, Vancouver, 1976.

——*Das Prinzip der spirituellen Ökonomie im Zusammenhang mit Wiederverkörperungsfragen. Ein Aspekt der geistigen Führung der Menschheit* [The principle of spiritual economy in relation to questions of reincarnation. An aspect of the spiritual guidance of mankind], Rudolf Steiner Verlag, Dornach, 1979, (GA 109/111).

——*Die Sendung Michaels, Die Offenbarung der eigentlichen Geheimnisse des Menschenwesens*, (*The Mission of the Archangel Michael*), Rudolf Steiner Verlag, Dornach, 1977, (GA 194).

——'Der Streit Michaels mit dem Drachen' [Archangel Michael's battle with the dragon], part of *Der Goetheanum-Gedanke inmitten der Kulturkrisis der Gegenwart*, Verlag der Rudolf Steiner-Nachlaßverwaltung, Dornach, 1961, (GA 36).

——*Die tieferen Geheimnisse des Menschheitswerdens im Lichte der Evangelien* [The deeper secrets of the evolving of mankind in the light of the Gospels], Verlag der Rudolf Steiner-Nachlaßverwaltung, Dornach, 1966, (GA 117).

——*Vorstufen zum Mysterium von Golgotha* [First stages to the mystery of Golgotha], (partly in *Pre-Earthly Deeds of Christ*), Verlag der Rudolf Steiner-Nachlaßverwaltung, Dornach, 1964, (GA 152).

Suess, Eduard, *Das Antlitz der Erde*, Freytag, Leipzig, 1888.

——*The Face of the Earth*, Clarendon, Oxford, 1904.

Testament of the Twelve Patriarchs (Ed. R. H. Charles), SPCK, London, 1917.

Wachsmuth, Guenther, *Die ätherischen Bildekräfte in Kosmos, Erde und Mensch*, (*The Etheric Formative Forces*), Philosophisch-Anthroposophischer Verlag, Dornach.

——*Die Entwicklung der Erde* [Evolution of the earth], Philosophisch-Anthroposophischer Verlag, Dornach, 1960.

——*Erde und Mensch, ihre Bildekräfte, Rhythmen und Lebensprozesse* [Earth and man, their formative forces, rhythms and life processes], Philosophisch-Anthroposophischer Verlag, Dornach, 1965.

——*The Etheric Formative Forces in Cosmos, Earth and Man*, Anthroposophical Publishing Co, London, and Anthroposophic Press, New York, 1932.

Wette, Wilhelm Martin Leberecht de, *Lehrbuch der Hebräisch-Jüdischen Archäologie nebst einen Grundriss der Hebräisch-Jüdischen Geschichte* [Textbook of Hebrew-Jewish archaeology with an outline Hebrew-Jewish history], Leipzig 1814.

Woolley, Leonard, *Ur of the Chaldees, A Record of Seven Years of Excavations*, Benn, London, 1950.

Index

Abel 49–55
Abimelech (king of Gerar) 107
Abraham, Abram 87f, 92–111, 114f, 118–26, 129–41, 146, 147, 154, 160
Achilles 143
Adam 14f, 23, 25f, 34ff, 41–44, 47, 56f, 66, 113, 115ff
Adam, Book of 42ff, 46, 56ff, 59, 64f, 77, 82, 98, 112, 133, 144
Adam, Garment of 144, 146, 161
Adam Kadmon 26, 29, 31
Adam, second 66, 77
Adonis 68, 166, 168
Adoni-Sedek (Melchizedek) 111
Africa 39
Agathodaimon (Seth) 59
Ahriman 83
Amfortas (king of Holy Grail) 78f
Amraphel (king of Shinar) 93n
ankh (♀) 54, 63
Anthroposophy 9, 16
Apis Bull (Egyptian cult) 167
Apocalypse (Book of Revelation) 14, 46n, 65, 66
Arabia 29f
ark of Noah 67f, 116
Armageddon 176
Arnon, Valley of, 131
Artemis of Ephesus 52
Asenath (wife of Joseph) 168
Asia 39
Asia Minor 31, 39
Asphalt Sea (Dead Sea) 131
Atlantic Ocean 18
Atlantis 18f, 35, 38, 53, 58, 61, 64, 67, 70–74, 103, 116
Atrachasis (Utnapishtim) 69
Audhumla cow (of Nordic mythology) 52
Augustine, St 64

Babel, Tower of 91–95, 102
Babylon 96, 98, 102
Babylonia 31, 88–93, 95, 98n, 100–06, 121, 141, 148–53, 156f, 163
Baptism in the Jordan 117, 173
Beer-sheba 141

Behemoth (monster) 83f
Benjamin (son of Jacob) 160, 174f
Berossus (Babylonian historian) 12, 21
Bethel 155ff
Bethlehem 129
Beth-Shemesh 168
bread and wine 52, 76, 109, 111, 116, 118ff, 173ff

cabbala 15, 98
Cain 49–54, 59f, 76, 118, 119, 147
Caleb (ruler of Hebron) 133
Canaan (son of Ham) 76
Chaldea, Chaldean 12, 97ff (*see also* Babylonia)
Christ 67, 108, 119, 140, 175, 176
Christian Community 8
Christopherus 117
circumcision 121ff, 164
Clemens Romanus 150n
Cleopatra 128

Damascus 31
David (king) 141
days of creation 13f
Dead Sea 37, 39f, 128, 131, 132
death 47ff, 52–56, 137
death, mystical 55, 63
deserts 37
Deucalion (Noah of Greek mythology) 68, 69, 88
Dinah (daughter of Jacob) 150, 163f
Dionysus (Greek god) 75f, 117
dolmen 155
dove 77
Druids 155

earth stage of evolution 17f
Eden (*see* paradise)
Egypt 92, 100–04, 106ff, 141, 165–76
Egyptian-Babylonian cultural period 90f, 138n, 167
El-elyon (God Most High) 109f, 119, 122
Eliezer (servant of Abraham) 106, 121, 141
Elihu (friend of Job) 81

Elijah 58, 133, 139
Elohim 51
Enoch (son of Cain) 15, 54, 57
Enoch (descendant of Seth) 57ff,
    61–67, 77, 79, 82f, 113 (*see also*
    Hermes Trismegistos)
Enoch, Book of, 63ff
Enosh (son of Seth) 60f, 65, 70
Ephraem of Syrus, St, 42, 115
Ephrath (wife of Caleb) 133
Ephron (Hittite prince of Hebron) 133
Erech (Uruk) 87
E Sag Ila (Marduk sanctuary) 102, 156
Esau 124, 142–49
Euphrates 29f
Europe 39
Eve 32, 38, 41, 49, 115, 116

Fall 38f, 44–47, 50, 60
Flood 68–71, 72, 88, 89, 116

Gabriel (archangel) 65, 99, 130f
Galilee 31, 39f, 101, 129
Galilee, Sea of, 40
Gethsemane 108
Gihon (river of paradise) 29f
Gilgal (near Jordan) 155
Gilgamesh 92f, 98
Giza, pyramids of 102, 103
Gobi Desert 72
Goethe, Johann Wolfgang, 27
Golgotha 117
Golgotha, mystery of, 138n, 173, 176
Gomorrah (*see* Sodom)
Gondwana 28
Goshen, Land of, 108
Greece 39

'h' in Abraham and Sarah 122
Habiri of Samothrace 134
Hagar (maid of Sarah) 107, 135
Ham (son of Noah) 76, 111, 116, 147
Hammurabi (Amorite prince) 93
Haran (brother of Abraham) 105f, 147
Haran (city) 97, 98, 104ff, 149–53
Hasidim 98n
Hathor (Egyptian goddess) 136
Havilah (land of gold) 29
Hebers (tribe) 133f
Hebron 129, 133f
Heliopolis (On) 168f
Hermes (of the Egyptians) 92, 167
Hermes (of the Greeks) 59, 64, 117
Hermes Trismegistos 59, 92
Hiddekel (Tigris) 29

Hindustan 29
Hur (son of Ephrath) 133
Hyperborea 18f, 27f, 40, 50, 101

Idris (Enoch) 59
India 73
Indian Ocean 18
Isaac 107, 123f, 134–41, 143, 146, 147,
    151
Iscah (daughter of Haran) 106n
Ishmael (son of Abraham) 107, 121,
    135f, 139, 147, 165, 171, 172
Ishtar (Babylonian goddess) 107, 136
Isis 136
Islam 135
Israel (Jacob) 158, 159
Israel, Land of, *see* Palestine
Israelites 112, 148, 160, 171–76

Jabal (son of Lamech) 53
Jabbok (ford) 158
Jacob 100, 124, 141, 142–62, 164, 166
Japheth (son of Noah) 111f, 116, 147
Jared (father of Enoch) 61, 63
Jebel Usdum (near Dead Sea) 128
Jebus, Mount of, 123
Jehoshaphat Valley 108
Jericho 128
Jerusalem 30, 39, 103, 111, 117, 123f
    (*see also* Salem)
Jesus of Nazareth 66, 173
Job 79–85, 100
Jordan 100, 125, 128, 131, 154, 157ff
    (*see also* Baptism, Rift)
Joseph (son of Jacob) 100, 148,
    161–176
Joseph's garment 161ff, 166
Joshua 155
Jubal (son of Lamech) 54
Judah (son of Jacob) 165, 167, 173
Judas Iscariot 166, 173
Judas Maccabeus 176
Judea 37, 39f, 101, 128f, 132

Kadmonite Sea (Dead Sea) 39
Kali Yuga (Dark Age) 89–93, 95, 97
Karnak (in Egypt) 166
Kidron Valley 108

Laban (father of Rachel) 149–153
Lagides dynasty 107n
Lamech (descendant of Cain) 53f, 77
Leah (first wife of Jacob) 151f
Lemuria 18ff, 24, 28ff, 32–41, 44, 47,
    50ff, 58, 64, 71, 116, 131ff

INDEX

Levi (son of Jacob) 164
Leviathan 83f
Levites 98n
Liber Adami 42
Lot (nephew of Abraham) 106, 125ff, 128, 129, 132
lotus flower (two-petalled) 139
Lucifer 36, 46n, 83
Luz (Bethel) 155f

maçebhah 155f
Mahanaim 157
Mamre (grove) 129f, 132, 134
manoach 73
Manu 69f, 71ff, 110–17, 119 (*see also* Noah)
Marduk 156f, 159
matriarchy 35
Megiddo 176
Melchizedek 108–11, 114f, 116–21, 122ff, 139f, 160, 175
Memphis 102, 166
Menahem (Noah) 77
menhir 155f
Mercury (Roman god) 59
Mesopotamia 88, 91, 92 (*see also* Babylonia)
Mesozoic era 33, 36
Michael (archangel) 36, 43, 46, 65, 130f, 134f, 156, 158ff, 173, 175
Michelangelo 23, 152
moon-stage of earth (Old Moon) 17, 51n
moon separation 17, 18, 32, 34, 36, 40
Moriah (in Jerusalem) 30, 31, 123f, 137
Moses 67f, 133, 138, 140, 152, 172, 176

Nahor (brother of Abraham) 105
Natura (goddess) 52, 129
Neit (Isis) 168
Nile 29f, 101, 166
Nimrod (grandson of Noah) 92–95, 98f, 121, 144f
Noah 66, 67ff, 73–78, 94, 98, 110, 114–17, 118, 119, 120

obelisks 156, 169
Odysseus 143
On (Heliopolis) 168
Origen 13
Osiris 68

Pacific Ocean 33

Palestine 30f, 34, 39ff, 98, 100, 176
Paraclete 77
paradise (Eden) 26–31, 34, 37–41, 47, 56, 115, 139
Peniel 158
Perez (son of Judah) 167
phallic cult 121
Pharaoh 107f, 169, 170, 174
Philo of Alexandria 15, 97
Pishon (river of paradise) 29f
Plato 27, 169
Polarean cycle 18, 30
post-Atlantean epoch 18, 71, 84f, 110
Potiphar (Egyptian captain) 167f
Potiphera (priest of On) 167f
Praxiteles (Athenian sculptor) 117
pyramids 102f, 166

Rachel 142, 151ff
Rahab (Egypt) 102
Raphael (archangel) 44, 65, 78, 130
Rebekah 107, 124, 142, 146
Reuben (son of Jacob) 148, 165
Revelation, Book of, *see* Apocalypse
Rift, East African/Syrian, 34
rishis, seven holy, 73

Sabians 104
Sais (in Egypt) 168f
Salem 108 (*see also* Jerusalem)
Samaria 163
Saqqara pyramids 102
Sarah, Sarai 106ff, 122, 124, 131, 135, 136
Sargon (king of Assyria) 151
Saturn stage of earth (Old Saturn) 17, 30, 51n
Saul (king) 141
Semites 112
Sepher Hayashar 153
Sepher Yetzirah 98
sephirot, ten, 84
Seth (son of Adam) 55–60, 113, 147
sex, hermaphroditic 25
sexes, separation of, 32
Shechem (city) 163ff
Shechem (ruler) 164
Shem 94, 111–14, 116ff, 119, 120, 121, 124, 137, 147, 150
Shinar (Babylonia) 104
sickness 56, 61
Simeon (son of Jacob) 164
Sinai Peninsula 34, 37, 39
Sodom 125–28

Sodom and Gomorrah, destruction of, 130–34
Solomon (king) 141
standing stones 155f
Steiner, Rudolf, 8
Sumerians 90f, 97
sun stage of earth (Old Sun) 17, 27, 40, 43, 51n
sun separation 17, 18, 29, 40
Syria 31
Syrus (*see* Ephraem)

Tabor, Mount 40
Talmud 15
Tamar (wife of Judah's sons Er and Onan) 167
Tammuz (Accadian god) 161, 166
temple in Jerusalem 30, 123
Terah (father of Abraham) 79, 94, 104ff
teraphim 153
Thebes 166, 170
tholedoth 13f
Thoth (Egyptian god) 59, 64
Thutmose III 176

Tigris 29f
Titurel (king of Holy Grail) 78f
Tree of Knowledge 41, 44f, 51, 56
Tree of Life 51, 56, 139
Tubal-cain (son of Lamech) 54

Ur (in Chaldean) 86ff, 98, 102
Uriel (archangel) 65
Uruk (city) 87, 98, 102
Utnapishtim (Atrachesis) 69, 110

vine 74ff (*see also* bread and wine)

Woolley, Sir Charles L. 86

Xisuthros (Chaldean Noah) 69

Yahweh 51, 109f, 118f, 121–24, 138
Yanhamu (?Joseph) 170

Zarathustra 73
Zerah (son of Judah) 167
ziggurat 102f, 156
zodiac 160, 167
Zohar (father of Ephron) 133

Emil Bock

The Three Years
The Life of Christ between Baptism and Ascension

How can the scientifically orientated man of today approach the healings and miracles of the Gospels, least of all such events as the raising of Lazarus and the Resurrection itself? Emil Bock shows with conviction how he can do this without feeling untrue to himself or the age in which he lives. He does not smooth the path by minimizing the significance of these events or explaining away the difficulties. Rather, he leads more deeply into them through creating an understanding of the implications of such a unique event as the incarnation of a divine cosmic being into the body of Jesus on earth.

Emil Bock examines the four Gospels both as historical documents and as profound spiritual records of the incarnation of Christ. Each of these aspects, in his vivid presentation, is seen to throw light on the other; he regards the Gospel of John as that which gives the most precise record of the progression of events in the three years of Christ's ministry as well as being that of the deepest esoteric significance.

Floris Books

Emil Bock

The Apocalypse of Saint John

Few people read the last, culminating book of the New Testament, the Revelation to John, or Apocalypse. It is often regarded as dealing in harsh, mysterious language, with problems of the early Christian Church, which are now irrelevant. Emil Bock, however, shows that the whole Bible helps us to interpret John's rich, concentrated pictorial language; and that we can then see that he is dealing with great problems of human spiritual development which are particularly relevant to the difficulties of our time.

This book is much more than a detailed commentary on the Apocalypse; it is a profound and encouraging examination of the present needs of man, which shows that in the Revelation to John we can find an understanding of the being of Christ as leader of mankind through the dangers of the present and the future.

Floris Books

Oliver Mathews

The Bible – Unclaimed Legacy

Compiled out of the experience of the early disciples of Christianity, the Bible is a revelation of the past, present and future of the human race. It is the one book in the world depicting the close relationship of the creation of the earth and of humanity and describes an unfolding drama leading to a consummation in the re-creation of both.

In the twentieth century man is awakening from the material interpretation of the universe adopted in the last three centuries. He begins to recognize himself as a spiritual being with the freedom to say yes or no, able to destroy as well as to create. The author shows how the Bible is not only a book of history but also a book that tells of the birth-process of the human self — the creation of the creator.

The Bible describes the painful emancipation of mankind from the heavenly father and an earthly mother towards the freedom, initiative and responsibility of a Sonship demonstrated in Jesus Christ, the recognition of a common humanity and a common ideal.

Floris Books

Evelyn Francis Capel

The Making of Christianity and the Greek Spirit

In their own style the Greek myths are a preparation for Christianity, as real as the stories of the Old Testament. Their magnificent pictures carry the central ideas of human evolution which are brought down to earth in Christian history. Myths are not to be treated lightly; they are history in its cosmic aspect, revealing the creative activity of gods. Charles Williams wrote of the mysterious kingdom of Arthur that the historic relationships lie eastward, the mythical to the west. In the mystery of Christianity, the chronicles that form the Old Testament come from the east, the Greek myths from the west. The Greek contribution shows us the essentially cosmic aspect: the gods dominate the myths, whereas in the Old Testament it is the human factor that is stressed. Classical Gods and Hebrew prophets share together in the making of Christianity. The old Greek tales are worth recalling if forgotten, well worth discovering for the first time.

Floris Books